PANGS OF
THE MESSIAH

PANGS OF THE MESSIAH

THE TROUBLED BIRTH
OF THE JEWISH STATE

Martin Sicker

Westport, Connecticut
London

Library of Congress Cataloging-in-Publication Data

Sicker, Martin.
    Pangs of the Messiah : the troubled birth of the Jewish state /
Martin Sicker.
        p.   cm.
    Includes bibliographical references (p.   ) and index.
    ISBN 0–275–96638–0 (alk. paper)
    1. Palestine—History—1917–1948.   2. Jews—Palestine—
History—20th century.   3. Palestine—History—Arab rebellion,
1936–1939.   4. Jewish-Arab relations—History—1917–1948.
I. Title.
    DS126.S475   2000
    956.94′04—dc21   99–28482

British Library Cataloguing in Publication Data is available.

Library of Congress Catalog Card Number: 99–28482
ISBN: 0–275–96638–0

First published in 2000

Praeger Publishers, 88 Post Road West, Westport, CT 06881
An imprint of Greenwood Publishing Group, Inc.
www.praeger.com

Printed in the United States of America

The paper used in this book complies with the
Permanent Paper Standard issued by the National
Information Standards Organization (Z39.48–1984).

10 9 8 7 6 5 4 3 2 1

For Avi, Adam, and Hanna

Contents

Introduction

For many centuries, Jews all over the world ended their traditional celebrations of the festival of Passover, commemorating the redemption of the Israelites from servitude in Egypt, with the cry "Next Year in Jerusalem." This expression reflected the indelible faith, maintained by the Jewish people since the destruction of their state by the Romans in the first century, that the time would come when the dispersed people of Israel would be gathered together once again and reconstituted as an autonomous nation in their own land. However, as historical circumstances seemed to conspire relentlessly against the realization of this aspiration, it soon became transformed into a dream that was expected to be realized only in a far-off messianic time to come.

There had always been a remnant of the nation living in Palestine, the name given to the land of Israel by the Romans to efface its memory as the national patrimony of the Jewish people. There also had always been a trickle of hardy individuals who immigrated there to immerse themselves in the sanctity of the Holy Land. Nonetheless, the idea of a political restoration of the ancient Jewish state seemed rather far-fetched to a people the vast majority of whom had lived in the Diaspora for some eighteen centuries. By the beginning of the nineteenth century, however, the course of history had taken some unanticipated turns that slowly made realization of the dream of Israel's restoration appear once again to be within the realm of historical possibility. The story of those unanticipated turns is told in an earlier work of mine, *Reshaping Palestine: From Muhammad Ali to the British Mandate,*

1831–1922 (Praeger, 1999). This book relates the story of how, in the thirty-year period following World War I, that historical possibility was incrementally transformed into a reality with the founding of the modern state of Israel in 1948.

But, one may ask, has this story not been told innumerable times over the last half-century? What conceivable justification can there be for yet another book on such an overworked subject? The sad truth, however, is that the story has only rarely been told as it actually happened in any language, and never completely in English. The reasons for this are several. Much historical writing on modern Israel is essentially apologetics and, as someone once remarked, apologetics is history with a purpose and without a conscience. Similarly, much historical writing on Israel is evaluated editorially through the filter of a traditional historiography that tends to obscure as much as it reveals. Finally, the emergence of modern Israel is shrouded in a mythology that has little or no place for inconvenient facts or dissonant voices.

This book does not claim to be a work of original scholarship, presenting information hitherto unavailable to the reading public. It is, rather, a synthesis of information already available from a wide range of published sources that have not previously been integrated to present an unromanticized recapitulation of the events and personalities that led to the troubled birth of modern Israel.

It hardly needs to be said that all history is written from a point of view and that the events described are selected in light of that perspective. This work is no exception. The underlying premise of this book is that virtually every major problem faced by contemporary Israel, a half-century after it came into existence, was foreshadowed by the events and circumstances that precipitated and conditioned its emergence onto the stage of history. This is especially so with regard to its internal affairs and its relations with the Arabs of Palestine. A host of current problems have their roots in earlier times. These include the seemingly irreconcilable differences between the left and right extremes of the political spectrum; between the religious community and the secular; between the Zionists and the anti-Zionists; between democracy and Judaism. There are also the problems of integrating diverse ethnic Jewish communities into a common social fabric, defining the appropriate role of a Labor syndicate such as the Histadrut in a democratic society, and determining the political and social status of non-Jewish minorities in a Jewish state. All of these volatile issues remained unresolved at the time of the creation of modern Israel. Today, a half-century later, these same issues are causing an increasing polarization of Israeli society, with uncertain ramifications for the future. In other words, to understand Israel's present, and possibly its future, one must truly understand its past.

In culling the seemingly limitless material available to demonstrate this thesis, I have sought to extract those items that seemed to me to best explain the struggles within the Zionist community over the national idea and its implications, and the evolving interactions of that community with the external political environment. This has led to my assigning a far more significant role to the so-called right-wing movements than is usually allotted to them in the traditional left-oriented historiography, and to a more critical assessment of the Zionist leadership than is to be found in the conventional Zionist mythology.

An ancient Jewish teaching suggests that the arrival of the messianic era and Israel's restoration will be accompanied by much travail, the "birth pangs of the Messiah." There is an ongoing debate within the contemporary Jewish religious community about whether the emergence of the modern state of Israel represents the dawn of the messianic era and the long-awaited redemption and restoration of the Jewish people to their appropriate place in the divine scheme for the universe. Although this avowedly secular book can shed no light on this question, it does attest to the very troubled birth of the modern state of Israel.

1

British Military Government, 1918–1920

In the winter of 1917–1918, an agreement was reached between the Zionist Organization and the British government to establish a Zionist Commission, under Chaim Weizmann's leadership, that would assist the British authorities in carrying out their commitments to the Jews concerning Palestine that were embodied in the Balfour Declaration. The commission was defined officially as "an advisory body to the British authorities in Palestine in all matters relating to Jews, or which may affect the establishment of a National Home for the Jewish People."[1]

The immediate task for the Zionist Commission was to go to Palestine to begin to lay the foundations for the forthcoming Jewish national home. On March 2, 1918, Arthur Balfour informed the chief political officer in Palestine, General Gilbert Clayton, about the functions and status of the commission. He told Clayton that the commission was being sent by the government "in order to assist you in carrying into effect such measures as can be taken, consistent with your operations, to give concrete form to this Declaration."[2]

In his capacity as the first chairman of the Zionist Commission, Weizmann went to Palestine in the spring of 1918. The tasks before the commission were staggering. The *Yishuv* (settlers) had suffered greatly during the war years. It had lost about one-third of its 1914 numbers through forced deportations, voluntary evacuations, and death from disease. The economy was in a shambles, and unemployment was high and increasing rapidly as refugees and exiles began to return from abroad. The serious shortage of medical personnel made it very difficult to cope with the epidemics that ravaged the country. Distress was particularly great among the Yishuv in the towns, where as many as 4,000 orphans needed care out of an overall remaining Jewish population of approximately 60,000. Moreover, although there was relatively little physical damage to the settlements as a result of military operations during the war, they were generally in very poor condition as a consequence of four years of economic hardship and neglect.

Undeterred by the enormous challenge before it, the commission lunged into its work, in the spring of 1918, with remarkable gusto. Since it also represented the Zionist Organization, it was anxious to accomplish much in a very short period, so as to create a favorable impression at the forthcoming peace conference, at which the fate of Palestine would be formally determined.

The leaders of the Yishuv were not entirely comfortable with the notion of placing its future in the hands of Weizmann and the Zionist Commission, which did not actually represent the Jews of Palestine except insofar as they were members of the Zionist movement. They also wished to present their own ideas and preferences for the future of the country before the peace conference. As a result, in December 1918, the Eretz-Israel Conference was convened to consider the future of the Yishuv. Much of the five-day meeting was spent in discussion of a "Plan for the Provisional Government of Palestine" prepared by Akiva Ettinger (1872–1945), Yitzhak Wilkansky (1880–1955), and, attending on behalf of the Zionist Commission, Vladimir Jabotinsky (1880–1940). A primary concern of the conference was to assure national and communal autonomy in all matters of religion, education, courts, and social welfare. The participants insisted upon complete equality between Arabic and Hebrew, both of which were to be official languages. Above all, it sought international support of a pro-Zionist government in Palestine that would facilitate the rapid expansion of the Yishuv until the Jews became the majority in the country.

There was no disputing the fact that the Arab population constituted the overwhelming majority in the country. The question that had to be resolved was how it would be possible to build the Jewish national home without obstruction by the Arab majority. It seemed clear that for the promises of the Balfour Declaration to be realized, it would be necessary to redefine the popular concept of national self-determination insofar as it applied to Palestine. In view of the newly independent Arab state in the Hejaz and the newly emerging Arab state in Syria, the conferees felt it was not unreasonable that Arab national goals should find fulfillment outside Palestine. As Jabotinsky put it:

We must pose this matter not as a "question" between the Jewish people and the Arab inhabitants of Palestine, but between the Jewish people and the Arab people. The latter, numbering 35 million, has [a territory as large as] half of Europe, while the Jewish people, numbering ten million and wandering the earth, hasn't got a stone. . . . We should stress the perspective of the "Jubilee Year": He who has nothing, give to him; he who has too much, take from him.[3]

Although the plan under discussion was considered too audacious and unrealistic by some, David Ben-Gurion, Yosef Sprinzak (1885–1959), and others argued that it did not go far enough. Ben-Gurion, ignoring two decades of Zionist diplomatic rhetoric, wanted to know why the plan spoke in terms of a Jewish national home rather than asking forthrightly for a Jewish state. As a result of his intervention, an editorial committee composed of Ben-Gurion, Ettinger, and Jabotinsky subsequently revised the wording of the document to make its message unambiguous—the Yishuv wanted the establishment of a Jewish state. The position taken by the Yishuv in its proposed submission to the peace conference was maximalist in character, overriding the concerns of those who believed that it was necessary to seek Arab goodwill and accommodation on this fundamental question.

It was evident that the conference, which approved the plan by a vote of 55–1, intentionally ignored Arab claims or interests with regard to the future of Palestine. It was certainly not the case that they had not given the Arab question any thought. They understood the nature of the Arab position on the matter very well. It was simply clear to them that Arab and Jewish national interests in Palestine were diametrically opposed. Since the Arabs had other lands and the Jews did not, Arab claims would have to be subordinated to Zionist needs. At one point in the discussion, the question of the possibility of a transfer of the Arab population out of the country was raised, something that was to be suggested again a few weeks later in England by Israel Zangwill. Wilkansky responded that he thought it impossible, as a practical matter, to evict the fellahin, even if the Jews wanted to. Nevertheless, he stated, if it were possible, he would be fully prepared to commit an injustice toward the Arabs. He readily acknowledged that there were those who opposed such an approach on moral grounds. However, he insisted,

[W]hen you enter into the midst of the Arab nation and do not allow it to unite, here too you are taking its life. The Arabs are not salt-fish; they have blood, they live, and they feel pain with the entry of a "foreign body" into their midst. Why don't our moralists dwell on this point? We must be either complete vegetarians or meat-eaters: not one-half, one-third, or one-quarter vegetarians.[4]

In late January 1919, a five-man delegation headed by David Yellin (1864–1941) left for Europe with the newly revised version of the "National Demands" of the Yishuv. When the delegation arrived in London, it was shocked to learn that the proposals of the Zionist Organization had already been submitted to the peace conference. Their dismay at realizing that the Yishuv had not been consulted with regard to its own future was further exacerbated when they reviewed the official Zionist submission. They correctly considered it to be far weaker than the "National Demands" they had brought with them. For their part, the official Zionist spokesmen considered the demands of the Yishuv to lack all political realism and to be a potential embarrassment for Zionist diplomacy. It was made unmistakably clear that, at least at this point in time, Zionist policy and the political future of the Yishuv were firmly in the hands of Weizmann and his supporters, and were being decided in London rather than Jerusalem.

Working in conjunction with the Palestine Office of the Zionist Organization, the Zionist Commission sought to overcome the numerous intercommunal differences that had effectively prevented the Yishuv from acting in concert. It attempted to establish a Constituent Assembly of Palestine Jewry, to serve as a legally recognized body representing all the Jews of Palestine that could assume the functions of a legislature. The effort proved fruitless. Once again, internal divisiveness precluded common action even when it appeared to serve the interests of all factions. It was therefore decided to establish a more limited *Asefat haNivharim* (Elected Assembly), representative of the broad spectrum of parties and communal groups in the Yishuv.

Elections eventually took place in April 1920, with some 20,000 voters participating. The Assembly, consisting of 314 members representing 20 different parties, finally met in October and elected a *Vaad Leumi* (National Council) of 36 members to serve as its executive body. The first presidium of the Vaad Leumi consisted of Itzhak Ben-Zvi, David Yellin, and Jacob Thon (1880–1950). Although the Asefat haNivharim and the Vaad Leumi were not given formal recognition by the British as representative institutions of the Yishuv until 1928, they were immediately treated as such for all practical purposes. The cornerstone of the infrastructure for Jewish self-government had been laid.

Because the Zionist Commission's highest priority was to repair the damages to the Yishuv that resulted from the war and Turkish misadministration during that troubled period, little attention was given to issues of Zionist settlement during its brief tenure. Nonetheless, some developments took place that would prove to be of significance in the years ahead. For one thing, there had been a dramatic growth in the number of collective settlements—from eleven in 1914 to twenty-nine by the end of 1918. The war had actually encouraged the growth of the *kvutzah* (collective group) movement because life had become difficult for the individual as a result of government repression, a failing economy, unemployment, and shortages. Many came to recognize that their situation would improve substantially if they lived in a collective environment.

Most of these new settlements were expected to be temporary entities. Indeed, many of them could not reasonably be seen as potentially viable over the long run because of objective factors such as having insufficient land to sustain a successful agricultural program. Nevertheless, the desperate situation of many young people provided an impetus for the continued growth of the kvutzah movement and the strength of the *Hapoel Hatzair* (The Young Worker) organization, with which most of these settlements were affiliated. In addition, a number of *kvutzot* founded during the war period were intended from the outset to become permanent settlements. Between 1916 and 1917 such prospectively permanent settlements were established in Upper Galilee at Ayelet Hashahar, Kfar Giladi, and Tel Hai, and at Tel Adashim in the Jezreel Valley. The settlement at Mahanayim, established in 1899 and abandoned a decade later, was resettled.

With the increase in the number of such settlements, and the onset of a new wave of Zionist immigration that began to arrive from Europe (1,806 entered in 1919) even before the country was officially reopened for immigration in 1920, the influence of the Labor movement continued to grow. As the country was about to enter a new era of development under a presumably benign British administration, efforts were made to unite the Labor parties into a common front to guide the development process. The distinctions between Hapoel Hatzair and *Poalei Zion* (Workers of Zion), however, remained as sharp as ever. Hapoel Hatzair rejected Marxism as inapplicable to Palestine because it was an undeveloped country, and did not have classes in the Marxian sense. By contrast, the Poalei Zion remained a Marxist-oriented party affiliated with the Second International. This latter affiliation was particularly offensive to the Hapoel Hatzair, which maintained that its entire reason for being lay exclusively in its duty to the Jewish people and their regeneration in Palestine. As a consequence, cooperation between the two parties was restricted primarily to their joint participation in the Agricultural Workers' Federation.

In the meanwhile, a third component of the Labor movement emerged, a group of workers who were nonpartisan and unaffiliated with either Labor party. Berl Katznelson, disenchanted with the perennial interparty squabbling, became one of the guiding lights of the nonpartisan group. It was his suggestion that, in view of the tasks for the nation that lay ahead, all elements of the Labor movement should unite in a single federation, *Ahdut Ha'avodah* (Unity of Labor).

The founding conference of the Ahdut Ha'avodah was held in February 1919 at Petah Tikva. Hapoel Hatzair ultimately declined to join the federation, allegedly because of its fundamental differences with Poalei Zion on a number of issues aside from the latter's continued membership in the Socialist International. Foremost among these was the Poalei Zion's declared aim of establishing a mass movement to engage as many people as possible in the building of Jewish Palestine. Hapoel Hatzair, by contrast, was principally concerned with quality rather than quantity. It wanted to build the country more methodically and conservatively—and, in its view, more solidly. However, it is equally likely that Hapoel Hatzair would have lost its freedom of action as a minority faction within the federation, and that it was this prospect that led to its decision not to join. As a consequence, the Ahdut Ha'avodah turned out to be little more than a slightly extended version of the Poalei Zion.

It was not long before circumstances renewed the pressure on the Labor parties to find some means of institutionalizing practical cooperation among them. Relatively large numbers of Russian immigrants were arriving in the country and, to a considerable extent because of Joseph Trumpeldor's formidable influence, they refused to join either the Ahdut Ha'avodah or the Hapoel Hatzair. Both parties now became concerned about how to cope with this grassroots revolt, and began to make new efforts to find common ground between them. At Trumpeldor's suggestion it was finally agreed to form a nonpartisan federation of trade unions, within which each party could retain its separate identity. In December 1920, the *Histadrut Haklalit Shel Ha'ovdim Ha'Ivrim be-Eretz Yisrael* (General Federation of Jewish Labor in the Land of Israel) came into being, with Ben-Gurion appointed general secretary of the organization. Under his leadership the Histadrut was to become the most powerful economic institution in Palestine, having enormous impact on the social and political life of the country.

Ben-Gurion's most pressing initial concern was to make certain that the capital resources of the Yishuv were expended primarily on industrial development that would assure the economic viability of the future

Jewish state. From his perspective this required that the Zionist component of the Yishuv, which for him meant the Labor parties, had to have the dominant voice in the communal financial decision-making process. As a way of achieving this, he wanted the Histadrut itself to accumulate large amounts of capital and thereby dominate investment in the country. This created the dilemma of how the Histadrut could serve as the voice of the workers if the organization also represented capital and management.

Ben-Gurion solved this problem by organizing the *Hevrat Ovdim* (Workers' Society). The Hevrat Ovdim would be comprised of all the individual members of the Histadrut and would become the holding company for the industries in which the Histadrut would invest its capital. Thus, in theory, the members of the Histadrut would own the companies they worked for and would therefore be working for themselves, eliminating any potential conflict of interest. Of course, notwithstanding the theory, the individual members of Histadrut could never act in their own best interest as they saw it, instead of as it was seen by the officials of the organization that acted in their name. They became, in effect, members of a large commune with very little autonomy of decision in matters that directly affected their livelihood and economic well-being. As a result, preferment and success in this organizational context were contingent upon discipline, and the membership of the Histadrut became a highly disciplined group. With such a power base the Histadrut would become the dominant institution in the Yishuv, and whichever political party could control the majority of the members of the Histadrut would also effectively control the Yishuv. This was Ben-Gurion's formula for assuring Labor's dominance over the Yishuv, a formula that proved remarkably successful for more than fifty years.

The success of the Zionist Commission ultimately depended on the cooperation of the British military administration in Palestine, and this was problematic from the first. Weizmann, who had invested a number of difficult years in working and developing relationships with British statesmen, tended to place a generally exaggerated faith in the expectation that the British government would honorably carry out the commitments it made in the Balfour Declaration. It was not long, however, before it became abundantly clear to other Zionist leaders that this was an illusion.

Several weeks after Weizmann's arrival in the country, General Clayton, Britain's chief political officer in Palestine, wrote to Balfour about his views regarding the aims of the Zionist Commission and the problems that would be faced by the British administration in Palestine in assisting in their achievement. Clayton reported on April 18, 1918, that it was inevitable that the British officials "should experience some difficulties in consequence of the fact that up to date our policy has been directed towards securing Arab sympathy in view of our Arab commitments. It is not easy therefore to switch over to Zionism all at once in the face of a considerable degree of Arab distrust and suspicion." Moreover, he suggested, "in the interest of Zionism itself, it is very necessary to proceed with caution." He indicated that he had explained this to Weizmann so that the latter might better appreciate why the military administration found it necessary "to turn down, or delay, some of the schemes put forward by the Commission. . . . Arab opinion both in Palestine and elsewhere is in no condition to support an overdose of Zionism just now." Clayton concluded his report with an urgent request that the government allow the local officials to deal with the Zionist Commission according to their best judgment, and not force them "into precipitate action which might well wreck our whole policy, both Arab and Zionist."[5] In essence, the report reflected Clayton's considered judgment that Zionist aims were in direct conflict with Arab aims and that the two were essentially irreconcilable.

Clayton's views, however, were not fully shared by other British Arab affairs experts in the region. Two days after Clayton transmitted his report to Balfour, Major Kinnahan Cornwallis, director of the Arab Bureau in Cairo, sent a confidential report to his superior on the state of Arab opinion regarding the Zionist Commission. He flatly contradicted Clayton's assertion that the military administration in Palestine was fully informed about the Zionist program and the commitments of the British government in that regard. He noted that since the arrival of the commission, "the Palestinians tend more and more to divorce themselves from Syria and most of the criticisms are now coming from Syrians, who having no direct interest in the matter, seek to disguise the fact by an exaggerated expression of concern."[6]

Captain William Ormsby-Gore, who was liaison officer to the commission, transmitted a similar more positive assessment to the head of the cabinet secretariat on April 19. There evidently was a sharp divergence of views among the British experts regarding the feasibility of proceeding with the Zionist enterprise. It was the perspective of Clayton, however, whether well founded or not, that prevailed and set the policy of the British administration in Palestine and later in London as well. Reflecting the preeminence of Clayton's point of view is the fact that the British military administration did not permit the formal publication of the Balfour Declaration in Palestine until after the San Remo Conference in 1920.

From the outset, the military administration in Palestine proceeded methodically to undermine the Jewish position in the country. Weizmann, well aware of this but still having an abiding confidence in the British government, tended to rationalize the military's obstructionism by suggesting that it was primarily due to their preoccupation with the war and their unfamiliarity with Zionism. Nonetheless, he was offended by the self-righteous argument of the British officers responsible for Palestine that while the Jews were demanding, and often receiving, especially favorable treatment, it was the responsibility of the military administration to be scrupulously and equally fair to all. He wrote of his concerns to Balfour on May 30, 1918.

Weizmann expressed the view that the vaunted fairness and impartiality of the British military in dealing equally with all the components of Palestinian society proved in fact to be advantageous to the Arabs and discriminatory to the Jews, since the Arabs outnumbered the latter severalfold. The policy tended to treat all as equals rather than equals as equals. "This system," he argued, "does not take into account the fact that there is a fundamental qualitative difference between Jew and Arab," and was, in the name of fairness, attempting to reduce the status of the Jews to the lowest common denominator. He asserted that if the military authorities persisted in pursuing such a policy, it "would necessarily tend towards the creation of an Arab Palestine if there were an Arab people in Palestine. It will not in fact produce that result because the fellah is at least four centuries behind the times, and the effendi . . . is dishonest, uneducated, greedy, and as unpatriotic as he is inefficient."[7]

It is evident that Weizmann had a rather low opinion of the state of development of the Arabs in Palestine. However, it is also clear that many key British officials held identical views and patronized the Arabs as primitives, notwithstanding the web of romanticism spun around them by T. E. Lawrence and other Arabists. They tended to like the relatively backward Arabs, one might suggest, because it fed their self-image of superiority. They felt quite different about the Jews, who were in fact their equals in most respects. The Jews rejected their patronization and insisted on being treated as the British themselves were treated—not as natives. Douglas Duff, who served with the British Army in Palestine, observed:

The official glories in the subservience of the Arab and resents the independent attitude of the Jew. Most of the Palestine Government officials are men

whose only claim to distinction was the holding of a temporary commission in
Allenby's armies. . . . This type of official liked the manner in which the Arab
approached him. He cringed and fawned, praised the official to the skies, flat-
tered and cajoled him, pandered to his vanity, paid him the utmost deference,
and made him feel "no end of a fine chap."

This was very different from the Jew, who approached the official as "a
business man, and expected to be dealt with and met on a business
footing."[8]

Apologists for Britain's regime in Palestine tend to argue that if the
British authorities were occasionally at fault in their administration of
affairs there, it was because of their commitment to fair play and impartiality. This argument is both disingenuous and absurd. The responsibility of the British officials was to carry out the policy of their
government, and that policy intended that they discriminate between
Jew and Arab in order to facilitate the development of a Jewish national
homeland in Palestine. The British cabinet was well aware of the fact,
both at the time they approved the Balfour Declaration and when they
had it included in the Mandate, that the vast majority of the residents of
Palestine were Arabs. They surely understood that the Declaration
clearly intended that the Jews be given preferential treatment over the
other inhabitants of the country.

The simple truth seems to be that General Edmund Allenby and the
senior officers at British military headquarters in Cairo thought the decision of the cabinet was wrong, and they were determined not to assist
in its implementation. While the war was still on, the military justified
its opposition on the basis that the discontent among the Arabs which
was likely to result from the government's pro-Zionist policy would be
exploited by the Turks in a way that could impede the war effort. Clayton wrote to the Foreign Office on June 16, 1918:

Any real development of the ideas which Zionists hold to be at the root of the
declaration made by His Majesty's Government entails a measure of preferential treatment to Jews in Palestine. This is bound to lead to some feeling on the
part of other interested communities, especially the local Arabs, and may give
rise to a measure of discontent and unrest of which advantage cannot fail to be
taken by enemy propagandists.[9]

While Clayton makes an ostensibly plausible case, it is a somewhat
disingenuous argument. The Arabs in those parts of Palestine that had
not yet been captured by the British Army were fully cooperating with
the Turks. Moreover, there was little likelihood that Turkish propa-

ganda would have any great effect on the Arabs who had been released from subjection to the Turks and were now under the more benign British control. Clayton's plausible case was nothing more than the kind of bureaucratic argument typically made by a staff official, civilian or military, to justify any deviation from policy that might be decided upon by his immediate superiors.

After the war, the same deviation from the government's policy would be justified on the basis of other plausible arguments, not the least of which was the disarming appeal to the British sense of fair play. In essence, this was not the first time, nor would it be the last, that bureaucrats, both military and civilian, would undertake to ignore or deliberately sabotage a governmental policy with which they disagreed, and ultimately succeed in creating facts that caused the policy to be formally revoked or modified. In the case at hand, the government itself later adopted the "fairness" argument for reneging on its 1917 policy when it no longer served its interests to be perceived as pro-Zionist. However, this was not to happen for some time, at least not while Lord Balfour was still foreign secretary.

Balfour was well aware that the policy of the Declaration contradicted the idea of self-determination for the Arabs of Palestine, but was not troubled by this fact. Indeed, the concept of self-determination was by no means considered by Britain—or by Woodrow Wilson, who elevated the idea to a principle—then or at any time after, to apply universally and indiscriminately. Balfour was quite explicit about his view that the idea of self-determination did not apply to the people of Palestine. He wrote to David Lloyd George on February 19, 1919: "Our justification for our policy is that we regard Palestine as being absolutely exceptional; that we consider the question of the Jews outside Palestine as one of world importance, and that we conceive the Jews to have an historic claim to a home in their ancient land."[10] In August, Balfour addressed this issue again in a "Memorandum respecting Syria, Palestine, and Mesopotamia," where he dealt with the problems of reconciling British policy with the principle of self-determination enshrined, at American insistence, in the League of Nations Covenant. He acknowledged that there was a fundamental contradiction, but nonetheless insisted: "The four powers are committed to Zionism. And Zionism, be it right or wrong, good or bad, is rooted in agelong traditions, in present needs, in future hopes, of far greater import than the desires and prejudices of the 700,000 Arabs who now inhabit that ancient land."[11]

Weizmann was convinced that he had to proceed on the assumption that this position would be maintained by the British government, although he should perhaps have been more open to the idea that it eventually might be changed to the detriment of the Zionist cause. Suffice it to note that this restatement of policy by Balfour was made after the war was over, but that the anti-Zionist policy of the military administration remained unaffected. London did nothing to make its agents conform to its official policy.

Jabotinsky, while still in uniform as an officer of the Jewish Legion, began to represent the Zionist Commission before the British administration in September 1918, just prior to Weizmann's return to England that same month. Jabotinsky had long experience with British officials at the operational level, gained during the years of his struggle to create the Jewish Legion and his subsequent acquaintance with the military bureaucracy from within the army. He quickly surmised that the future Jewish state was being undermined by the British military bureaucrats in Palestine. He wrote to Weizmann on November 12, 1918:

The local situation is not good. Precedents are being established that will later be used against us. Everything that is now being done here against us will serve as a precedent. I never thought that our National Home will emerge by miracle. But we believed in one thing: that the Government will conduct in Palestine a clear policy earnestly aiming at the establishment of a Jewish National Home, and that when the British Administration will take over, there will be equality between Jews and Arabs.[12]

Two weeks later he wrote to Weizmann again: "If the Arabs try a pogrom I will not hold them responsible; responsible are those whose policy leads, nay—forces savage minds to believe that such acts will be tolerated and even welcomed."[13] Jabotinsky, who was the chief political officer of the Zionist Commission at the time, stated in yet another letter to Weizmann, dated January 22, 1919: "[T]he Palestine authorities are acting in a manner which clearly tells the Arabs that the Declaration need not be fulfilled." He also noted that "the Foreign Office has not lifted a finger to remedy the situation."[14] Thirty years later, Weizmann was to write of this period in his autobiography.

Whether the Arabs got positive encouragement to oppose the Allied policy from one or two of the British officials, or whether they just drew their own conclusions from the day-to-day conduct of these gentlemen, it is impossible to say, much less to prove. Nor does it much matter. The fact was that Arab hostility gained in momentum as the days passed; and by the time a civil administration under Sir Herbert Samuel took over, the gulf between the two peoples was already difficult to bridge.[15]

Jabotinsky's reports from Palestine regarding British malfeasance were not what Weizmann wanted to hear. Jabotinsky had told the Zionist Commission at the end of February 1919 that the Balfour Declaration "had the effect of excellent propaganda in the Allied countries, but the promises therein contained had not been fulfilled . . . and the situation had developed in such manner that the Arabs believed that the British would welcome massacres of the Jews."[16] Weizmann was not prepared to accept the validity of this argument. He still preferred to believe that in the end the British government's declared policy would prevail. As a result of the disagreement, Jabotinsky was fired from his position with the Zionist Commission.

Nonetheless, it was becoming increasingly apparent that Britain's Palestine policy was being directed not from the Foreign Office in London but from Allenby's headquarters in Cairo, and the latter had no intention of supporting implementation of any of the policies that would achieve the stated goals of the Balfour Declaration. The rationale used to underpin the military's position in this regard was its ostensibly primary obligation to preserve the status quo in Palestine. The military argued that until a peace treaty was signed, the country remained under martial law and had to be administered in accordance with the "Laws and Usages of War." According to the army's *Manual of Military Law*, the occupant of enemy territory "should only exercise such powers as are necessary for the purpose of the war, the maintenance of order and safety, and the proper administration of the country."[17] Allenby and his subordinates interpreted this as authorizing them to ignore the policies of their government if they concluded that such policies conflicted with the maintenance of the status quo. One student of the history of the period observed:

It is apparent . . . that the Military Administration had taken up a decided view in opposition to the Balfour Declaration policy. Outwardly their attitude was justified by reference to the *Status Quo*—to the duty of a Military Administration to confine itself to "care and maintenance" and to avoid anticipating any future political settlement. Behind the scenes there is no doubt that they were attempting to influence the nature of the future political settlement and to persuade the British Government to abandon the policy of the Balfour Declaration.[18]

The anti-Zionist policy of the military administration became fully evident in the matter of the disposition of the Jewish Legion that had served in Palestine during the war. Allenby clearly understood that the presence of thousands of trained and disciplined Jewish soldiers in Pal-

estine, as intended by Jabotinsky from the very outset, would constitute a potential military infrastructure for assuring the security of a
Jewish national home. However, this would contradict his policy of
bolstering the Arab position in the country. Accordingly, he cabled the
War Office on June 6, 1919:

I am strongly opposed to any increase of Jewish troops in Palestine. The measure would be interpreted as a preparation to enforce the claim of the Jewish
minority on rest of population. The present distrust of Zionist aims among
non-Jewish population would be greatly increased. There have been already
incidents between Jewish soldiers and non-Jewish inhabitants, especially Moslems, and increase in number of Jewish troops would certainly lead to riots and
widespread trouble with the Arabs.[19]

The greater likelihood, however, was that an increase in the number
of trained British troops in the country, Jewish or other, would have
had a quieting effect and would have increased the probability that no
riots or trouble would take place at all. Nonetheless, the War Office accepted Allenby's bogus argument. There was another way, however,
that would have permitted the Zionists to achieve the same goal, and
that would come about if the Jewish Legion were disbanded and its
members elected to remain in Palestine. This would have permitted
them to reconstitute themselves quickly into a Jewish militia. Yet, for
reasons that are still obscure, Weizmann opposed this idea. On July 23,
1919, he wrote to Eric Forbes-Adam: "I realize that nothing can be
done until the Mandate to Palestine has been granted. Moreover, it is
not our desire to increase the Jewish population by means of an undue
proportion of soldiers or ex-soldiers." At the same time he acknowledged "that a strong militia will be needed in Palestine for some years
after the political settlement has been effected." However, Weizmann
entertained the notion of using thousands of young Russian Jews who
had served in the Russian army instead of proposing to build a militia
out of the veterans of the Jewish Legion. His assessment was that the
Russians would make "an excellent type of immigrant for pioneer work
in Palestine and at the same time as material for a militia."[20]
    Why did Weizmann prefer new Russian immigrants to the members
of the Jewish Legion for the purpose of establishing a militia in Palestine? As a practical matter, why did he prefer to build a militia out of
Jews who were not in the country rather than from those who were already in place? One possible answer is that Weizmann's problem with
the legionnaires was that most of them were Americans who had experi-

enced "real freedom and might therefore prove less tractable when confronted with the subtle erosion of the meaning of the Balfour Declaration, and with the curtailment of their human rights."[21] Furthermore, the numerous American legionnaires who intended to remain in Palestine were not at all interested in the slow absorption process contemplated by the Zionist Commission, and many were not interested in pursuing careers in agriculture. The American Zionists had been discussing large-scale immigration and settlement schemes (Jacob de Haas had spoken in December 1917 of a plan to raise $100,000,000) to absorb and provide employment for the legionnaires and thousands of others in all sectors of the economy. The American approach to development of the country had led to conflicts between Weizmann and Louis Brandeis and their supporters. For the London-based Zionist establishment, this kind of thinking meant trouble with the British and was therefore undesirable. Consequently, the Zionist Executive remained silent in the face of the British decision to disband the Jewish Legion and repatriate the legionnaires to their countries of origin.

In the meanwhile, the British military administrators in Palestine were pursuing an increasingly pro-Arab policy. According to a one-time civil servant in the Palestine government, as a general rule the British military officers "regarded the Balfour Declaration as damn nonsense, the Jews as a damn nuisance, and natives into the bargain; and the Arabs as damn good fellows."[22] This pro-Arab bias was particularly blatant under the administration of Major General Arthur W. Money. He is quoted as having asserted: "I have asked many people in position—in England and elsewhere—why England has capitulated to the Zionists, but none of them has been able to give me a straight answer."[23]

Money refused to consider Hebrew as an official language, and had all tax forms and receipts printed only in Arabic and English. His military governor of Jaffa insisted on addressing Jews in Arabic. Even though Jews constituted the majority in Jerusalem at the time, they were allotted only one-third of the seats in the municipal corporation. Money's pro-Arab administration was brought to a close as a result of intervention by Brandeis. Following his visit to Palestine in the early summer of 1919, Brandeis complained vigorously to Balfour that the administration of General Money was sabotaging the efforts to develop the Jewish homeland, making Money's conduct an international political liability at a time when the Mandate was under negotiation. As a result, Money and a number of his senior officers were recalled. It is noteworthy that the protests that caused Money's removal came from

Brandeis rather than Weizmann and his associates in the Zionist Executive in London.

Brigadier C. F. Watson replaced Money in July 1919. By August, the new military administration had had its fill of having to deal with the Zionist representatives, who spoke and acted as if they, and not the British, were the governing authorities. The chief political officer of the Palestine administration urged Allenby's headquarters in Cairo to take steps to have the Zionist Commission abolished. Frustrated and chagrined by the license taken by Allenby and his officers in thwarting its declared policy, the British government once again made its intentions clear to the military administration. On August 4, the government advised that it envisaged that the Mandate for Palestine would be given to Britain and that "the terms of the Mandate will embody the substance of the Balfour Declaration."[24] Accordingly, there was no longer any justification for maintaining the status quo so as not to affect the nature of the final settlement. The government had advised the military what that settlement was to be. In fact, however, Allenby ignored the government and continued to pursue his anti-Zionist policy.

That this was the case becomes evident from the memorandum sent by Brigadier Watson, on September 26, 1919, to the new chief political officer, Colonel Richard Meinertzhagen. The letter concerned the status of the Muslim-Christian Association, which had been established in mid-1918, with the direct political and financial support of the military administration, as an Arab counterpart to the Zionist Commission. The association would soon play a major role in the effort to thwart implementation of the Balfour Declaration and in fomenting anti-Jewish violence. Watson wrote:

The main object of this society is to oppose the Zionist aims and they claim to be representatives of the majority of the population. . . . On taking this Administration I was advised to keep the balance of all parties, and in view of the fact that the Administration is known to be in close touch with the Zionist Commission, it is well to be in touch with the body representing the other parties in the country, although the body is not officially recognized beyond registration.[25]

The advice given to Watson surely came from Cairo rather than London.

Things were destined to become worse for the Jews with the appointment of Major General Sir Louis Jean Bols to replace Watson as chief administrator of the Palestine government in November 1919. It is noteworthy that the selection of Bols was unopposed by Weizmann and the Zionist leadership in London. The fact that Bols, a rabid anti-

Zionist, was appointed to such a position without protest was but another explicit example of the pattern of British anti-Zionist actions abetted by official Zionist passivity. Colonel John Patterson, the British commander of the Jewish Legion, was mortified by what had taken place.

The moment I heard that a certain officer was to be appointed to an important post in Palestine I felt it my duty to warn the chief Zionist leader of the evil that would follow such an appointment, and told him that in the interests not only of Jewry, but of England, it was necessary that he should make a public protest against the appointment of this official. Although I warned Dr. Weizmann of the dangers that would follow, he was loath to believe that a British officer would be disloyal to the policy laid down by the Government.[26]

In the winter of 1919, a number of the settlements in Upper Galilee suddenly found themselves isolated from the rest of Palestine as a consequence of the partial implementation of the Sykes-Picot Agreement in the establishment of the Occupied Enemy Territory Administrations (OETA). The boundaries of the OETAs had been drawn according to the Sykes-Picot map, which placed the northern border of OETA South (Palestine) at the Huleh. When Britain turned OETA North (Syria) over to the French, British forces were withdrawn from the Upper Galilee to south of the Huleh. This left the settlements of Metulla, Kfar Giladi, Tel Hai, and Hamara isolated and devoid of protection in an area that was claimed by Britain, France, and Faisal's Syria, but in fact had become a no-man's land. The Christian Arab villages there favored France, while the Bedouin supported Sherif Hussein, in whose name Faisal was ruling Syria. The area became the scene of Bedouin massacres of the Christian Arabs, and of struggles between Syrian irregulars and the Arab villages over tax collections and other issues. The French forces that were occasionally sent in to restore order were too small to be effective, and the area was reduced to anarchy and chaos. In addition to this inter-Arab strife, the Jewish settlements became the targets of raids by both Syrian irregulars and Bedouin, often at the instigation of the Syrian nationalists in Damascus.

On December 12, 1919, the settlement at Tel Hai came under heavy attack. In view of the lack of security in the region, most of the Jewish settlers withdrew by mid-January except for a small group under the leadership of Trumpeldor that decided to remain at Tel Hai and Kfar Giladi. Trumpeldor wrote to a provisional defense committee in Tel Aviv: "We lack armed men: not every one has a rifle. We need 1,000 cartridges per rifle and we haven't even got one hundred. We have no hand grenades and no machine guns and our food supplies are diminishing. In another week we will be starving."[27]

Ahdut Ha'avodah published an appeal to its members to go and help defend the endangered positions in Upper Galilee, but the response was inadequate. Jabotinsky took the position that unless the purpose of the proposed mobilization of volunteers was to make a political point—namely, that Jews had a right to the territory—and the volunteers were prepared to become martyrs to emphasize that point, it would be a senseless effort. Indeed, it would probably have proved pointless in any case. Since, in Jabotinsky's opinion, it was not within the power of the Yishuv at the time to establish order in the French zone of Upper Galilee, it would not be possible to defend the settlements successfully. He therefore urged that they be temporarily abandoned. Trumpeldor and his fellow settlers, however, refused to abandon the villages and decided to hold out at all costs. Since Trumpeldor was a seasoned soldier, he was surely well aware of the untenability of his position from a military perspective. He may have believed, however, that his determination to make a stand despite the risks would force the Yishuv to mobilize in his support.

The issue came before the Provisional Committee (the predecessor of the Vaad Leumi) on February 24, 1920. Jabotinsky, who was not a member of the Committee, was nonetheless invited to present his views. Underlying his stance on the question was his belief that neither the Zionist Commission nor the Provisional Committee was capable of organizing the resources necessary for the successful defense of the settlements. He appealed to the representatives of the Labor movement to recall their people from the threatened settlements. Jabotinsky argued that "a systematic defense of the northern settlements is under the present conditions impossible," and that defending the settlements "will therefore inevitably result in a tragedy, or, at best, in the defenders of the northern colonies being captured and abused by the Arabs." He pleaded that "Trumpeldor and his comrades must be recalled while it is not too late to do so."[28]

The Labor leaders—Berl Katznelson, Ben-Gurion, and Eliahu Golomb (1893–1945), among others—insisted that the settlements had to be held at all costs. Menahem Ussishkin also agreed with this position, even though the Jewish community could not get the settlements the help they needed to survive. The Provisional Committee, chaired by Ussishkin, therefore rejected Jabotinsky's arguments and decided overwhelmingly that defense of the settlements was needed as a matter of national honor. Within a few days, a handful of volunteers—forty-four in all, including about twenty Legion veterans who had come from the United States, but who were not all armed—arrived at Kfar Giladi. Neither the outspoken Labor leaders nor the Provisional Committee did anything further to provide the necessary levels of assistance to Tel Hai and Kfar Giladi. The Provisional Committee sent a study group of six to examine the situation. However, when it arrived at Ayelet Hashahar, some twenty kilometers from Tel Hai, on March 1, it was already too late. That same day, Trumpeldor and five others (including two women) were killed in an attack. The following day, the remaining settlers were evacuated to Ayelet Hashahar with the assistance of Khamil al-Asad, a friendly local sheikh.

Regardless of what motivated Trumpeldor and his colleagues to attempt to defend Tel Hai and Kfar Giladi, Trumpeldor and Tel Hai became highly valued symbols of national heroism, and the stuff of legend. Indeed, as it turned out, it was Jabotinsky who was to make the greatest use of these symbols in the years to come. The tragedy of Tel Hai also led the Zionist leaders to continue to press even harder for a more favorable border that would include, at a minimum, the Upper Galilee as far north as Metulla. While the final border demarcation was generally unfavorable for Palestine, the inclusion of the Metulla salient was finally agreed to by the Anglo-French boundary commission in February 1922, and formalized by both governments in March 1923. However, it remains a mystery as to whether Zionist pressure had any impact on the outcome of the negotiations.

The tragic results at Tel Hai clearly demonstrated the vulnerability of the Yishuv and the need to develop a substantial self-defense capability. The first steps in this direction had already been initiated at a conference of Zionist leaders in Palestine at the end of 1919. After protracted debate, a decision was reached to proceed with the organization of a self-defense corps. Although the Labor representatives strongly believed that such a body should be clandestine in nature, they eventually yielded to Jabotinsky's insistence that it must be an open and officially recognized organization within the Jewish communal infrastructure. Jabotinsky also wanted all the Arabs to know that the Jews were taking steps for their self-defense, hoping that such knowledge might have a deterrent effect on Arab aggressiveness. It was also decided that once the initial recruitment was completed, the British authorities would be approached with a request to legalize and arm the organization. The proposal was submitted to the Zionist Commission, which gave its stamp of approval to the idea.

At about the same time, the nucleus of such a defense force came into existence independently when some youngsters spontaneously formed a clandestine group called *Haganah* (Defense). The group turned to Jabotinsky to become its leader, a position he readily accepted. Haganah thus became the self-defense force of the Yishuv. Jabotinsky and Pinhas Rutenberg (1879–1942) subsequently approached the British authorities repeatedly with requests for legal status and arms. Ronald Storrs, the military governor of Jerusalem, turned down these requests with assurances that the authorities were fully aware of the danger of an outbreak of Arab violence and were taking every precaution to ensure public safety. The Haganah proceeded to obtain some weapons illegally from an Armenian arms smuggler.

With the approach of the Muslim holiday of *Nebi Musa*, which coincided with Easter and Passover, there were persistent rumors of an impending large-scale pogrom that would be directed against the Jews of Jerusalem. It was suspected that the incident was being staged at this time in anticipation of the San Remo Conference of the Allied powers that was to take place several weeks later. (On February 27, 1920, nonviolent demonstrations had taken place in Jerusalem, Jaffa, and Haifa; on March 8, another demonstration in Jerusalem turned violent and five Jews were injured before the police took effective action.) It was widely anticipated that the Balfour Declaration would come up for consideration as the Allies reached final decisions on the dismemberment of the Ottoman Empire. Some Arab leaders believed that if serious disturbances directed against the Jews were to take place, the conferees might think twice before giving international sanction to a Jewish homeland in Palestine in the face of obviously strong local Arab opposition.

The Haganah, which had attracted some 500 volunteers in the wake of the earlier Arab demonstrations, wanted to position itself for the defense of the Old City in Jerusalem by setting up strong points within the Jewish quarter, but they were thwarted in this by the Orthodox residents. The latter refused to allow the secular Jewish youth into their homes or synagogues, believing that their presence would of itself bring disaster upon them. Because of this the Haganah units could be deployed only outside the Old City walls, standing by to rush in should it become necessary. At the same time, Jewish members of the police force were unaccountably reassigned outside and away from the Jewish quarter of the Old City, leaving only Arab police on duty there. In the New City, however, Haganah patrols covered all the Jewish residential sections.

On April 4, as anticipated, the fervor of the Arab celebrants was whipped up by inflammatory speeches, and anti-Jewish rioting broke out. Notices appeared all over Jerusalem that read: "The Government is with us, Allenby is with us, kill the Jews; there is no punishment for killing Jews."[29] Large numbers of Arabs gathered at the Dome of the Rock mosque in the Old City to begin the traditional procession to the nearby hill that Muslims believe to be the burial site of Moses. As the procession began, an Arab mob suddenly rushed into the Jewish quarter. When the alarm was sounded, two companies of Haganah men were sent to enter the Old City, as planned, through the Damascus and Jaffa gates. However, when they arrived at the gates they found them closed and guarded by British troops who prevented anyone from entering or leaving the Old City.

The Jews of the Old City paid dearly for their refusal to be defended by the irreligious youth of the Haganah. The pogrom lasted two days and resulted in the death of five Jews and four Arabs, with 211 Jews and twenty-one Arabs wounded and two Jewish girls raped. Colonel L. R. Waters-Taylor, the chief of staff of the military administration, who had been collaborating with the local Arab extremists, sent for the mayor of Jerusalem, Musa Kazim Pasha, two days after the rioting. He said to him: "I gave you a fine opportunity; for five hours Jerusalem was without military protection; I had hoped you would avail yourself of the opportunity but you have failed."[30] In the New City, which was guarded by Haganah patrols, there was not a single casualty.

As soon as the pogrom ended, the British administration began reprisals against the Haganah for their defense of the Jews of Jerusalem. Jabotinsky and nineteen members of Haganah were arrested. The subsequent trial was a travesty of justice. The British military governor wanted to try Jabotinsky on the charge of having organized and armed a self-defense unit. However, he soon discovered that this was not illegal under either British military law or the regulations of the British military administration. Consequently, Jabotinsky was tried under the provisions of the Ottoman Penal Code. He was found guilty notwithstanding the lack of any evidence, and sentenced to fifteen years' imprisonment, the same sentence that was imposed on the two Arabs found guilty of rape, and to deportation from Palestine after completing his term of incarceration. Each of the remaining Haganah men received the sentence of three years at hard labor. Haj Amin al-Husseini, whose inflammatory articles in *Suriyah al-Janubiyah* contributed to setting off the rioting, was charged with inciting violence. Since he had violated his bail by running away to Trans-Jordan, where he went into hiding, he was tried in absentia and sentenced to ten years' imprisonment.

The report (which was never published) of the Military Commission of Inquiry sent to look into the disturbances concluded that the Zionist Commission was mainly responsible for the crisis. Accordingly, on April 20, General Bols recommended the abolition of the Zionist Commission. "My own authority and that of every Department in my Administration is claimed or impinged upon by the Zionist Commission and I am definitely of opinion that this state of affairs cannot continue without grave danger to the public peace and to the prejudice of my Administration." He argued that "it is manifestly impossible to please partisans who officially claim nothing more than a National Home but in reality will be satisfied with nothing less than a Jewish State and all that it politically implies."[31]

Once again, official Zionist rhetoric was turned against its authors, who were being characterized as duplicitous because they were saying one thing but obviously meant something rather different. It would be another twenty years before the Zionist leaders began to articulate what they had generally meant from the very beginning.

The sentencing of Jabotinsky and the Haganah men to long terms of imprisonment for trying to defend Jewish lives provoked cries of outrage and protests around the world. The British military administration, however, was impervious to all of this, and refused to budge. What was needed was an approach to the British government at the policy level that would insist on the replacement of the capricious military administration that was betraying British commitments under the Balfour Declaration. Making such an approach, however, was the prerogative of the Zionist Executive in London and the Zionist Commission in Jerusalem. Once again, Weizmann seemed constitutionally incapable of accepting the idea that British actions in Palestine were perfidious, and that they had no serious intention of honoring their wartime commitments to the Zionists. He consequently tried to play down the importance of the affair. He would not publicly acknowledge that the British military had in fact aided and abetted the pogrom and had interfered with the defense of the Jews of the Old City. In effect, he did nothing. While he was prepared to condemn the sentence given to Jabotinsky as equivalent to judicial murder, he also told the *Manchester Guardian* on April 26, 1920, "[T]echnically he is guilty, no doubt. . . . He organized the Jewish Defence Corps against an occurrence which the British assured us would never occur." Weizmann conceded that Jabotinsky was "guilty of the political offense," but condemned the fact that he was given the same sentence as the rapists. Instead of defending Jabotinsky and the Haganah, Weizmann threw himself at the feet of the government with his plea that it "was a blot on British justice that this man should remain a day longer in the prison of Acre. We respectfully pray the Prime Minister to set Jabotinsky and his colleagues free at once."[32]

The extraordinary timidity of Weizmann and his colleagues in both Britain and Palestine brought Jabotinsky to address a "Letter to the Jewish Community" in which he charged:

Weizmann has never understood the political position in the country, never realized the significance of previous events as precedent for the future; during those two years of continuous pogrom he had stifled the outbursts of protest until the impudence of our enemies grew and ripened and took deep roots, and we became *hefker* [ownerless property] in their eyes. During last Passover he saw for himself the results of his tactics—but even after the slaughter he did neither learn nor forget. And now he is continuing his blind policy that is bound to bring us ever greater damage.[33]

The Zionist leadership had effectively abandoned Jabotinsky and the Haganah. With the disbanding of the *Hashomer* (The Watchman) in May, the Yishuv was left without any organized defense capability. At this time, the Ahdut Ha'avodah stepped into the breach. In June 1920 it decided to assume responsibility for the defense of the Yishuv and the reorganization of the Haganah on a new populist model, although it was to take some time before anything resembling a defense force actually came into being. Immediate relief was to come only as a consequence of the decision of the San Remo Conference, on April 25, to assign the Mandate for Palestine to Britain, and the subsequent decision by the latter to replace the military government in Palestine with a civil administration.

The decision to restructure the administration in Palestine did not come about by mere coincidence. When General Money was replaced as chief administrator in the summer of 1919, the chief political officer at headquarters in Cairo, General Clayton, was removed as well. His replacement was Colonel Richard Meinertzhagen, one of the few British officers wholeheartedly committed to carrying out the policy of the Balfour Declaration. Meinertzhagen noted in his diary on June 2, 1920: "Zionism need not waste its thanks on British Officials out here. They have all worked against it, hoping to crush it at its birth. I was sent out by the Foreign office on this very account and found on my arrival that every man's hand was working against Zionism, some openly, others clandestinely."[34] His known support of the government's policy placed Meinertzhagen in an awkward position within Allenby's command and, as a consequence, his superiors routinely rejected many of his recommendations.

As a political officer, however, Meinertzhagen had a direct reporting channel to the Foreign Office, whereas his military superiors reported to the War Office. Outraged by British complicity in the Jerusalem riot, on April 14 Meinertzhagen undertook to communicate his views on the matter directly to Lord Curzon, who had replaced Balfour as foreign secretary, and who received his memorandum while at San Remo. He informed Curzon that he had received ample warning about the forthcoming riot and had advised both Allenby and Bols about it. Moreover, he had warned them that another official of the military administration, Waters-Taylor, had been surreptitiously encouraging Haj Amin al-Husseini and Aref al-Aref to stir up trouble. Neither Allenby nor Bols took any measures to prevent the outbreak. Meinertzhagen told Curzon: "The officers of the Administration are, almost without exception, anti-Zionist in their views. . . . I am convinced that if our British Administration were imbued with an understanding of and sympathy for Zionism which your Lordship has a right to expect, the risk of anti-Jewish riots might have been minimized, if not altogether avoided."[35]

Curzon and Lloyd George were sufficiently influenced by Meinertzhagen's memorandum to conclude that it was time to replace the military administration by a civil government under a high commissioner. The memorandum also ended Meinertzhagen's career on Allenby's staff.

NOTES

1. Alex Bein, *The Return to the Soil*, p. 180.
2. Jon Kimche, *The Unromantics*, p. 52.
3. Neil Caplan, *Palestine Jewry and the Arab Question, 1917–1925*, pp. 26–27.
4. Ibid., p. 29.
5. Kimche, *The Unromantics*, pp. 53–54.
6. Ibid., pp. 55–56.
7. John J. McTague, *British Policy in Palestine, 1917–1922*, p. 50.
8. Douglas V. Duff, *Sword for Hire*, pp. 156–157.
9. McTague, *British Policy in Palestine*, p. 52.
10. Ibid., pp. 72–73.
11. *Documents on British Foreign Policy, 1919–1939*, vol. IV, p. 345.
12. Joseph B. Schechtman, *Rebel and Statesman: The Early Years*, p. 295.

13. Caplan, *Palestine Jewry and the Arab Question*, p. 59.

14. Schechtman, *Rebel and Statesman*, pp. 295–296.

15. Chaim Weizmann, *Trial and Error*, p. 224.

16. Schechtman, *Rebel and Statesman*, p. 296.

17. John Marlowe, *The Seat of Pilate*, p. 66.

18. Ibid., pp. 70–71.

19. *Documents on British Foreign Policy, 1919–1939*, vol. IV, enclosure 2 in no. 209.

20. Ibid., enclosure in no. 231.

21. Elias Gilner, *War and Hope*, p. 331.

22. Horace B. Samuel, *Unholy Memories of the Holy Land*, p. 37.

23. C. R. Ashbee, *A Palestine Notebook*, p. 90.

24. *Documents on British Foreign Policy, 1919–1939*, vol. IV, p. 329.

25. Yehoshua Porath, *The Emergence of the Palestinian-Arab National Movement, 1918–1929*, p. 33.

26. John H. Patterson, *With the Judeans in the Palestine Campaign*, p. 264.

27. Gilner, *War and Hope*, p. 339.

28. Schechtman, *Rebel and Statesman*, pp. 314–315.

29. Richard Meinertzhagen, *Middle East Diary 1917–1956*, p. 82.

30. Ibid.

31. J.M.N. Jeffries, *Palestine: The Reality*, p. 359.

32. *Jewish Chronicle*, June 4, 1920.

33. Schechtman, *Rebel and Statesman*, p. 355.

34. Meinertzhagen, *Middle East Diary*, p. 89.

35. Marlowe, *The Seat of Pilate*, pp. 80–81.

2

The Jewish High Commissioner

At the beginning of 1920, in anticipation of Britain's acceptance of the Mandate for Palestine, the Foreign Office requested that Sir Herbert Samuel go to the country and report on its financial and administrative condition. Samuel arrived in Palestine at the end of January and remained there for some ten weeks. His final report from the country, which he submitted on April 2, just prior to the outbreak of anti-Jewish violence in Jerusalem, was quite optimistic and evidently not grounded in a realistic appraisal of what was taking place before his eyes.

Echoing the views of the Zionist leadership in London, Samuel suggested that the apparent hostility of the Arabs toward the Zionists was based on misperceptions that could be overcome. In his memorandum to Lord Curzon he suggested that the key to success in treading the delicate path between the competing interests of Arabs and Zionists would be for the latter to decelerate implementation of their goals: "On the supporters of Zionism lies the duty to allay apprehension by not being over-eager in the execution of their policy, and by offering to the Moslem and Christian inhabitants of Palestine opportunities of participating in their enterprises."[1]

Samuel repeatedly emphasized the importance of being solicitous of Arab sensibilities, and implicitly suggested that he himself was particularly sensitive to the problems that would have to be overcome for there to be a viable accommodation between the Arabs and the Jews. Nonetheless, at the same time that he was apparently promoting himself as a candidate to replace the military administrator in Palestine, he evidently harbored an objective reservation regarding the qualifications of the person who might be chosen to administer the country on behalf of the British government. He wrote to his son on February 22, "[I]t would be inadvisable for any Jew to be the first Governor."[2]

Samuel stopped at San Remo on his way home from his mission and, on April 24, met with Lloyd George. The prime minister discussed Meinertzhagen's letter with Samuel and informed him of his decision to replace the military administration in Palestine with a civilian government. He then offered Samuel the post of high commissioner for Palestine. Pleased by the offer and inclined to accept the appointment, Samuel nonetheless told the prime minister about his concern that placing a Jew in that sensitive position might make it more difficult to obtain Arab support and cooperation. He suggested that it might be best if he consulted with the Zionist leaders before accepting the appointment. The next day, after having spoken with Chaim Weizmann and Nahum Sokolow, he advised Lloyd George:

I am quite clear that if the Government decide to invite me to fill that post it is my duty to accept it. The objection which I mention to you, that measures which the majority of the population would accept from a non-Jew would be resented if they came from a Jew could, I believe, be overcome. In the long run their attitude would depend upon the reasonableness of the measures themselves and upon the manner in which they were represented.[3]

From the moment Samuel took up his new office, it was evident that he had assumed a role that placed him, an avowed Zionist sympathizer, in an obvious conflict of interest. He could not conceivably carry out the policy of the Balfour Declaration in the manner intended by its framers and at the same time satisfy the claims of the Arabs. To accommodate the demands of the latter, he would have to compromise the interests of the Zionists.

It is perhaps not surprising that Samuel was prepared to believe that he somehow could satisfy both sides; it is easy for one's ego to interfere with sound judgment. What is surprising is that Weizmann and Sokolow encouraged him in his self-delusion, a colossal misjudgment on their part. They evidently failed to understand that, as a Jew, his extreme need to appear evenhanded to the Arabs might have incalculable consequences for the Zionist cause. However, what is perhaps most intriguing is the question of why Lloyd George, who surely understood the implications of appointing a Jew to such a position, offered him the post in the first place.

Samuel had emerged as one of the bright stars of the Liberal Party in Britain. He had risen to cabinet rank as home secretary during the war and had served in that post with distinction. At the end of the war Samuel's reputation and standing were such that he seemed destined to become Lloyd George's rival and successor as leader of the Liberal Party. Thus, as one writer put it in discussing the appointment of Samuel as high commissioner, "[T]here was a stroke of genius about Lloyd George's move; it caught Herbert Samuel in his one vulnerable point, in his Jewishness, that double existence from which no Jew can free himself."[4] Samuel, who should have known better, could not resist the temptation of being the first Jewish ruler of Palestine since the first century. For Lloyd George, the appointment was ideal because it virtually guaranteed the elimination of Samuel as an effective political rival.

Were Samuel to pursue the course of rigorously carrying out the Balfour Declaration, which Lloyd George would agree was the obligation the government had undertaken, he would be seen by critics as having been partisan, favoring his own religious and ethnic community against the Arabs. This would have been a mortal blow to his reputation for fairness. On the other hand, should he attempt to be impartial and evenhanded, as he had been with regard to Jewish immigration into England during the war years, he would undoubtedly offend both the Jews and the Arabs, since he would satisfy the demands of neither. Because he was Jewish, it was evident that in order to placate the Arabs he would have to be accommodating to an extent that would surely antagonize the Jews. He therefore would find himself in a politically untenable position as he vainly tried to harmonize the interests of the two communities. As a result he would satisfy neither constituency in Palestine, and would appear weak and indecisive in carrying out the government's official policy, possibly raising questions about his competence. No matter what Samuel did in Palestine, Lloyd George would benefit from the standpoint of domestic British politics. As it turned out, Samuel's tenure as high commissioner effectively destroyed his chances for any high political position in Britain. Upon his return from Palestine, he found himself removed by his party from the arena of high politics and relegated to the honorific but politically insignificant position of chairman of the Royal Commission on the Coal Industry.

News of Samuel's pending appointment, which was to take effect in July 1920, immediately elicited a negative reaction from Allenby, who cabled Curzon on May 6:

I think that appointment of Jew as first Governor will be highly dangerous. The Mahometan population are already in a state of great excitement owing to news that Mr. Balfour's declaration is to be included in treaty of peace, the only restraining factor being assurance which has been given by Chief Administrator that Government of country would be a British Government. They will regard appointment of a Jew as first Governor, even if he is a British Jew, as handing the country over at once to a permanent Zionist Administration.

Allenby suggested that Samuel's appointment would probably trigger "outrages against Jews, murders, raids on Jewish villages, and raids into our territory from East if no wider movement."[5] He also anticipated objections from the Christian community about having a Jew placed over them.

Given the violence that had recently taken place in Jerusalem, it appears that Allenby's objections to the appointment of Samuel caused the foreign secretary to have second thoughts about the matter. On May 12 Curzon met with Samuel and told him of Allenby's views. He suggested to Samuel that it might be best if he were to delay taking up his post for a year or so, to allow the situation in the country to stabilize. Samuel, however, was encouraged by the Zionist leaders to take up his appointment without delay, and he decided to do so. He was full of enthusiasm for the task ahead. He wrote to his niece that same month:

For the time being, there will be no Jewish state; there will be restricted immigration; there will be cautious colonisation. In five years, the pace will probably accelerate, and will grow after that progressively in speed. In fifty years there may be a Jewish majority in the population. Then the government will be predominantly Jewish, and in the generation after that there may be what might properly be called a Jewish country with a Jewish state. It is that prospect which, rightly, evokes such a fine enthusiasm, and it is the hope of realizing that future which will make me ready to sacrifice much in the present.[6]

The announcement of Samuel's appointment was the cause of a good deal of rejoicing in Zionist circles. Perceived as having good Zionist credentials, he seemed a godsend, the ideal person to carry out the policy of the Balfour Declaration. However, the military administrator, General Bols gave what proved to be a more prescient assessment of the situation: "A leading Western European Jew, a Zionist, sums up the attitude of the Palestinian population with regard to Mr. Herbert Samuel as follows: 'For the first six months he will require a British bodyguard to protect him from the Moslems and Christians, after six months he will require a doubled British bodyguard to protect him from the Zionists.' "[7]

Samuel arrived in Palestine to take up his post on July 1, and within days demonstrated his intention of governing with evenhandedness toward both Arabs and Jews. One of his first acts was to declare an amnesty for all those who had been imprisoned in connection with the Nebi Musa riots in Jerusalem. In doing so, as might have been anticipated, he pleased the Arabs and offended many Jews, who resented the fact that he had effectively drawn a moral equivalence between the Arab perpetrators and the Jewish defenders.

The amnesty specifically excluded Haj Amin al-Husseini because he had violated his bail and fled across the Jordan to avoid arrest. Seven weeks later, however, while addressing a group of Arab notables in Amman, Samuel declared: "Let Haj Amin come to Jerusalem; he will not be molested; we have pardoned him."[8] Singled out for special treatment by the British authorities, Haj Amin returned to Jerusalem as an important and respected public figure in Arab eyes. Samuel thus initiated his term as high commissioner on a most inauspicious note for Zionism and the Yishuv.

From the beginning, with few exceptions, the senior staff assigned to Samuel were holdovers from the previous military administration that, for one reason or another, tended to be hostile to the Balfour Declaration and its incorporation in the Mandate. At the secondary staff level, especially in the police force and the intelligence department, Arabs filled most of the key non-British positions. The anti-Zionist structure of the administration was so patent that a number of Jewish officers resigned their positions out of frustration, explaining that there did not seem to be room for Jewish officials in the Jewish national home.

Samuel's general approach to governing Palestine, at least in theory, was to proceed gradually and with extreme caution in all matters of contention between Arabs and Jews. In this way he hoped to be able to get the two communities to develop mutual confidence in the possibility of constructive coexistence. While his expectations reflected great faith in the ability to solve most human problems through rational discourse, they were not well grounded in reality. By late November, as far as Berl Katznelson was concerned, Samuel's honeymoon period was at an end. Serious problems that would disturb the superficial calm, which characterized his initial period of tenure, were about to surface. As Katznelson put it, despite the "new era" supposedly brought about by the high commissioner, the Jews of Palestine were "still living in a country atop a volcano. True, it is in a quiet state at the moment, but the political intrigue around us will not sleep nor slumber."[9]

The problems of governance in Palestine were significantly exacerbated in February 1921 as a consequence of wide-ranging criticism in Britain over the inefficient administration of its mandates in the Middle East. Responsibility for carrying out the provisions of the mandates had been shared among the Foreign, War, and India Offices, engendering much duplication of effort and incurring unnecessary expenditures. To eliminate such deficiencies, a major reorganization of the bureaucracy took place that awarded unified control over the mandates to the Colonial Office, headed by Winston Churchill. While this made a good deal of sense from a British administrative perspective, it was to prove disastrous from a Zionist viewpoint. Nonetheless, the Zionist leadership in London was too unfamiliar with the administrative aspects of Britain's colonial system to understand the implications of the reorganization, and therefore made no attempt to prevent the change from taking place. Moreover, since the foreign secretary, Lord Curzon, was an opponent of Zionism from the first, and the new colonial secretary was an outspoken supporter of Zionism, the change seemed to be for the best.

Palestine thus came to be governed under the Crown Colony Code, which had been designed primarily for the control of the primitive and non-Westernized indigenous peoples of the tropics and subtropics. Even relatively backward India had been removed from the rule of a colonial regime as early as 1909. The British were later to admit that, with regard to the Jews, it "is not a suitable form of government for a numerous, self-reliant, progressive people, European for the most part in outlook and equipment, if not in race."[10] The British personnel who were brought to Palestine to serve in the colonial administration were of a special stamp. They were oriented by training and experience to deal with a particular kind of situation, one in which a small number of Englishmen lived in an essentially primitive territory that was to be administered and exploited for the benefit of Great Britain. The idea of a mandate to further the development of a country for its own sake was alien to them and remained a peculiar notion that they intuitively rejected. Moreover, it was far easier for these bureaucrats to deal with the Arabs than with the Jews, who were very European in appearance and demeanor. The unfortunate consequence of this approach to governing Palestine was a growing hostility between the colonial regime and the Yishuv.

Following the Nebi Musa riots in Jerusalem in April 1920, the mayor of the city, Musa Kazim al-Husseini, was dismissed from his post and was replaced by Ragheb Nashishibi. The Husseinis and Nashishibis were the two most prominent clans in Palestine and had long dominated local politics. In March 1921, Kamal al-Husseini, the mufti of Jerusalem, died. The high commissioner, in what was intended as a clear display of his sensitivity to the nuances of Arab interests, decided that it was important to appoint another member of the Husseini clan to the position in order to maintain the local political balance between them and the Nashishibis. The procedure for appointing a mufti, however, had long been specified in the Ottoman law, which was still operative in Mandatory Palestine. A Muslim electoral college was to recommend three competent and qualified candidates, one of whom would be selected for the position by the sheikh al-Islam, the spiritual head of the Muslims of the Ottoman Empire. Since the Ottoman regime was now defunct, the British high commissioner assumed the authority to make the appointment.

The Husseinis chose to promote the candidacy of Haj Amin, who less than a year earlier had received a pardon from the high commissioner for his role in inciting the riots in Jerusalem. Haj Amin had already been rejected as a candidate by the electoral college because he was not deemed qualified to serve as a Muslim religious leader and jurist (as a student at al-Azhar University in Cairo, he had failed his qualifying examination). Nonetheless, his name was added to the list of nominees at the insistence of some British officials. In the electoral college poll, Haj Amin (the only Husseini candidate) received only enough votes to rank fourth on the roster; that meant his candidacy would be discarded, since the college would recommend only the top three names, all of which were Nashishibis.

At this point Samuel intervened in the electoral process to ensure the outcome he desired. As noted by Norman Bentwich, legal secretary of the civil administration at the time, "[I]t is true that Amin was not among the first three elected candidates from whom, according to the Turkish regulation, the High Commissioner, as Governor, had to choose. Some manipulation was required to bring him into the list."[11] Samuel somehow induced Sheikh Husam ad-Din, the Nashishibi candidate with the most votes, to decline consideration, thereby bringing Haj Amin into the range of consideration. He was then awarded the position of mufti, which traditionally had life tenure. In his diary entry of June 27, 1921, Meinertzhagen wrote that Samuel had placed Haj Amin

in a position where he can do untold harm to Zionism and to the British; he hates both Jews and British. His appointment is sheer madness. I am particularly annoyed about this as before I left Palestine in 1920, I left a memorandum with Samuel warning him of appointing the man when it was obvious his predecessor was in failing health and also warning him that Storrs [Sir Ronald Storrs, governor of Jerusalem] would press for his appointment purely on the grounds of hostility to Zionism.[12]

In August 1920, the civil administration issued an Immigration Ordinance that officially opened Palestine to immigration for the first time since the war. All persons of independent means, as well as dependents of Palestinian residents, were permitted to enter the country. The ordinance specified a "labor quota" of 16,500 immigrants per year that was allocated to the Zionist Organization, which became responsible for the financial support of such immigrants for at least the first year after their arrival. Jewish immigration picked up at once, and between September 1920 and April 1921, nearly 10,000 Jews entered the country. The number of immigrants was less than that hoped for by the Zionists, but the Zionist Commission lacked the necessary resources to ensure a livelihood for the additional immigrants authorized under the ordinance. Nonetheless, the sudden influx of a large number of Jews into the country aroused concern among the leaders of the Arab community. From their perspective, the increase in the Jewish population would contribute to transforming their fears of a potential domination of the country by the Jews into a reality. That spring, portions of the notorious anti-Semitic tract *The Protocols of the Elders of Zion* began to appear in the Arab press, at the same time that the Arab public was being harangued by anti-Zionist agitators who were spurred to action by the mufti.

As long as King Faisal appeared to be in control of Syria, the Arab leaders in Palestine sought to bring the country under his regime. However, once the French dislodged Faisal from Damascus in the summer of 1920, the Arab leaders turned inward and began to seek recognition by Britain of their demand for Arab self-determination in Palestine. On December 13, 1920, with the assistance of the Muslim-Christian Association, the Third Palestine Arab Congress (the first two were meetings of the Syrian National Congress) convened in Haifa, marking the resurgence of Arab troublemaking in Palestine. Among the resolutions passed at the meeting was a call for British recognition of the Arab right to self-determination and the establishment of a national government responsible to a council elected by those Arabic-speaking persons who were resident in Palestine at the start of the war in 1914. The congress proclaimed its unequivocal rejection of the

Balfour Declaration, and demanded revocation of concessions already granted to the Jews in implementation of the provisions of the document.

Musa Kazim al-Husseini and Aref ad-Dajani were chosen to head the Executive Committee of the Palestine Arab Congress, and to carry on the struggle for Arab national aims. The Executive Committee undertook the first organized protest demonstration in Nablus in January 1921 and strengthened the existing anti-Jewish boycott in that city. In February the Executive Committee began to flood the League of Nations with documents challenging the legitimacy of the Balfour Declaration.

At the end of March 1921, the Executive Committee of the Palestine Arab Congress presented a petition to Churchill, during his visit to Jerusalem, that demanded a repudiation of the Balfour Declaration and a cessation of Jewish immigration. Churchill, however, would not make concessions under pressure, and told them flatly that Britain could not, and did not, wish to renege on its commitments to the Jews. As for their other demands, he stated: "Step by step we shall develop representative institutions, leading to full self-government, but our children's children will have passed away before that is completed."[13]

The Arab response to Churchill's rejection of their demands came a month later. On May 1, 1921, an outbreak of anti-Jewish violence took place in Jaffa that closely followed the pattern of the Nebi Musa riots of the previous year. The day coincided with the Orthodox Easter. The few Jewish policemen in the city were unaccountably reassigned to the boundary line between Jaffa and Tel Aviv. Although there were warnings of impending trouble issued by the Criminal Investigation Department in Jerusalem, the district commandant of police decided to go on a trip to Gaza, leaving his Arab assistant, Abdin Bey, in charge.

The authorities had granted permission to Ahdut Ha'avodah to hold a May Day parade in Tel Aviv but denied a similar permit to the radical leftist *Mifleget Poalim Sozialistit* (Socialist Workers Party), a small group affiliated with the Communist International. Undeterred, the latter group gathered at the Borochov Club in Manshieh, a mixed Arab-Jewish neighborhood in Jaffa. The police arrived at the clubhouse and ordered the crowd of some fifty people to disperse. The group reconstituted itself on the beach and, eluding the police, made its way to Tel Aviv, where it ran into the Ahdut Ha'avodah parade. A brief scuffle between the two groups took place but did not result in any serious injuries. The problem was strictly between the Jews and took place in Tel Aviv, the all-Jewish suburb of Jaffa.

Nonetheless, ostensibly because of alleged Jewish provocations against the Arabs, wholesale looting and violence directed against the Jews broke out in Manshieh and other sections of Jaffa. On the outskirts of the town, a well-known author, Yosef Hayyim Brenner, and five other Jews were found literally butchered to death. Eyewitnesses saw Hanna Effendi Bardcosh, an Arab police inspector, throw a bomb into Immigrants' House, where about 100 recent arrivals were being housed temporarily. There were thirty-seven dead and injured in that incident alone. The total casualties that day included twenty-seven Jews and three Arabs killed, and another 104 Jews and thirty-four Arabs wounded. The violence continued the following day with another thirteen Jews and ten Arabs killed, and twenty-six Jews and eleven Arabs wounded. Two days later there were another seven Jewish and five Arab casualties. Order began to be restored only after Samuel finally consented to declare martial law, and after a Major Montefiore, the British commandant of the Palestine Police Training School, replaced Abdin Bey.

The violence came to an end in Jaffa but, in large measure because of false claims made by the mufti's agents that the Jews were attacking Arabs, it spread to the nearby countryside. On May 5 and 6, Arab gangs attacked the Jewish settlements at Petah Tikva, Kfar Saba, Rehovot, and Hadera. Petah Tikva and Hadera suffered extensive damage. At Petah Tikva four Jews and at least twenty-eight Arabs were killed, and twelve Jews and at least fifteen Arabs were wounded. The settlement was saved from far greater losses by the fortunate intervention of an Indian army cavalry unit that happened to be in the vicinity when the attack took place. It was clear that the Zionist leadership in Palestine had failed to take the steps necessary to ensure the security of the Yishuv, a deficiency they would soon begin to correct.

Horace Samuel, a member of the British administration and in a position to know what the public could not, repeatedly implicated the government as bearing significant responsibility for the riots and their aftermath. He noted with some bitterness that the government "refrained from publishing the number of the Arabs who had been killed in the attack on Petach Tikvah, for fear presumably of unduly depressing and discouraging Arab susceptibilities." The bias of the police was evident. When Shakir Ali Kishek, one of the Bedouin chiefs who attacked Petah Tikva, was arrested, he "was immediately released on bail as a graceful gesture; while . . . the chief notable of the colony, one of the most respected Jewish colonists in the whole of Palestine, Abraham Shapiro, was arrested by order of the same officers, not on any charge, but administratively, and carted off to Jerusalem in a motor lorry." Since the authorities refused to make any serious investigation of what had precipitated the riots, the Zionist Commission undertook to do so on its own. It hired a British investigator "who, immediately after he had gotten on the track, was promptly ordered by the military authorities to leave the Jaffa district."[14]

Another commission of inquiry was formed under the chief justice of Palestine, Sir Thomas Haycraft, but it refused to investigate the role of the mufti in promoting the violence. It did agree that the Arabs committed the actual aggression, but the blame for the disturbances was once again placed primarily on the Jews, whose pursuit of Zionist aims and the British government's own commitments had outraged the Arab populace. Particularly egregious, in their view, was the continuing Jewish immigration into the country. The commission found that "the fundamental cause of the Jaffa riots and the subsequent acts of violence was a feeling among the Arabs of discontent with and hostility to the Jews due to political and economic causes and connected with Jewish immigration and with their conception of Zionist policy as derived from Jewish exponents."[15] The commission flatly rejected the charge that the Arab violence had been premeditated and organized.

In response to the report of the commission, Samuel conceived of a series of steps calculated to appease the Arabs, all at the expense of the Jews. These included the temporary suspension of all immigration (which went into effect on May 14) and the imposition of new restrictions when it was resumed. He also proposed the deportation of all Communist immigrants, although the Haycraft Commission (notwithstanding its preoccupation with the dangers of communism) made clear that it did not believe that the May Day demonstrations were the real cause of the bloody rioting. Finally, he recommended that a legislative assembly be convened to provide the Arabs with a suitable means of peaceful expression of their concerns. This last proposal was particularly repugnant to the Jews because it meant having formal minority status in a representative institution dominated by the Arabs. The proposal was correctly perceived as a clear threat to the viability of the Zionist development program, which could be impeded at will by the Arab majority. It also would have constituted a de facto repudiation of the Balfour Declaration. Interestingly, the proposal was rejected by Churchill not because it contradicted the government's commitments to the Jews, but because the colonial secretary was unwilling to risk being seen as making political concessions to the Arabs under duress.

Especially infuriating to the Jews was the fact that Samuel had effectively made further Jewish immigration into Palestine subject to an Arab veto. By temporarily suspending such immigration because of Arab violence, he sent an unmistakable message to the Arabs that they could manipulate the British administration into sabotaging the Zionist program simply by taking up arms and rioting. It seems clear that the Jaffa riots frightened Samuel, and he reacted by moving sharply away from his earlier support of the Zionist aims reflected in the Balfour Declaration. He was now prepared to impose a series of restrictive definitions on the declaration that he hoped would appease the Arabs sufficiently to allow the Jews in the country to live in peace. On May 27, two days after the Fourth Palestine Arab Congress met in Jerusalem and reaffirmed its unshakable opposition to British policy, Samuel proposed to Churchill that the government redefine the policies set forth by the Balfour Declaration in a more restrictive manner. He suggested that the declaration be interpreted to mean the following: "Jewish people scattered throughout the world but whose hearts always turn to Palestine should be enabled to found here a spiritual centre and that some of them within the limits fixed by numbers and the interest of present population should be allowed to come help by capital, labour, and intelligence to develop country to advantage of all its inhabitants."[16] In this formulation Samuel clearly revealed how far he had distanced himself from the Zionist mainstream. His proposed reinterpretation of the meaning of the Balfour Declaration was not only pro-Arab; it was unmistakably anti-Zionist.

With Churchill's blessing, Samuel announced the new British position in a speech to Jewish and Arab notables on June 3, 1921. In preparing his remarks he recognized that his originally proposed formulation, limiting the Balfour Declaration to the creation of a "spiritual centre," would be vehemently rejected by the Zionists, and he therefore reverted to speaking of a "home." Nonetheless, his intent was unmistakable. His statement merits citation at length.

I am distressed that the harmony between the creeds and races of Palestine, which I have desired most earnestly to promote, has not yet been attained. . . . Let me in the first instance refer to the unhappy misunderstanding that has existed with reference to the phrase in the Balfour Declaration "the establishment in Palestine of a National Home for the Jewish people." I hear it said in many quarters, that the Arab people will not agree to their country, their Holy Places, their lands being taken from them and given to strangers; that they will never agree to a Jewish Government being set up to rule the Moslem and Christian majority. . . . That is not the meaning of the Balfour Declaration. It may be that the translation of the English words into Arabic does not convey their real sense. They mean that the Jews, a people that are scattered throughout the world but whose hearts are always turned to Palestine, should be enabled to found there their home, and that some among them, within the limits that are fixed by the numbers and interests of the present population, should come to Palestine in order to help by their resources and efforts to develop the country, to the advantage of all the inhabitants. If any measures are needed to convince the Moslem and Christian population that these principles will be observed in practice and that their rights are really safe, such measures will be taken. For the British Government, the trustee under the Mandate for the happiness of the people of Palestine, would never impose upon them a policy which the people had reason to think was contrary to their religion, their political and their economic interests.[17]

In this statement Samuel reasserted the principle previously employed by the military administration for setting limits to Jewish immigration: the absorptive capacity of the country. As a practical matter, the Zionist Organization was in accord with the need to restrict immigration to the level that could reasonably be absorbed without putting too great a strain on the economy of the Yishuv. However, it was one thing for it to make the determination as to what constituted the limits of absorptive capacity; it was quite another matter for such limits to be decided by the British administration, perhaps in collusion with the Arabs. Leon Eder, acting chairman of the Zionist Commission, was furious. In a letter to the Zionist Executive, dated June 5, Eder expressed his outrage and recommended that the Vaad Leumi (the National Council) break off all relations with the Palestine government in protest, that all Jewish members of the Advisory Council resign, and that the Zionist Commission leave Palestine.

The leaders of the Yishuv were ultimately convinced not to take any of these steps despite the evident betrayal of their legitimate interests by the high commissioner. The sole exception among the Jewish leadership was Itzhak Ben-Zvi (a future president of Israel), who had already resigned his seat on the Advisory Council on May 11. The Vaad Leumi formally responded to Samuel's statement of policy, characterizing it in both form and content as "an indictment not of those who have committed crimes and organised disorder, but of those who have been victims of those crimes and that disorder. . . . The general impression made by the statement is that it is an endeavor to protect the Arabs from the 'Jewish Peril.' "[18] The deeply felt disappointment of the Yishuv with Samuel's performance was more clearly stated in the private memorandum that the Vaad Leumi sent to him on June 27. "We did not imagine," they wrote, "that a non-Jewish High Commissioner could have cast upon us blows such as those which we have taken from Your Excellency. We cannot imagine that such a High Commissioner could have found the strength, as Your Excellency has done, to influence the central Government to nullify the contents of the Mandate."[19]

Shortly afterward, Weizmann noted with some bitterness in a letter to Churchill that he drafted but never sent: "I can attach no meaning to these [Samuel's] words but this, that the Jewish National Home of the war-promise has now in peace-time been transformed into an Arab national home."[20] It had finally dawned on Weizmann that he had made a horrendous blunder in encouraging Samuel to accept the position of high commissioner. On August 10, 1921, Weizmann penned a letter in which he lamented Samuel's appointment: "The latest and most terrible disappointment is Herbert Samuel. . . . It is a terrible tragedy. . . . Whenever you think you have won a man, a real support . . . it proves at the end to be a mirage."[21]

Ten days after his speech, having concluded that there was still the possibility of some further disturbances by the Arabs, Samuel wrote to Churchill, "[A] serious attempt must be made to arrive at an understanding with the opponents of the Zionist policy, even at the cost of considerable sacrifices. The only alternative is a policy of coercion, which is wrong in principle and likely to prove unsuccessful in practice."[22] Since it was deemed necessary to placate the Arabs, the sacrifices alluded to by Samuel would have to be made by the Zionists.

It was evident that the high commissioner, with the approval of the British government, had formulated and put into effect a policy of equal obligation to both Jews and Arabs in place of the preferential treatment of Jews unquestionably intended by the Balfour Declaration. However, as observed by one writer in discussing the ultimate viability of Samuel's policy:

Such a Program, based upon recognition of equal obligations to Arabs and Jews, could have a satisfactory outcome only in the creation of a unitary, binational state, and that goal was entirely foreign to the desires of either community in Palestine. Every new attempt to reconcile the incompatible purposes of Arabs and Jews embittered their relations with one another and with Great Britain and made more difficult a clear decision in favor either of a Jewish autonomous home or of an Arab state.[23]

Samuel categorically refused to acknowledge that no matter how much he might force compromises upon the Zionists, the Arabs would remain unplacated. Nothing would satisfy them except a total British repudiation of the Balfour Declaration and everything it implied. Contrary to Samuel's intentions and wishes, every attempt he made to further appease the Arabs only strengthened their resolve to oppose the equal obligation policy that was the hallmark of his administration. This became fully evident in July 1921. Musa Kazim al-Husseini, who had been removed from his position as mayor of Jerusalem because of his role in the Nebi Musa riots of 1920, led an Arab delegation to England and Europe to mount a propaganda campaign against both the Balfour Declaration and the British Mandate. This campaign had some success in Britain, as the Arab cause in Palestine began to gain support from a number of conservatives opposed to the coalition government, anti-Semites, and a few people who were genuinely sympathetic to the Arab cause.

In August, the Crown lawyers drafted an order-in-council that provided for the administration in Palestine to consist of a British high commissioner, an official executive council, and a partially elected legislative council. The high commissioner retained an absolute power of veto, and no provision was made for a legislative override of his disapproval. Moreover, the legislative council was to be structured in a way which assured that the high commissioner could always command a majority of its members. The Arab delegation in London was permitted to review the draft document, and it informed the government that unless the Balfour Declaration were repudiated, immigration stopped, and full self-government promised, the Arabs would not enter into formal discussions of the proposed draft constitution.

It is of interest to note the confusion that reigned in British government circles about just what its policy was with regard to Zionist aims in Palestine. On November 7, John Shuckburgh of the Colonial Office wrote that Weizmann had recently told him of a conversation with the prime minister in which he asked for an explanation of what the British government meant by the phrase "Jewish National Home" in the Balfour Declaration.

The Prime Minister replied: "We meant a Jewish State," and I understand that Mr. Balfour, who was present on the occasion, corroborated the Prime Minister's statement. I do not know what may have been the original intention, but it was certainly the object of Sir Herbert Samuel and the Secretary of State to make it clear that a Jewish State was just what we did not mean. It is clearly useless for us to endeavor to lead Doctor Weizmann in one direction, and to reconcile him to a more limited view of the Balfour pledge, if he is told quite a different story by the head of the government.[24]

The increasingly pro-Arab orientation of the British government, not to speak of the high commissioner, aroused serious concern among the leaders of the Yishuv regarding the security of the Jews and Jewish settlements in the country. This concern was no doubt heightened by the blatantly pro-Arab letter sent by General Sir Walter Congreve in Cairo to the commandant of British forces in Palestine, a letter that undertook to explain the government's policy to the British garrison in the country. Congreve stated in part: "Whilst the Army officially is supposed to have no politics, it is recognized that there are certain problems such as those of Ireland and Palestine, in which the sympathies of the Army are on one side or the other. In the case of Palestine these sympathies are rather obviously with the Arabs."[25]

The Nebi Musa riots of April 1920 made the Yishuv acutely aware of its vulnerability to organized Arab militancy, a concern that was further heightened as a result of the virulently anti-Zionist stance that emerged from the Palestine Arab Congress held at Haifa in December. That same month, at its founding convention, the Histadrut (the general labor federation) took over from Ahdut Ha'avodah the responsibility for establishing and maintaining a clandestine defense force for the Yishuv. But the relative quiet that characterized the first few months of the new civil administration engendered complacency among the Histadrut leadership, and little of any significance was done to bring such a force into being. Ben-Zvi warned the Histadrut Council in the spring of 1921, in reaction to what he saw as a new but false sense of security: "Despite the apparent quiet in the country, we are well aware how complicated and dangerous the situation actually is. . . . If the danger is not as great as it was last year, nevertheless the balance of forces in the country and along the frontiers obliges us to be on guard constantly. We are not prepared."[26]

As a result of this complacency, when anti-Jewish violence broke out in Jaffa at the beginning of May 1921, there was no organized defense capability in place to deal with the threat to the Yishuv. Subsequently, Eliahu Golomb of the Histadrut took the lead in reestablishing the Haganah (defense force) and preparing for the defense of Jewish life and property, spurred on by a number of incidents of Arab violence against Jews in Jaffa during June and July. A first training course for Haganah officers took place in August. At the same time the Haganah began to smuggle small arms into the country for use by the new defense force.

The issue of the security of the Yishuv and the militancy of the Arabs dominated the proceedings of the Twelfth Zionist Congress, which met at Carlsbad (Karloy Vary), Czechoslovakia, in September 1921. Weizmann set the tone in his opening address:

Our policy in regard to the Arabs, as in regard to all our other problems, is clear and straightforward. We intend to abate no jot of the rights guaranteed to us by the Balfour Declaration, and recognition of that fact by the Arabs is an essential preliminary to the establishment of satisfactory relations between Jew and Arab. Their temporary refusal to recognize that fact compels us to give thought to the means by which we can best safeguard our Yishuv against aggression. Self-protection is an elementary duty.[27]

The congress spent a good deal of time deliberating how to convince the Arabs that the Zionist enterprise was no threat to them, and a number of resolutions were passed reaffirming the Zionist commitment to respect legitimate Arab rights in Palestine. However, there was also a growing exasperation on the part of the Yishuv with what many considered Samuel's betrayal of the Zionists, and with those who placed the burden of moral responsibility for improving Arab-Jewish relations on the Jews. In uncompromising and unadorned language, Berl Katznelson categorically rejected this sort of self-flagellation. He denied that the Jews bore a moral responsibility to appease the Arabs. As far as he was concerned, the moral burden fell squarely on the Arabs. "During the forty years of the New Yishuv," he declared, "Jews have yet to attack an Arab village and there has yet to occur a case where a Jew has attacked an Arab." As for Samuel's emasculation of the meaning of the Balfour Declaration, Katznelson was similarly outspoken. "We cannot concede our aspiration to become a majority in the country. . . . Our most crucial political activity must be: to renew our immigration; to strengthen our pioneering spirit; to reinforce *hagana*; and to fortify our positions in the country."[28]

As the third anniversary of the Balfour Declaration, November 2, 1921, drew near, the Haganah became aware of a strong possibility that there would be Arab disturbances in the country to protest the occasion. As a result, defense committees in the major Jewish centers were placed on alert, but the country remained generally peaceful except for Jerusalem. There, Arab shops were closed and crowds milled around, shouting anti-Jewish slogans. All the accounts by Jewish eyewitnesses noted that the police did not appear to be concerned about the demonstrators. However, after a gathering of Arab protesters in the Temple

Mount area, a meeting at which the governor of Jerusalem, Ronald Storrs, was present, a nearby Jewish house was attacked and two of its occupants killed. Another Jew was killed in the street while escorting a group of women and children to the safety of a police station. The mob then converged on the main street of the Jewish quarter and prepared to carry out a pogrom there. However, unknown to the Arabs, a contingent of armed Haganah men had infiltrated into the quarter the preceding day. When the few police who were there could not restrain the Arabs, the Haganah men opened fire and eventually dispersed the mob by throwing several hand grenades. Subsequently, order was restored throughout the city. The extent of the casualties suffered by the Arab rioters, including the sheikh who led the mob, was to contribute significantly to the relative quiet in the country for the next seven years.

The British authorities attributed the outbreak to hooligans and denied that it had been a premeditated and planned attack. Leaders of the Yishuv, however, openly condemned the authorities for their complicity in the affair, which was seen by some as a repetition of the Nebi Musa riots of the previous year, except that this had taken place under the administration of a Jewish high commissioner. David Ben-Gurion accused Samuel directly of responsibility for the outbreak because he had chosen to retain a number of openly anti-Zionist officials of the earlier military government, such as Storrs, in his administration. This, he suggested, helped convince the Arabs that the civil administration was with them as much as its military predecessor had been. Others blamed Samuel's blatant appeasement of Arab extremism as a contributing factor to the disturbances. The Vaad Leumi and other communal bodies called insistently for the removal of Storrs from his post.

However, the outrage of the Yishuv's leaders against Samuel's administration did not sit well with the Zionist leaders in London, who were fearful of antagonizing the British government. They called repeatedly for the Yishuv to exercise self-restraint, a plea that Ben-Gurion categorically rejected. He wrote in the Labor weekly *Kuntres*, on November 11: "This time the moderates and 'notables' among us will not be able to restrain themselves. Out of national sorrow and insult they call upon the successor of Pontius Pilate, the Governor of Jerusalem: Step down! . . . The very fact of Storrs' presence in Palestine is a danger to the life of the Yishuv."[29]

The new assertiveness of the Yishuv in taking concrete steps to defend itself, instead of merely pleading for the British to do something, brought a significant change in the attitude of the administration. The British clearly did not relish the idea of a Jewish military force emerging in the country, and therefore sought to reach an understanding with the Yishuv regarding the maintenance of its security. A tacit agreement was reached under which the British undertook to exercise greater control over Arab extremists, in return for which the Haganah would significantly reduce its public visibility. However, it was also understood that the Haganah would maintain its vigilance and would take action to defend the Yishuv if the authorities did not.

In December 1921, perhaps to assuage their feelings after the blow they received from the Haganah in November, Samuel took another step to convince the Arabs of his fidelity to their intrinsic interests. He established a Supreme Muslim Council that assumed control of the *wakf* (religious trusts) and the *shariah* (religious courts with full jurisdiction over matters of personal and family status). By so doing, Samuel unwittingly created another institution of extreme importance in the lives of the Palestinian Arabs, one that would soon be exploited to the detriment of the British administration. To the consternation of many, Haj Amin al-Husseini became the council's president in March 1922. Since the Supreme Muslim Council had the power to appoint the preachers in all of Palestine's mosques, the mufti used this power to build up a cadre of religious leaders who were personally loyal to him. As a result, the mufti was now indisputably the most powerful Arab leader in the country.

Samuel sought to deal with the intercommunal problems in the country through the implementation of a limited self-government charter that would clearly have favored the Arabs. But the Arab leaders simply refused to participate in the political process unless their demands for a repudiation of the Balfour Declaration were satisfied. Accordingly, Samuel went to London in May 1922, determined to press the Colonial Office for an official interpretation of the Balfour Declaration that would placate the Arabs sufficiently to allow implementation of the limited self-government charter. His recommendations were accepted, and the necessary policy document was prepared for Churchill's signature. The document was submitted to an Arab delegation on May 30 and, with a minor change insisted upon by the Arabs, was presented to the Zionist Executive on June 3 for their assurances regarding its acceptability. The Zionist leadership, led by Weizmann to believe that a rejection of the policy statement would seriously damage its relations with the British government, gave the requested assurances on June 19. However, they did not specifically endorse Samuel's concept of equal obligation that was incorporated in the document. The Arabs, on the other hand, evidently not overly concerned about how the British would react to their intransigence, rejected the formulation as not going far enough to meet their demands.

With the Zionists endorsing the effective emasculation of the original intent and meaning of the Balfour Declaration, the Arabs had achieved much of their purpose without conceding anything. The policy document, which became known as the Churchill White Paper, was published on July 1, 1922, along with the correspondence between the Colonial Office and the Arab and Zionist groups. It took note that "Phrases have been used such as that Palestine is to become 'as Jewish as England is English.' His Majesty's Government regard any such expectation as impracticable and have no such aim in view. Nor have they at any time contemplated . . . the disappearance or the subordination of the Arabic population, language or culture in Palestine." Then, using the same circumlocutions employed over the years by the Zionists to obscure their true intent, the White Paper drew attention to the fact that the terms of the Balfour Declaration

do not contemplate that Palestine as a whole should be converted into a Jewish National Home, but that such a Home should be founded *in Palestine.* . . . When it is asked what is meant by the development of a Jewish National Home in Palestine, it may be answered that it is not the imposition of a Jewish nationality upon the inhabitants of Palestine as a whole but the further development of the existing Jewish community, with the assistance of Jews in other parts of the world, in order that it may become a center in which the Jewish people as a whole may take, on grounds of religion and race, an interest and a pride.[30]

Samuel, the inspiration behind, and to some extent author of, the White Paper, had succeeded in scuttling the Balfour Declaration and Britain's commitment to a Jewish state in Palestine, not only for the moment but also for any time in the future. The fact that the Zionist leadership meekly went along with the policy is a tribute to the extent of Weizmann's influence on the movement. It had, in effect, repudiated Herzl's purpose in creating the Zionist Organization. In a sense, what they had agreed to was a reversion to the situation that existed under the Ottoman Empire, except that the autonomous development of the Jewish *millet* (religious community) would be guaranteed by the British government under international law. But since the Arabs refused to accept the policy of the White Paper, the Zionist politicians had outwitted themselves, acceding to significant concessions in return for nothing. The Yishuv would once again have to revert to the pursuit of its nationalist interests through subterfuge and circumvention of the restrictions of the Mandatory regime, since the latter implemented the self-defeating policy that the Zionist leadership had formally accepted.

On August 10, 1922, on the heels of the ratification of the Mandate for Palestine by the League of Nations, the Palestine Order-in-Council was enacted. In accordance with Article 4 of the Mandate, the Zionist Commission, which had been renamed the Palestine Zionist Executive earlier in the year, now became transformed into the Jewish Agency for Palestine. The Arabs were offered a similar opportunity to establish an Arab Agency to look after their interests, even though such was not contemplated by the Mandate. The Fifth Palestine Arab Congress, which met in Nablus on August 22, rejected the limited self-rule constitution and refused to participate in the political process that it established. It resolved to boycott the forthcoming elections to the legislative council. Notwithstanding this, Samuel proceeded to promulgate the order-in-council on September 1 and began preparations for the primary elections to the legislative council that were to be scheduled early the following year.

In October 1922, Lloyd George's coalition government was replaced by a Conservative regime under Andrew Bonar Law. Since their main source of support in England was the Conservative Party, the Arabs scurried back to London, hoping to get the new government to reverse its policy entirely. Their erstwhile supporters, however, were now content with the constraints imposed on the Balfour Declaration by the Churchill White Paper and Samuel's policy of appeasement. In January 1923, the new colonial secretary informed the Arab delegation that the government contemplated no further revisions to its Palestine policy.

The question of Jewish participation in the elections to the legislative council had by no means been settled. There was concern that if the Arabs chose to participate, the two Jewish members of the council would consistently be outvoted by the Arabs and British acting in concert. Moreover, participation would imply a readiness to abide by the decisions of the council. Was the Yishuv prepared to lend this sort of legitimacy to a body that by its very makeup would likely oppose Jewish interests in the development of the national homeland? The Vaad Leumi debated the issue a week before the elections in early 1923. Only Meir Dizengoff expressed categorical opposition to participation in a vote for an institution that was obviously inimical to Jewish interests. The other speakers gave a variety of rationalizations for participation that reduced to two considerations: a refusal to participate would align the Jews with the rejectionist position of Musa Kazim al-Husseini and the Arab extremists, and the dubious assumption that their participation would earn the gratitude of the British administration.

These discussions were followed by some heated negotiations with the Ahdut Ha'avodah and Hapoel Hatzair. The Labor parties demanded that there should be a prior British acceptance of two conditions before they would agree to the Yishuv's participation in the election. First, they wanted approval of the long-discussed Communities Ordinance that would give the Jewish community legal autonomy. Second, they demanded that control of immigration be placed in Jewish hands. After a long debate, the Vaad Leumi passed the following somewhat awkwardly composed resolution: "The Vaad Leumi regards as a prior condition to its participation in the elections the sanction of the Communities [Ordinance] and its autonomous rights before the convening of a Legislative Council; otherwise it is certain that there will not be the desired participation in the elections, the abstention of important sections is to be feared, and the necessary moral prestige for Jewish participation in the elections will be lacking."[31]

A delegation went to see the high commissioner on February 16, 1923, to present the Yishuv's demands. Samuel was rather surprised by the strong position taken by the Vaad Leumi. However, he soon succeeded in convincing them that the Yishuv's failure to participate in the election would strengthen the hand of those elements in Britain that were agitating for an abandonment of the burdens of the Mandate. Although he made no commitments with regard to the specific demands presented to him, the Vaad Leumi backed off and agreed to support the election.

The mufti and the Executive Committee of the Palestine Arab Congress actively boycotted the legislative elections that were called for the week of February 20. Haj Amin let it be known that any Muslim participating in the election would be denied burial in a Muslim cemetery. As a consequence of the multiple pressures brought to bear on the electorate, only 107 out of the available 663 Muslim, and 19 of the 59 Christian, electoral seats were filled. The Jews and Druzes, who participated fully, seated 79 and 8 electors, respectively. Given the virtual nonparticipation by the Arab electorate, the administration was forced to defer establishment of the legislative council. On May 29, Samuel suspended the clauses of the constitution that called for a legislative council and revived the advisory council with an unofficial appointed membership of eight Muslims, two Christians, and two Jews.

The Arabs, however, were not satisfied with having scuttled the limited self-rule constitution. They now applied pressure on the Arabs selected to serve on the advisory council, and on June 12, all the Muslim and Christian nominees refused to accept their appointments. As a result, the government was forced to give up the idea of reestablishing the advisory council. Samuel now understood the immense power that he had given the mufti, and he never again attempted to challenge Haj Amin's authority.

On October 11, Samuel announced new concessions, which were rejected by the Executive Committee of the Palestine Arab Congress. Indeed, it made little sense for them to do otherwise, since by their intransigence they had virtually crippled the Zionist program and had forced Britain to accelerate its movement toward incrementally meeting their uncompromising demands. On November 9, the Colonial Office determined that it had gone as far as it could to placate the Arabs, and advised Samuel to cease further negotiations with them. Henceforth he would govern the country with the help of an all-British advisory council, without the benefit of any popular participation.

In the meanwhile, in October 1922, Emir Abdullah, accompanied by his advisers, arrived in London to negotiate a final settlement of the status of Transjordan. The country was populated mostly by Bedouin, and it sorely needed skilled personnel, initiative, development, and most especially capital investment. Abdullah believed that these might be forthcoming from the Jews of Palestine if he could come to some agreement with the Zionists. During his London visit he met five times with Weizmann and some of the latter's associates. He tried to determine whether it would be possible to get Zionist support for his extension of the emirate to cover all of Palestine, in exchange for his guarantee of support for the implementation of the Balfour Declaration and the Jewish national home policy. The reports of these conversations indicate that the members of the Zionist Executive who participated in the meetings with him approved of Abdullah's proposal. The Zionist leaders stipulated, however, that the plan had to have the approval of Britain before they could agree to it. The British, for reasons of their own, which probably included the consideration that such an alliance could well result in Transjordan's becoming too self-sufficient, and therefore less compliant with British goals in the territory, would not agree. The initiative came to nothing.

Once reports of the secret Abdullah-Weizmann meetings leaked out, both leaders were subjected to a torrent of criticism from their respective constituencies. Palestinian Arab leaders were suspicious of the new Hashemite ruler of Transjordan, fearing he might be as ready to sell out their interests, to further his own, as his brother Faisal had been. On the

Zionist side, Weizmann outraged the leaders of the Yishuv by undertaking diplomacy of this sort without consulting them. Ben-Gurion
took sharp issue with Weizmann's actions at a meeting of the Vaad Leumi at the beginning of January 1923. "No one," he insisted, "has the
authority to conclude any agreement with Abdallah [sic]. Dr. Weizmann has already failed once with Faisal, and he must be careful not to
do the same this time."[32]

Nevertheless, the Zionist leaders were anxious to find a representative of the Arabs with whom they might be able to negotiate a practicable arrangement that would serve their mutual interests. Weizmann
initially thought that perhaps Abdullah might be such an Arab leader.
His reassessment of Abdullah a few weeks later indicated that he no
longer harbored any such illusions. In February 1923, Weizmann reported that it was "very doubtful whether the Emir carries any weight
in Palestine or even in Trans-Jordania itself, and whether his promises
and guarantees do represent an asset of any real value."[33] Indeed, notwithstanding the earlier Zionist acceptance of the detachment of
Trans-Jordan from Palestine, the Thirteenth Zionist Congress, held at
Carlsbad in August 1923, passed a resolution that effectively repudiated the earlier position: "Recognizing that eastern and western Palestine are in reality and de facto one unit historically, geographically, and
economically, the Congress expresses its expectation that the future of
Transjordan shall be determined in accordance with the legitimate demands of the Jewish people."[34]

Given the repeated blows that the Yishuv experienced as a result of
Samuel's equal obligations policy and the White Paper of 1922, one
would assume that it would be pleased to be rid of the Jewish high commissioner. It is therefore remarkable that when it came time for Samuel
to leave Palestine, there was a great deal of Jewish sentiment, both
popular and official, in favor of prolonging his stay in office. The Vaad
Leumi went so far as to circulate a memorandum on the subject
throughout the Zionist world, in an effort to get support for an extension of Samuel's term as high commissioner. This time, however, the
Zionist leadership, and most particularly Weizmann, had a rather different view of the desirability of retaining Samuel in his post. They were
relieved to see him go, despite the public praise they heaped on him.
They recognized that from a Zionist perspective, the appointment of a
Jewish high commissioner had been a tragic mistake. However, there
was sharp disagreement from the Vaad Leumi on this point. For reasons
of its own, even though it was disenchanted with many aspects of Samuel's governance, it clearly hoped that he would be followed by another

Jewish high commissioner, presumably one who might be more sensitive and responsive to the needs and interests of the Yishuv.

NOTES

1. *Documents on British Foreign Policy, 1919–1939,* vol. XIII, p. 241.
2. John J. McTague, *British Policy in Palestine, 1917–1922,* p. 106.
3. Lord Russell of Liverpool, *If I Forget Thee,* p. 62.
4. T. R. Feiwel, *No Ease in Zion,* p. 113.
5. *Documents on British Foreign Policy, 1919–1939,* vol. XIII, pp. 255–256.
6. Evyatar Friesel, "Herbert Samuel's Reassessment of Zionism in 1921," *Studies in Zionism,* Autumn 1984.
7. Doreen Ingrams, *Palestine Papers 1917–1922,* p. 107.
8. John Gunther, *Inside Asia,* p. 579.
9. Neil Caplan, *Palestine Jewry and the Arab Question, 1917–1925,* p. 74.
10. Palestine Royal Commission, *Report,* pp. 121–122.
11. Norman Bentwich, *My 77 Years,* p. 73.
12. Richard Meinertzhagen, *Middle East Diary 1917–1956,* p. 97.
13. *The Times,* April 2, 1921.
14. Horace B. Samuel, *Unholy Memories of the Holy Land,* pp. 72–75.
15. John Marlowe, *The Seat of Pilate,* p. 89.
16. McTague, *British Policy in Palestine,* p. 159.
17. *Zionist Review,* July 1921, p. 53.
18. Caplan, *Palestine Jewry and the Arab Question,* p. 90.
19. Neil Caplan, "The Yishuv, Sir Herbert Samuel, and the Arab Question in Palestine, 1921–25," in Elie Kedourie and Sylvia G. Haim, eds., *Zionism and Arabism in Palestine and Israel,* p. 18.
20. Complete text in Richard Crossman, *A Nation Reborn,* pp. 153–163. Citation is on pp. 155–156.
21. Chaim Weizmann, *The Letters and Papers of Chaim Weizmann,* series A, vol. X, p. 247.
22. Christopher Sykes, *Crossroads to Israel,* p. 163.
23. Paul L. Hanna, *British Policy in Palestine,* p. 108.
24. Ingrams, *Palestine Papers,* pp. 146–147.
25. Ibid., p. 158.
26. *Sefer Toldot haHaganah,* vol. II, pt. 3, pp. 1265–1266.
27. Zionist Organization, *Reports of the Executive to the XIIth Zionist Congress,* p. 44.
28. Caplan, *Palestine Jewry and the Arab Question,* p. 116.
29. Ibid., p.120.
30. Government of Palestine, *A Survey of Palestine,* vol. I, p. 88. Full text of Cmd. 1700 is included.
31. Caplan, *Palestine Jewry and the Arab Question,* p. 157.

32. Ibid., p. 174.

33. Neil Caplan, *Futile Diplomacy: Early Arab-Zionist Negotiation Attempts 1913–1931*, p. 53.

34. Aharon Cohen, *Israel and the Arab World*, p. 190.

3

Internal Developments During the Samuel Regime

The period of Herbert Samuel's tenure as high commissioner for Palestine (1920–1925) not only saw the groundwork laid for the effective repudiation of the Balfour Declaration by the British government. It also witnessed developments within the Yishuv and the Zionist Organization that would have long-term consequences for the Zionist enterprise.

In addition to the two major Labor parties, Ahdut Ha'avodah and Hapoel Hatzair, there were a number of religious and other parties that played a significant role in the political organization of the Yishuv. One of the more prominent of these was the *Mizrahi* (a contraction of *Mercaz Ruhani*, Spiritual Center), a world organization of religiously Orthodox Zionists founded in Vilnius, Lithuania, in 1902, by Rabbi Isaac Jacob Reines. The organization was brought into being largely as a reaction to the resolution passed at the Fifth Zionist Congress, in 1901, that called for the obligatory education of the Jewish masses in the spirit of nationalism. The religious Zionists understood this to mean the promotion of a secular outlook they feared would be destructive of traditional Judaism. The Mizrahi was intended to provide the alternative of a religiously oriented nationalist perspective. Mizrahi established a bureau in Palestine in 1912 but did not become active there until after World War I, when it began to organize branches throughout the country. The central executive of the world organization moved its headquarters to Jerusalem in 1920.

The Mizrahi spun off its own Zionist youth movement, *Tzirei Mizrahi* (Mizrahi Youth), which was founded in Poland in 1918. The Tzirei Mizrahi developed a concept of *Torah va'Avodah* (Torah and Labor), which became the organizing principle of the religious labor movement that soon arose in Palestine. Rejecting the effective monopoly wielded by the secular Labor parties over practical nation-building activity in Palestine, in the spring of 1922 *Hapoel HaMizrahi* (The Mizrahi Worker) was founded as a religious labor movement to "endeavor to build the country in accordance with the teachings of Tora and tradition through labor. Its aim is to put its members on a firm material and spiritual footing, to develop and strengthen religious sentiment among workers, and to make it possible for them to live as religious workers."[1]

The anti-Zionist counterpart of the Mizrahi was the *Agudat Israel* (Society of Israel), which was founded at Katowice, Poland, in 1912, to a large extent in reaction to a decision of the Tenth Zionist Congress (1911) to include cultural projects within the scope of the Zionist movement. It established a branch in Palestine that same year but did not become active there until 1919, under the leadership of Rabbi Moshe Blau. The Agudah was fundamentally opposed to the concept of a Jewish national home or a Jewish state that was not founded on Jewish law and tradition. It was also opposed to the Zionist call for the return to Zion, which the Agudah maintained could not be separated from the messianic redemption—and the latter clearly was not yet at hand or anywhere in sight. At the same time it could not ignore the reality that for many Jews in Europe, resettlement in Palestine provided an alternative to a life of persecution and anguish. Accordingly, the Agudah established its own institutions for assisting the settlement of its adherents in Palestine. However, it sought to achieve complete social and political separation of Orthodox Jews from the Zionist Yishuv.

The majority of the other political parties that emerged after the war tended to fall in a broad center group between the secular left and the religious right. The fundamental differences between these various parties, already reflected in the difficulties encountered in organizing the Yishuv into a Jewish communal political force before the war, made communal cohesion equally tenuous afterward. Among the most divisive of the issues confronting the Yishuv were those that touched on religion and religious values. One of the most intractable of these issues that repeatedly threatened the dissolution of the community was that of female suffrage.

The Yishuv became caught up in the question of extending electoral suffrage to women that was being debated throughout the Western world after World War I. This, perhaps more than any other single issue, exemplified the fundamental differences between the Old Yishuv and the New. There had never before been a question of female suffrage throughout the long history of traditional Jewish communal life. In that social framework women played a crucial role, but it was limited exclusively to the context of the family. Women, with a few notable exceptions, had no active public role that would effectively remove them from the confines of the home. Furthermore, the Old Yishuv was seriously troubled by what they saw as the destruction of morals by the New Yishuv, particularly the immigrants of the Second Aliyah (emigration), who appeared to them as sexually promiscuous. The suffrage issue was seen as another manifestation of this uprooting of traditional values. The secular Zionists, by contrast, were imbued with the modern Western ideals of democracy, social justice, and equality of the sexes, and quickly became ardent advocates of female suffrage.

It is of interest to note that the strong opposition of the Orthodox community to female suffrage was not engendered in the first instance by the rabbis. The initial impetus came from traditionalist family heads who saw the implications of suffrage as highly threatening to their way of life. They began to pressure their rabbinic leaders to do something to prevent the erosion of traditional Jewish religious and family life. Y. G. Horowitz, rabbi of the Mea Shearim district of Jerusalem, recorded this pressure in September 1919. Although he at first hesitated to take any steps against the extension of the suffrage to his small community, perhaps more than a thousand disturbed and angry people came to his house, demanding to know whether he would sanction participation in elections along with women. He noted, "I saw that the feelings of the congregation were opposed to it."[2]

The suffrage issue became serious and highly divisive because it was widely believed that the establishment of autonomous political institutions by the Yishuv would be followed shortly by the establishment of the Jewish national home. Consequently it was considered essential that the issue of public morality be addressed immediately. The rabbis originally hesitated to leap into the fray because, from the standpoint of Jewish law, it was not absolutely clear that female suffrage violated any halakhic precept. Rabbinic authorities' strongly differing views on the matter threatened to seriously divide the Ashkenazi Orthodox community into three camps. The conservative Orthodox (often mistakenly characterized as ultra-Orthodox) denied the permissibility of extend-

ing the franchise to women, whether actively or passively, that is, either
to be eligible to vote or to be elected to office. A centrist group was prepared to allow women to vote but not to be elected. Finally, the liberal
Orthodox group was prepared to grant both active and passive electoral
rights to women.

The Agudah represented the conservative position: "According to
the Law of the Torah, women have no right of suffrage in the community"; "it is forbidden to elect women to govern the community its institutions"; and "it is forbidden to participate in an election based on
the principle of granting the franchise to women."[3] The Mizrahi originally maintained the centrist position for some time but finally adopted
the more liberal approach. This permitted the majority of Orthodox
Zionist Jews in Palestine to participate in the electoral process.

The older Sephardi community, effectively embracing all non-
Ashkenazi Jews, had been larger than the Ashkenazi community until
1870. The Ashkenazi community had refused to unite with the Sephardim because of traditional differences in Jewish religious practices and
perspectives, as well as for practical reasons involving the issue of extra-
territoriality with respect to the jurisdiction of the Ottoman regime.
When the Ashkenzim became the majority, the Sephardim similarly refused to join them, not only because of the differences in religious practice and tradition, but also because the Sephardim had enjoyed a long
history of formal communal recognition by the ruling Ottoman authorities. This situation had not changed very much with the arrival of the
British, although some accommodations between the two communities were made from time to time. For example, in the first general election for a council of the Jerusalem Jewish community, they acted in
concert and elected a slate of mixed Ashkenazi and Sephardi candidates
in proportion to the communities' sizes. As a rule, however, there was
little connection or even communication between the two religious
communities.

To complicate matters further, as the Sephardi community grew in
numbers, it split several times along subcommunal lines because of differences in traditional religious and customary practices among its constituent groups. Thus, in Jerusalem, which was the only one of the holy
cities of Palestine to have sustained growth in population from internal
migration, the Moroccan communal congregation became autonomous as early as 1845. The Persian, Sudanese, and Yemenite communities became autonomous in 1907; the Bukharan, in 1912; and the
Georgian, Kurdish, and Mesopotamian communities, in 1929. The existence of these as well as other small religious communal congrega-

tions, all extremely protective of their religious autonomy, helped to impede the emergence of a common structure for the general religious community.

A serious but fruitless attempt to unite the broad Ashkenazi and Sephardi communities was made in 1891 and again in 1895. In the latter instance, a short-lived joint committee of two members from each community was constituted to deal with "matters concerning the whole Jewish community residing in Jerusalem and its relations with the government . . . without any distinction between Sephardi and Ashkenazi."[4] Although the communities did cooperate in times of crisis, such as during the cholera epidemic of 1902, the joint Central Committee for Conserving Health in the City disbanded as soon as the crisis was over. A number of subsequent attempts at unification were made between 1910 and 1915, all to no avail. The situation in the smaller holy cities of Hebron, Safed, and Tiberias was comparable with that in Jerusalem.

The disparate components of the Yishuv were compelled to acknowledge a critical need for a united Jewish front by the Arab attacks in the Galilee during March 1920, which resulted in the death of Trumpeldor and his companions. The need was further reinforced by the Nebi Musa riots in Jerusalem that took place two weeks before the election of the *Asefat haNivharim* (Elected Assembly). At the time, even the conservative Orthodox agreed to participate along with the secularists, albeit in separate special elections in which women were not permitted to vote. More than 70 percent of the 28,765 registered voters took part in the election that was finally held on April 19, 1920. As a consequence of the intracommunal divisions among the religious components of the Yishuv, Labor emerged from the election as the dominant bloc. It is worth noting that in this election, for the first and last time, the Orthodox parties, including both Ashkenazi and Sephardi groups and factions, actually elected a greater number of representatives than the Labor bloc. They could have determined the future course of the Jewish homeland had they been able to act in unison or even in coordination as a bloc. However, narrow partisan interests prevented any such development.

The Elected Assembly was scheduled to convene on May 26. But for reasons that were never clearly articulated, the British military administration prohibited the meeting. The civil administration of Herbert Samuel, which took office on July 1, finally authorized the inaugural session to take place on October 7. However, on September 26, at virtually the last minute, Eliezer Ben-Yehuda, editor of *Doar haYom*, attempted to block the convening of the assembly on the grounds that

the Labor bloc of parties had succeeded in capturing control of an un-
justifiably large plurality of the delegates. He suggested that the election results should be voided, and that delegate committees from the
local communities meet and elect a central representative body. Although this attempt to forestall Labor dominance of the Elected Assembly received some initial support from the independent farmers, it
proved ineffective. The assembly convened as scheduled and asserted
that it "had laid the foundation of the self-government of the Jewish
people in Palestine." Moreover, it proclaimed itself to be the "supreme
organ in conducting the communal and national affairs of the Jewish
people in Palestine and its sole representative internally and externally."[5] It then elected a thirty-six-member *Vaad Leumi* (National
Council) to act on behalf of the Elected Assembly between sessions and
to implement its decisions regarding the conduct of the public affairs of
the Yishuv.

One of the first tasks of the Vaad Leumi was to draft an internal constitution for the Yishuv ("Regulations for the Jewish Community")
that could be presented to the British government for ratification. It
would take seven years to get government approval of the communal
constitution. The major problem was that the Colonial Office did not
know how to cope with what was being proposed. What the Jews of
Palestine were asking for was something unprecedented in British
colonial experience. The concepts of self-government and home rule
were understood as applying to the entire people of a territory. In Palestine, however, they were being asked to grant self-rule to a segment
of the population that was diffused throughout the entire territory
and that, with the exceptions of the all-Jewish settlements and municipal suburbs, was a minority everywhere. Furthermore, the Jews of
Palestine themselves were not universally supportive of the proposed
constitution.

The Vaad Leumi soon found that it could not function effectively
without resources and that it was imperative to find sources of income
to cover its operating budget. Accordingly, the Vaad Leumi wrote to
the high commissioner on February 5, 1921, requesting that it be
authorized to impose taxes on the local Jewish communities within the
limits of the budget approved by the Elected Assembly. The high commissioner rejected this proposal on the recommendation of Norman
Bentwich, the legal secretary of the civil administration. He urged that
"the National Council not be permitted to impose special taxes on the
local Communities, but that it should be supported by voluntary con-
tributions from the Committees of the local Communities and other

Jewish institutions that possessed public representation."[6] As a result, the ambitious plans of the Vaad Leumi were stymied from the outset.

The next session of the Elected Assembly had been scheduled for May 1921, but it was delayed for about a year because of the rioting in Jaffa that month, the Zionist Congress at Carlsbad in September, and further rioting in Jerusalem that November. By early 1922, the resurgence of parochial issues once again threatened the cohesion of the Yishuv. The Ashkenazi conservative Orthodox leaders met on February 6 and passed a resolution that called for no further participation in the assembly unless the female suffrage provisions of the electoral regulations were eliminated. The resolution they presented to the Vaad Leumi on February 8 claimed that the assembly was unrepresentative of the Yishuv. This was because Orthodox Jews constituted the majority in the country but nonetheless were not adequately represented in the Elected Assembly as a consequence of the arbitrary imposition of female suffrage on the electoral process, a provision that was fully exploited by the secular parties. Accordingly, it asserted, "[T]he Elected Assembly has no right or power whatever to enact statutes or to institute regulations governing the affairs of the Hebrew Yishuv in Eretz Israel, such as the organization of the congregations, the levying of taxes, education, and so forth."[7]

A few days later, the Sephardi delegates, joined by the representatives of the independent farmers, objected to the progressive taxation system for the Yishuv proposed by Arthur Ruppin and threatened to secede from the Elected Assembly unless its next session, rescheduled for February 21, were postponed. The Sephardim also demanded that their delegates be enabled to appoint one of their number to become a member of the governing presidium of the Vaad Leumi.

The Sephardi demands were satisfied quite easily. However, an impasse developed between the presidium of the Vaad Leumi and the general Orthodox community over the female suffrage issue. As a consequence, the second session of the First Elected Assembly convened on March 6, 1922, with many Orthodox delegates refusing to attend. The assembly adopted the draft of the constitution prepared by the Vaad Leumi and immediately ran into new problems with the Orthodox community. The Agudah, which would not participate in the Elected Assembly, was certainly not going to permit itself to be bound by a constitution approved by that body. Accordingly it wrote to the high commissioner, expressing its wish not to be subjected in any manner to the authority of the Vaad Leumi. The Agudah gave as grounds for rejecting the draft constitution its opinion that the document deposed God and

His Torah from sovereignty over the Jewish nation (there was no reference to either in the document), and that it sought to attribute such sovereignty to a secular regime.

Norman Bentwich, acting on behalf of the high commissioner, conducted extensive negotiations with the leaders of the Agudah in an effort to get them to agree to the concept of a single unified Jewish community. In a letter of May 6, 1922, Bentwich outlined a number of proposals intended to deal with their concerns. First, any minority within the community that numbered at least twenty persons, and represented at least 10 percent of the members of any congregation within the general Jewish community, would be assured of the freedom to conduct its religious and cultural affairs autonomously. Second, each autonomous subgroup would receive an allocation from the community according to its numbers, to enable it to conduct its affairs independently. Third, a joint board would be established, made up of representatives of the majority and minority factions of the congregation, to deal with matters of *shehitah* (ritual slaughter), *mikvaot* (ritual baths), and burial. Fourth, the congregation's funds would be divided in two; one part would be dedicated to secular affairs and the other to religious matters. Of the latter, each minority group would receive a proportionate share. Fifth, an acknowledged minority group would have its own official religious leadership that would be fully authorized to conduct marriages and divorces. Sixth and last, in the event of a matter of contention between members of the majority and minority factions of the congregation, the issue would be adjudicated before the congregational court with the participation of a jurist drawn from the minority.

Notwithstanding these assurances by the high commissioner that their religious interests would be protected, the Agudah remained dissatisfied and proceeded to make an international issue of the matter by turning directly to the Permanent Mandates Commission of the League of Nations for relief. The Agudah claimed that their "freedom of conscience," guaranteed by Article 2 of the Mandate, was being violated by the proposed constitution, which, they asserted, contained "clauses that are against Jewish morals and religion, such as giving women active and passive rights of election." They also argued that "Agudath-Israel regards the integral observance of the Jewish law as the first duty of universal Judaism and is therefore opposed to the Zionist programme, which is based solely on a nationalist conception of the Jewish community, religion being regarded as a private and individual concern."[8] (It should be noted that much of the turmoil in Israel's religious community at the end of the twentieth century hinges on this very identification by the Orthodox of religion with nationality.)

The Agudah's appeal was considered at no fewer than four separate sessions of the Permanent Mandates Commission. The resulting pressure on the British government compelled Bentwich, who was now the attorney general of Palestine, to write again to the leaders of the conservative Orthodox community of Jerusalem. On September 10, 1922, he assured them once more that "no attempt is made under the proposed statute to the Jewish community to force all Jews to participate in the community. Your congregation, if it does not desire to enter the general community, will be at liberty to stand outside, and will enjoy its complete religious and cultural independence."[9]

The Mizrahi attempted to intervene with the other Orthodox groups to get them to participate in the third session of the Elected Assembly, scheduled for March of the following year. Again, the session was delayed repeatedly because of the protracted negotiations with the religious parties over their conditions for participation. In October 1923, the Mizrahi proposed an all-male national referendum of the Jews of Palestine on the issue of female suffrage as a vehicle for achieving a national consensus on the issue. The majority of the Vaad Leumi, however, sustained the view of the Labor bloc that because women had been elected to the First Assembly, nothing might be done to eliminate rights already granted. In February 1924, the Vaad Leumi made its proposed election regulations public, regulations that granted women full equality. When this happened, the Mizrahi felt it had no choice but to join the conservative Orthodox of the Agudah in boycotting the forthcoming session of the Elected Assembly. To avoid this, a rift that would have divided the Yishuv in half along religious and secular lines, the Vaad Leumi again postponed the assembly session. Negotiations to resolve the crisis continued for another year, without result.

The growing rift between the conservative Orthodox and the Zionists, with the Mizrahi and other moderate and liberal Orthodox groups caught in the middle, was seriously exacerbated by the activities of one of the most effective spokesmen for the Agudah, Jacob de Haan. De Haan was a brilliant though unstable personality who, originating from an Orthodox family, successively toyed with anarchism, socialism, and Christianity (he married a non-Jewish physician in 1907), and finally reverted to strict Orthodoxy shortly before World War I. He was also a writer whose first two semiautobiographical novels, published in 1904 and 1906, suggested homosexual tendencies that led to his dismissal from a teaching post and expulsion from the Dutch Socialist Party. He subsequently became a Zionist, joined the Mizrahi, and, in 1918, abandoned his family in Europe and settled in Palestine. There he became a foreign correspondent of the Amsterdam *Algemeen Handelsblad* and, in 1923, of the London *Daily Express*.

Having become disillusioned with both the secular and the religious leaders of the Zionist Yishuv, de Haan became a member of the Agudah and spokesman for the Ashkenazi Council of Jerusalem, headed by Rabbi Joseph Hayyim Sonnenfeld. He then began to circulate anti-Zionist articles and reports to the overseas press, and pro-Arab memoranda to the Permanent Mandates Commission and the British government. He sought to build a front consisting of all elements of the Old Yishuv to combat the New Yishuv, which he characterized to the foreign press as "Bolsheviks." De Haan's anti-Zionist propaganda activities raised the intracommunal hostility to a feverish level, bringing serious warnings from the Zionist camp that his activities were harming the Yishuv and that he had best cease and desist.

De Haan brought the anger of the Zionists to its apex when, in January 1924, he managed to arrange a meeting in Amman for Rabbi Sonnenfeld with King Hussein of the Hejaz and his sons, King Faisal of Iraq and Emir Abdullah of Transjordan. This was part of de Haan's ongoing effort to reach an accommodation between the Arab national leaders and the anti-Zionist Orthodox community. This brought charges of treason from the Jewish press and threats from Zionist circles. Jewish students boycotted his lectures at the government school of law. At the beginning of June 1924, he published a collection of poems that revealed his deep personal torment, again indicating his homosexual tendencies, something that caused consternation and extreme embarrassment to the leadership of the conservative Agudat Israel. He even considered returning to his non-Jewish wife and family in Holland. He had, in the view of many, gone far past the point of no return in his anti-Zionist activities. Joseph Hecht, the effective leader of the Haganah, issued instructions to eliminate him. On June 30, after leaving evening prayer services at a synagogue near the Shaarei Tzedek Hospital in Jerusalem, de Haan was assassinated by two members of the Haganah, acting on the orders of the commander of the Jerusalem branch, Zechariah Urieli.

This first political assassination of a Jew by coreligionists in modern times was generally greeted in Zionist circles with elation, reflecting the state of tension in the Yishuv at that time. Moshe Beilinson, however, publicly decried the act. He remonstrated that even though de Haan certainly was a traitor to his people, the shedding of blood, even guilty blood, could have serious moral consequences. "We are strong enough," he argued, "to allow our enemics to live . . . but we are not strong enough to undertake methods of struggle that will bring in their wake moral destruction within the movement."[10]

For the Agudah, the assassination simultaneously constituted a welcome relief, given the potential embarrassment to it from de Haan's alleged homosexuality, as well as a tremendous loss, since he was conservative Orthodoxy's most effective instrument in the struggle against the Zionists. De Haan's murder was mourned bitterly by the Agudah as well as by the Arab leadership that had benefited from his pro-Arab propaganda. Indeed, none other than Musa Kazim al-Husseini offered a eulogy that was published in the Agudah's *Kol Israel*. It asserted: "The murder of de Haan has had a shocking impact on all Palestinian Arabs, especially because he was well known for his singular outlook and his program that was to have brought about an agreement with the leaders of the Arab movement that would have guaranteed to orthodox Jews the rights denied them by the Zionists."[11]

The third and final session of the First Elected Assembly finally convened on June 15, 1925, without the participation of Mizrahi and the other Orthodox parties, although Mizrahi had agreed to send some representatives to present its proposal for a national referendum on the suffrage issue. However, before the proposal could be considered, a majority of the Elected Assembly succeeded in getting consideration of the proposal removed from the agenda. The following day, the Mizrahi, the other Orthodox parties, and some of the Yemenite and Sephardi groups convened separately; declared themselves the legal Elected Assembly; and attempted to obtain recognition as such from the Zionist Organization. However, the Palestine Zionist Executive effectively quashed this effort.

This incident was followed by a new round of negotiations with the Mizrahi that, at a meeting of the Vaad Leumi on October 14, succeeded in overcoming Labor's opposition to its proposal by a few votes. It was agreed to hold a referendum on female suffrage, with women voting. When this was announced, it created an outcry in both Labor and women's rights groups, which threatened to boycott the referendum. The new impasse was effectively resolved by the conservative Orthodox when a group of their prominent rabbis declared their utter opposition to the referendum and prohibited their followers from participating in it. This extreme position was rejected by the Mizrahi, which subsequently agreed to participate in the elections without preconditions, implicitly accepting the full participation of women in the political process.

Because of difficulties encountered in accommodating the religious concerns of the several Orthodox segments of the community in the establishment of representative Yishuvwide institutions, there was renewed interest in identifying a central Jewish religious authority to deal with matters of personal and family status. This would make the organization of the Yishuv compatible with the other religious denominations in the country.

Under Ottoman rule, the chief rabbis of the Sephardi community were formally acknowledged as heads of the community. However, there was never a central religious authority that was recognized as such by the diverse elements within the traditionalist segment of the Jewish population. In 1918, the Zionist Commission, under the chairmanship of Chaim Weizmann, attempted without success to create such a central authority. After the British civil administration took over three years later, the high commissioner appointed a committee under Norman Bentwich to study the problem and make recommendations for the establishment of a central religious authority for the Jews of Palestine. The committee recommended the formation of a Rabbinical Assembly that would in turn establish a Rabbinical Council as the highest Jewish religious body in Palestine.

The Rabbinical Assembly, consisting of sixty-eight rabbis and thirty-four laymen representing the local communities, convened in Jerusalem on February 23, 1921. The Ashkenazi conservative Orthodox of Jerusalem boycotted the conclave on ostensibly halakhic grounds. At issue was the fact that the Rabbinical Assembly had intended to transform the Rabbinical Council into a court of appeal for the various rabbinical courts in the country. The conservatives argued that there was no provision in Jewish law for an appellate court system that could override the rulings of jurists who had original jurisdiction. To demonstrate their concern about what they saw as a fundamental infringement of Jewish law and tradition, the conservative orthodox rabbis declared the day on which the Rabbinical Assembly met to be a day of fasting, and subsequently refused to have anything to do with the institution.

To avoid the inevitable conflicts over differences in the traditional customs and practices of the Ashkenazim and Sephardim, the Rabbinical Assembly decided to elect two chief rabbis, one for each of the two major communities. The chief rabbis, together with three Ashkenazi and three Sephardi rabbis, who also were chosen by the Rabbinical Assembly, constituted the Rabbinical Council. Three lay counsellors were elected to serve as advisers with regard to procedural matters, but they had no voice in its substantive deliberations. The Rabbinical Council was originally elected for a term of three years, but that time limitation was soon discarded as a matter of practice. Since the high commissioner had played a prominent role in bringing the Rabbinical Council into being, the British government decided to give it legitimacy as a matter of public law that was later adopted by the state of Israel.

The 1922 Palestine Order-in-Council stipulated (Article 51):

[I]nclusive jurisdiction in matters of personal status shall be exercised . . . by the courts of the religious communities. . . . For the purpose of these provisions matters of personal status means suits regarding marriage or divorce, alimony, maintenance, guardianship, legitimation and adoption of minors, inhibition from dealing with property of persons who are legally incompetent, successions, wills and legacies, and the administration of the property of absent persons.

It stipulated further (Article 53), "The Rabbinical Courts of the Jewish Community shall have . . . exclusive jurisdiction in matters of marriage and divorce, alimony and confirmation of wills of members of their community . . . [and] over any case as to the constitution or internal administration of a Wakf or religious endowment constituted before the Rabbinical Court according to Jewish Law."[12]

The Agudah refused to accept the authority of the chief rabbinate, which it saw as a Zionist institution. It was especially disturbed by the sympathetic position taken toward Zionism by the widely respected Ashkenazi chief rabbi, Abraham Isaac Kook (1865–1935). The Agudah therefore established its own parallel rabbinical institution under the leadership of Rabbi Sonnenfeld. This cleavage between the rabbinical institutions of the Agudah and of the rest of the nation persists in Israel to this very day.

The Twelfth Zionist Congress, the first to meet after the war, convened at Carlsbad in September 1921. At the time, the Zionist movement consisted of some 778,400 dues-paying members in 40 countries, who were represented by 445 delegates. The political makeup of the movement consisted of three major groupings that generally conformed to the same political configuration as the Yishuv. The most significant difference was that in the world organization, the Mizrahi had more than twice as many delegates as the Labor bloc, which consisted primarily of the Poalei Zion and the *Zeirei Zion* (Youth of Zion). The dominant voice in the Zionist Congress, however, was that of the General Zionists, with some 300 delegates representing the political center. This meant, in effect, that there was a fundamental difference in perspective between the leadership of the World Zionist Organization and that of the Yishuv, the latter being dominated by the Labor bloc. The differences were manifested most sharply in the matter of the approach to be taken with regard to the increasingly anti-Zionist policies of the British government.

Chaim Weizmann, who more than any other Zionist leader was responsible for the Balfour Declaration and the British Mandate, was still held in highest esteem by the Zionist movement and was able to dominate the congress. However, even at this early date, challenges to his leadership arose from both extremes of the Labor bloc, particularly in the mutually opposing positions taken by Berl Katznelson and Solomon Kaplansky. Katznelson took the Zionist leadership to task for their apparent readiness to go along with the policies of Herbert Samuel, who was sacrificing Zionist interests in order to appease the Arabs. Kaplansky, on the other hand, challenged the Zionist Executive for its failure to come up with a program designed to facilitate a rapprochement between the Zionists and the Arabs.

Weizmann responded to these challenges by attributing the failure of the Zionist Executive to be more effective in dealing with the British to the lack of adequate resources to support the pioneering activities of the settlers in Palestine. He argued that political gains could be achieved only as a result of more intensive agricultural and industrial development work; that growth in the Yishuv's economic importance to the country would in effect force the high commissioner to be more solicitous of Zionist concerns. Weizmann's practical Zionist position was upheld by an overwhelming majority of the delegates, effectively squelching any serious challenge to his leadership.

One issue on which the Zionist Congress was unanimous was its protest against the temporary cessation of immigration into Palestine in the wake of the May Day riots, as well as the restrictions imposed by the new immigration regulations promulgated by the high commissioner: "The Congress declares before the entire world that large immigration to Eretz Israel is an uncontestable right of the Jewish people of which under no circumstances it may be deprived. The internal regulation of immigration into Eretz Israel, according to the economic capacity of the country, is a matter for the Jewish people, represented by the Zionist Organization, in agreement with the Administration of Palestine."[13]

Notwithstanding its outspoken position on the immigration issue, the Zionist Executive continued to operate on the basis of Weizmann's insistence on full cooperation with the British government. For this reason it accepted the Churchill White Paper of 1922 with barely a murmur of open dissent. Moreover, the Zionist Executive convinced the Vaad Leumi to participate in the elections to the Legislative Council that had been proposed by the Palestine administration, in order to please the high commissioner. The Vaad Leumi went along with this even though it knew that this was a very dangerous step, since it could relegate the Yishuv to the status of a permanent minority under the effective dominance of the Arab majority. Fortunately for the Yishuv, the Arabs steadfastly refused to participate in the Legislative Council plan, eventually causing the matter to be dropped entirely.

Jabotinsky, after returning to London from a private visit to Palestine in the fall of 1922, during which he gained a new and distressing appreciation of the Samuel regime, submitted a memorandum to his colleagues on the Zionist Executive in which he argued,

The wobbling attitude of the present [British] Government is merely the logical consequence of the High Commissioner's policy in Palestine and of our own meekness in dealing with his administration. . . . Very often, as for instance after the Jaffa events, prominent officials of the Colonial Office admitted to us that the H C's panicky behaviour was entirely unjustified in their opinion, but so long as we Zionists wanted him to remain High Commissioner they naturally had to accept his views as approved or at least condoned by us.[14]

Weizmann and the Zionist Executive, however, were not prepared to admit their errors in judgment and to revise their policies for dealing with the British government. Jabotinsky characterized the fundamental differences between Weizmann and himself to a colleague in August 1922: "Weizmann believes that his way is that of a compromising realist, and mine is the way of a stubborn fantast, of a utopian; and I feel that his line is the line of renunciation, of subconscious Marranism, while mine is a difficult, stormy way, which will, however, lead more quickly to a Jewish State."[15]

Jabotinsky, who as a member of the Zionist Executive had reluctantly yielded to Weizmann's pressure for acceptance of the Churchill White Paper, no longer felt able to cooperate in what he saw as a self-defeating Zionist policy. He belatedly recanted his prior acceptance of the White Paper in January 1923, when he resigned from the Zionist Executive in protest over the anti-Zionist British policy that was clearly reflected in that document. In his January 18 letter to the president of the Actions Committee, Jabotinsky declared that the committee had "sanctioned a policy which threatens to bring the Movement to a decay and the Jewish work in Palestine to bankruptcy." Moreover, he wrote, he considered "the attitude of the Executive and the A.C. [Actions Committee] as incompatible with the interests and the principles of Zionism."[16]

When the Thirteenth Zionist Congress convened at Carlsbad in September 1923, the obvious timidity and demonstrably poor judgment of the Zionist Executive in stubbornly maintaining its conciliatory policies toward the British drew the ire of many participants. In fact this was one of the two primary issues considered by the congress. The second was the proposed expansion of the Jewish Agency to include non-Zionists. Isaac Gruenbaum (1879–1970), leader of the Radical Zionists, a General Zionist group in Poland, accused Weizmann of defeatism in his dealings with the British government and capitulation to the non-Zionists in the matter of the Jewish Agency. Menahem Ussishkin joined in attacking the Zionist Executive on the latter issue. Joshua H. Farbstein (1870–1948), a leader of Mizrahi in Poland, demanded the resignation of the Zionist Executive because of its acceptance of the 1922 White Paper. Kaplansky, representing the radical wing of Labor Zionism, once again made a sweeping attack on numerous facets of the leadership's policies that were having negative repercussions on the realization of Zionist aims in Palestine. He also indicted the leadership for having done nothing to prevent the separation of Trans-Jordan from Palestine.

Weizmann, however, still commanded the loyalty of almost two-thirds of the delegates and was easily able to ride out the storm. He summed up his position by stating: "The irrevocability of the Mandate, the good faith of the Mandatory, and the sympathy of the enlightened people throughout the world, are the foundations upon which we must rebuild our policy."[17]

The congress also approved the expansion of the Jewish Agency to include non-Zionist members. There were high hopes attached to the potential impact of the Jewish Agency on the building of the national homeland. Indeed, in 1923 a confidential circular issued by the Palestine administration recognized the special competence of the Jewish Agency by providing for a weekly meeting between the high commissioner and the representative of the Jewish Agency. The circular, which was given limited distribution, further specified:

The Chief Secretary [of the Palestine administration] will consult the Representative of the Jewish Agency on all matters appertaining to the "establishment of the National Home," and also on matters affecting the "development of the country" when Jewish interests are involved. Due weight will be given to the opinions expressed on behalf of the Jewish Agency, with a view to allowing that body to fulfill the role assigned to it by the Mandate.[18]

However, these undertakings were soon forgotten by the Palestine administration, the regular meetings were never held, and the Jewish Agency appears to have decided not to make an issue of it.

The two years following the Thirteenth Zionist Congress witnessed an unexpectedly high level of immigration and the opening of the Hebrew University in Jerusalem. There was also a new sense of optimism among the Yishuv in the wake of the visit of a Palestinian Jewish delegation to King Hussein of the Hejaz at Amman in January 1924 that seemed to suggest the likelihood of improved relations between Jews and Arabs. Taken all together, events seemed to augur well for the future of the Zionist enterprise. The Zionist Executive, in its report to the Fourteenth Zionist Congress, which convened at Vienna in August 1925, used the occasion to vindicate its original judgment in encouraging the appointment of Herbert Samuel, who had just retired from his post as high commissioner. It extolled, perhaps with tongue in cheek, the exemplary manner in which he carried out his difficult assignment:

Sir Herbert has, by common consent, acquitted himself of his historic task with dignity and distinction, and he carried with him in his retirement the enduring gratitude of the Zionist Organization and of the Jewish world at large. . . . Not only have the past five years brought Palestine peace, order and good government, but they have witnessed the successful completion of the first and most difficult stage in the establishment of the Jewish National Home.[19]

Criticism of the Zionist Executive at the Fourteenth Congress was more muted than at the earlier assemblies, presumably because of the general improvement of the situation in Palestine. Labor toned down its usual arguments and seemed resigned to following the leadership's line with regard to the benefits of full cooperation with the British government. The Mizrahi, however, continued to attack the Zionist Executive on a number of issues. It challenged its policy of showing partiality toward cooperative and collective forms of agricultural settlement, and accused the leadership of opposing middle-class immigration. Farbstein insisted that the Zionist Executive should have demanded a voice in the selection of Lord Plumer as Samuel's successor as high commissioner.

However, the most troublesome challenge to the Zionist leadership came from Jabotinsky. He appeared at the Congress as spokesman for a new Revisionist Party that presented a Herzl-style political Zionist program advocating that active measures be taken to secure British government support for a dramatic reassessment of the absorptive capacity of Palestine. His immediate goal was approval of an immigration level of 40,000 Jews a year for a twenty-five-year period. He called for the nationalization of all uncultivated lands and their subsequent lease to Jews, for purposes of colonization, on the payment of modest sums. He also insisted on the need for rapid industrialization of the country and the development and promotion of international trade, the latter requiring that the British government agree to the necessary promotional tariff policies. It was a far-reaching and dramatic program, a far cry from the gradualism and incrementalism that characterized official Zionist policy throughout Weizmann's tenure.

As expected, Weizmann's response to Jabotinsky's challenge was merely to reassert that the only viable course for the Zionist movement was the one that was being pursued by the Zionist Executive under his leadership. While Weizmann still prevailed in the final vote of confidence in his leadership, it was clear that the extent of his domination of the organization was shrinking. This was reflected in the fact that about half of the delegates to the Fourteenth Zionist Congress abstained from the vote on the confidence resolution.

NOTES

1. *Encyclopedia of Zionism and Israel*, p. 794.
2. Menachem Friedman, *Society and Religion: The Non-Zionist Orthodox in Eretz-Israel 1918–1936*, p. 147.
3. Moshe Burstein, *Self-Government of the Jews in Palestine Since 1900*, p. 87.
4. M. D. Gaon, *Yehudei haMizrah beEretz Yisrael beAvar ubaHove*, p. 136.
5. Burstein, *Self-Government of the Jews in Palestine*, pp. 100–101.
6. Ibid., pp. 157–158.
7. Friedman, *Society and Religion*, p. 175.
8. Burstein, *Self-Government of the Jews in Palestine*, p. 160.
9. Ibid.
10. *Sefer Toldot haHaganah*, vol. II, pt. 1, p. 253.
11. Friedman, *Society and Religion*, p. 248.
12. M. Chigier, "The Rabbinical Courts in the State of Israel," *Israel Law Review* 2.2 (1967).
13. Zionist Organization, *Reports of the Executive to the XIIth Zionist Congress*, pp. 149–150.
14. Joseph B. Schechtman, *Rebel and Statesman: The Early Years*, pp. 418–419.

15. Ibid., p. 424.

16. Ibid., p. 429.

17. Zionist Organization, *Reports of the Executive to the XIIIth Zionist Congress*, p. 356.

18. Ibid., p. 39, n. 23.

19. Zionist Organization, *Reports of the Executive to the XIVth Zionist Congress*, p. 16.

4

The Passfield White Paper

Field Marshal Lord Plumer, who succeeded Herbert Samuel as high commissioner in August 1925, was like a breath of fresh air for the Yishuv and the Zionist movement, notwithstanding the initial disappointment over his designation. It was widely expected by many in the Yishuv that another Jew would be appointed successor to Samuel, hopefully one less committed to the equal obligation policy stressed so one-sidedly by the latter. Although a military man, Plumer apparently inherited none of the biases displayed so visibly by his colleagues in the earlier military administration of the country. He was fully committed to carrying out the policies of the British government, as they were understood in London rather than in Cairo. He made economic development his highest priority, and was disinclined to allow himself to become ensnared in the complex internal politics of the country. Frederick H. Kisch (1888–1943), head of the political department of the Zionist Executive in Palestine, wrote in his diary after his first official meeting with the new high commissioner: "I conclude that Plumer's attitude to our submissions will be 'Is the request justified under the policy of H.M. Government?—If so, I must grant it, and carry it through.' The last High Commissioner's first reaction was: 'What will the Arabs say to this?' "[1]

Plumer's "no nonsense" approach to dealing with the Arabs made it clear to them that, unlike his immediate predecessor, he could not be pressured into unwarranted concessions. It was also understood that he was prepared to use military force to deal with any contingency that arose. Moreover, and probably of equal significance in contributing to the general calm that characterized the term of the Plumer administration, the Yishuv suddenly found itself in the midst of an economic crisis that brought further Zionist development work to a virtual standstill.

In 1925, an attempted currency reform in Poland helped precipitate an economic collapse in that country. This coincided with a general imposition of currency transfer restrictions in Eastern Europe. The impact on the Yishuv, with its large numbers of East European and Polish immigrants, was devastating. Many suddenly found themselves penniless. Numerous businesses owned by Polish and other East European immigrants failed because of the sudden loss of capital, and unemployment among Jews began to rise dramatically, increasing from 400 in 1925 to 8,500 two years later. As described by Robert Weltsch, at the time editor of the *Judische Rundschau* in Berlin: "Unemployment was a regular feature, workers lived on an appalling minimum, often on the dole, which was a heavy unproductive drain on the Zionist exchequer. There was genuine starvation in the communal settlements and elsewhere. Zionist money-chests were empty, officials and teachers did not get their salaries and were finally paid by some paperbills issued by institutions or even by private persons. Debts accumulated everywhere."[2] Although immigration from Poland was still high in 1926, nearly 14,000, it dropped dramatically to 3,034 in 1927. That same year, 5,071 Jews left Palestine. With the Yishuv apparently being seriously weakened, Arab leaders became optimistic that the Zionist tide had run its course and would soon reverse itself permanently.

Under Plumer's administration, the security situation in the country appeared to have improved even more than it had during the last two years of Samuel's tenure. The disturbances of May and November 1921, and the emergence of an effective self-defense capability in the new Haganah, led to an understanding between the administration and the Yishuv under which the British distributed rifles and ammunition to the outlying Jewish settlements, to enable them to defend themselves. These arms were kept in sealed armories that were to be opened only by a designated leader of each settlement in case of emergency. These designees were held personally responsible for the arms' appropriate use.

By June 1924, the security situation had improved so significantly that Samuel ordered the inventory of arms distributed to the Yishuv to be reduced, and during Plumer's term as high commissioner the Yishuv's armories were almost completely emptied. At the same time, in response to pressures from London to reduce overseas expenditures, Plumer agreed to decrease the number of British troops stationed in

Palestine, with the understanding that in case of emergency, reinforcements would be sent from Egypt. The Palestine Gendarmerie was disbanded and the British garrison was reduced to a squadron of armored cars. However, with the appointment of Sir John Chancellor, who took over as Plumer's successor in December 1928, the security situation in the country deteriorated rather significantly, at least as far as the Yishuv was concerned.

Chancellor was far more inclined to involve himself with partisan communal political matters than Plumer had been. He tended to give serious consideration to Arab complaints about the failure of the British to establish a parliamentary system in which the Arab majority would be fairly represented—that is, one that the Arabs would dominate. His approach to such questions was reminiscent of Herbert Samuel's. He unwittingly lent encouragement to those Arab leaders who were inclined to resort to the use of violence as a political instrument to achieve their nationalist aims, an orientation that began to become prominent once again toward the end of Plumer's term in office.

The Seventh Arab Congress had met in June 1928, and finally established a united front that included the Nashishibi and Husseini factions, thereby giving greater weight to the Arab nationalist movement's demand for self-determination and conversion of the Mandate to Arab self-government. Before long, there were clear indications that another outbreak of Arab violence against the Jews would soon follow to force the British to make further concessions toward that goal. The spark that ignited the explosion was provided by the local Muslim-Jewish conflict over rights of access to the Western Wall in Jerusalem.

The recognized customary right of the Jews to pray at the Western Wall long predated the Ottoman conquest of Jerusalem. The usual practice was for the worshipers to come to the wall to offer personal petitionary prayers, rather than to conduct regular communal prayer services. This pattern had evolved for practical reasons. The area in front of the wall had not been paved in earlier times, and there were no facilities there for the storage of the necessary synagogal paraphernalia.

During the second half of the nineteenth century, with the growth of the Jewish community in Jerusalem and the general increase of security in the city, the Jewish presence at the Western Wall became more regularized. Daily, Sabbath, and festival services began to be held there, and arrangements were sometimes worked out with the Arabs of the neighborhood to allow for the storage on their properties of materials necessary for the services. In the 1890s the area in front of the wall was paved, and the Jewish community assumed the responsibility for keeping the area clean. As the Jewish community continued to grow, and the flow of pilgrims increased, large crowds began to come to the wall to hold services, particularly during the High Holidays. On Yom Kippur (Day of Atonement), because of the fast, the heat, and the length of the service, people began to bring chairs and benches to the wall.

The Western Wall itself had long been considered part of the *wakf* of the Muslim community, the Jews being permitted to worship there as a matter of customary but not proprietary right. This second-class status of the Jews was reaffirmed by a decision of the Majlis of Jerusalem in November 1911, when it ruled that the Jews had no rights whatever at the wall other than prayer. It was forbidden for them to erect any permanent structures adjacent to the wall. Moreover, out of the simple vindictive desire to make things as difficult as possible for the Jewish worshipers, Jews were forbidden to bring any Torah scrolls, candelabra, benches, or partitions to the paved area in front of the wall. These onerous and arbitrary constraints were accepted by the British administration as the customary rules that were to be observed by the Jews in order to maintain the religious status quo at the site.

The prohibition against the use of partitions was especially irritating because Orthodox practice normally requires the separation of men and women in public prayer. On occasion, starting in Turkish times and continuing during the first years of British rule, a portable linen screen mounted on a wooden frame was brought to the wall to provide the required segregation. The portable screen was promptly removed at the conclusion of the service. However, with Samuel's establishment of the Supreme Muslim Council and the assumption of control of that institution by Haj Amin al-Husseini, every opportunity to create problems for the Jewish community was fully exploited. The mufti and his colleagues drew no distinctions between the secular Zionists and the anti-Zionist conservative Orthodox Jews who worshiped at the wall. It was sufficient that they were Jews. Thus, when chairs, benches, and partitions were brought to the wall for the Yom Kippur services on September 28, 1925, the Supreme Muslim Council protested to the British authorities that this constituted an unacceptable breach of the status quo that the British had committed themselves to uphold. Accordingly, the police removed the offending pieces of furniture from the immediate vicinity of the wall.

After a hiatus of several years, a partition was brought to the wall once again for the two days of Rosh Hashanah (New Year) in September 1928. It was removed after the holiday and brought back again ten days later, on September 24, for the Yom Kippur services. Once again the mufti charged that the presence of the portable screen constituted an infringement of Muslim rights and a violation of the conditions for Jewish worship at the wall. As observed at the time with unusual candor by the Arabic newspaper, *Al-Sirat al-Mustakim*:

The clique at the head of the Supreme Moslem Council did nothing for the benefit of the people and everything for its own. They did not prevent the sale of land to the Jews, but made a great noise about it and instigated trouble when the Jews brought a screen before the Wailing Wall to divide the male from the female worshipers. The truth is that the Supreme Moslem Council exploited this incident to demonstrate to the government its leadership of the Arab people, and the desire of the people that the office of the head of the Supreme Moslem Council should be made permanent.[3]

Responding to pressure from the mufti, the British forcibly removed the screen shortly before the service was concluded, to the outrage of the Jews and the delight of the Arabs. The Supreme Muslim Council deliberately transformed what would have been treated under ordinary circumstances as a petty squabble into a raging political controversy. Its agents spread the word among the Arab masses that the erection of the portable screen was part of a Zionist plot to destroy the Muslim holy places on the Temple Mount and to rebuild the Holy Temple there. Then, ostensibly to foil this nefarious plot, the Supreme Muslim Council began construction activities in the vicinity of the wall that were calculated to interfere with Jewish worship.

At one end of the paved area adjacent to the wall they undertook the painfully slow construction of a building that was supposed to house members of the Muslim religious courts. At the other end a *zawiyah* (hospice) was established in a house belonging to the *wakf*. A muezzin now called the faithful to prayer five times a day, frequently disrupting the Jewish services. Later the mufti introduced another provocative violation of the status quo by using the area opposite the wall, for the first time, for a religious ceremony, the *Zikr*, that involved repeatedly shouting the name of God to the accompaniment of drums, cymbals, and rattles. In addition, a passage was cut through an adjacent wall to allow Muslim worshipers to reach the mosques on the Temple Mount without having to go around the paved area in front of the wall, which had been a dead end alley for many centuries. This transformed the area immediately in front of the wall into a busy thoroughfare, littered with offal from donkeys, that interfered with the conduct of solemn Jewish services at the wall.

It is noteworthy that the authorization from the high commissioner for the construction activity in the area of the Western Wall specified that the grant of permission was contingent on there being no disturbance or annoyance to Jewish worshipers, a constraint the Palestine administration did nothing to enforce. Indeed, if the Palestine administration had displayed even a modicum of goodwill, the problems at the wall could have been resolved amicably. As it was, the local British authorities served as provocateurs who aggravated matters. An example of this was the White Paper issued by the Palestine administration on December 12, 1928, ostensibly to restore calm in the overheated atmosphere of Jerusalem. The policy reasserted the rights of the Jews to pray at the wall while reaffirming Arab ownership of the site. However, it permitted the Jews to bring to the wall only those items of religious paraphernalia that had been permitted under the Turkish regime, and further required the Jews to specify what those items were. The chief rabbinate refused to comply because it could not accept the principle of external restrictions on the Jewish right of prayer at the wall. This gave Harry Luke, the acting high commissioner (Chancellor had left Palestine for England in June and did not return until the end of August), the opportunity to castigate the Jews as obstructionists who were interfering with the resolution of the problems at the wall.

The events on and subsequent to September 24, 1928, had significant repercussions within the Yishuv. Prior to that time the anti-Zionist conservative Orthodox, led by the Agudat Israel, were opposed to any attempts by the Jews to alter the status quo in the regime of the Western Wall. It preferred to see the wall remain in the hands of the Muslims rather than under Zionist control. The wall carried a symbolic significance for both the religious and the secular Jewish communities that can hardly be overestimated. For the religious, the wall symbolized the exile of the Holy Presence that resulted in the destruction of the Temple and the dispersion of the Jewish people. They came to pray there for the redemption and the return of the Holy Presence, and the rebuilding of the Temple. The wall was thus a religio-national symbol that reached to the heart of Judaism. For the secular Zionists the wall symbolized something else. It provided a tangible link to the Jewish state of the distant past that they aspired to re-create. It thus came to symbolize the historic right of the Jews to the land, not from a religious perspective but from a historical-nationalist standpoint.

These two opposing perspectives were soon to merge in common cause against perpetuation of the status quo, as it became increasingly dangerous to pray at the wall because of escalating Arab hooliganism.

The Jews began to demand that the wall and its environs be returned to them as a matter of right; they could no longer allow Jewish rights at the wall to be determined by the highly politicized and anti-Jewish Supreme Muslim Council. This upsurge in Jewish activism was reflected most clearly in the decision of the Vaad Leumi to demand that control of the wall be transferred to the Jewish community. The representatives of the Ahdut Ha'avodah, however, were troubled by the use to which the mufti might put the challenge to Muslim control of Judaism's and the Jews' holiest site. Ben-Gurion and Eliahu Golomb warned that the mufti, with the support of the British, would transform the argument over the wall from an Arab-Zionist quarrel to a Muslim-Jewish religious conflict, thereby bringing a new and volatile dimension to the problem. However, they found themselves in the proverbial situation of trying to close the barn door after the cows had already gotten out. The mufti was already taking steps to employ the religious sensibilities of the Arab masses in a new effort to destabilize the situation and to force the British to meet the Arab demands for control of the country. There was in fact little that the Yishuv could do, short of abandoning the Zionist enterprise, that would make any difference to the Supreme Muslim Council and the Arab Executive, although many simply refused to believe that such was the case.

Anti-Jewish agitation was further accelerated in Palestine by reports that the Sixteenth Zionist Congress, which was convened at Zurich in late July, had decided to enlarge the Jewish Agency. This was done to ensure a new major influx of non-Zionist American wealth into the country to support the development of a Jewish national home. The feedback from Palestine was so worrisome that Kisch and a delegation left the Congress and went to London to warn the government of the imminent danger of violent disturbances.

On August 8 Pinhas Rutenberg (1879–1942), a prominent Yishuv figure, went to see Luke at the request of Chief Rabbi Kook. Rutenberg advised him of the Yishuv's concerns regarding the possibility of violence during the forthcoming religious fast of *Tisha b'Av*, the Jewish day of mourning over the destruction of the Temple, which traditionally brought large crowds to the wall. In the interest of forestalling the likelihood of clashes with the Arabs, Rutenberg proposed that Luke intervene to limit the numbers of Jews who might come to Jerusalem from other cities and settlements. He also urged him to increase the number of police at the gates of the Old City. On August 11, however, the Zionist Congress concluded in Zurich with a resolution that firmly rejected any change in the status quo at the wall and insisted on the unimpeded right of the Jews to worship there. The mufti seized upon this as additional grist for his agitation and propaganda mill, and now succeeded in obtaining support from the Arabs of Haifa, Nablus, and Hebron, which had previously been strongholds of opposition to the mufti. The government, however, paid no heed to these warnings or to the other numerous signs of growing hostility that had been plainly visible since the incident at the wall the previous year. No steps had been taken to ensure that adequate forces were on hand to maintain order. Indeed, Chancellor told the Permanent Mandates Commission on July 5: "There has been no serious breach of the peace since I became High Commissioner, and I consider that the resources at the disposal of the Government are sufficient to deal with any situation that is likely to arise."[4]

On Tisha b'Av, August 15, 1929, a group of some 200–300 Jewish youngsters, many of whom were followers of Jabotinsky, marched in procession to the wall under the leadership of Jeremiah Halpern. The government was advised of the march in advance and had provided a heavy police escort to prevent any incidents along its route. Upon arrival at the wall they read a number of resolutions regarding the Arab infringements on Jewish rights of worship at the wall, which they intended to present to the British authorities. They raised the Zionist flag, sang the Zionist anthem, and then left. It was later claimed, presumably because of Halpern's leadership role in the event, that the Brit Trumpeldor (Betar), the Zionist youth movement founded by Jabotinsky, had carried out this provocative demonstration. This was denied by Jabotinsky, although he stated explicitly that he wished it were true, since he considered it a most appropriate demonstration of Zionist interest in the wall.

The entire affair had taken place without incident. However, rumors soon spread like wildfire that the Zionist plot against the Muslim holy places, which the Supreme Muslim Council had previously warned about, was now being carried out. The following day a demonstration of about 2,000 Arabs took place at the wall. The small police contingent assigned to the demonstration cooperated by removing the dozen or so Jews who were praying there and by clearing the alleyways leading to the wall from the *Haram as-Sharif* (the Temple Mount), where the Muslims had gathered for their regular Friday worship. The mob destroyed the prayer books that were kept at the wall, beat up the beadle who was there to assist the worshipers, and later interfered with the Sabbath services that began just before sundown.

The government's patent complicity in the Muslim demonstration evoked a joint protest to Luke from the Zionist Executive, the Vaad Leumi, the Chief Rabbinate, Agudat Israel, and the Sephardi community. After their meeting with the acting high commissioner, the Zionist Executive protested the government's decision to allow a Muslim demonstration at the wall: "The government clearly knew beforehand of the intended demonstration as is sufficiently shown by their sending police to clear the place. The effect of allowing such a demonstration is in the first place a complete reversal of the doctrine of the status quo. . . . It also involved a breach of the assurance recently given by the government to the effect that no interference with or disturbance of the rights of Jewish worship at the Western Wall would be permitted."[5]

Following the Arab demonstration at the wall, tensions increased demonstrably throughout the country, most particularly in Jerusalem. On August 17 some Jewish boys were playing soccer in the Bukharan quarter of the New City when the ball fell into a tomato garden belonging to an Arab. When one of the youths went to retrieve the ball, an argument developed with the owner, and the boy was stabbed. This led to a scuffle in the neighborhood during which eleven Jews and fifteen Arabs were injured before the police restored order. The stabbed youngster was taken to the government hospital, where he died on August 20. The British authorities insisted that the burial take place secretly at night, contrary to Jewish custom, to avoid further provocation of the Arabs. The boy's parents categorically refused to do this, and the Zionist Executive had to intervene with the government to arrange for a burial very early the following morning.

The funeral procession grew to about 2,000, and before long an incident developed between some of the youngsters in the cortege and the British and Arab police. The latter had cordoned off some streets to prevent the cortege from following the usual route to the cemetery that passed by the Jaffa Gate of the old walled city. They had done this in order to avoid bearing of the body through an area that was filled with Arab shops. When a few marchers attempted to break through the cordon, the Arab police attacked the entire funeral procession, leaving twenty-four people injured. The pallbearers were forced to leave the corpse of the young Jew in the middle of the street and flee for their lives.

There was no doubt in anyone's mind that the police could have maintained order without using violence, and certainly without the excessive, indiscriminate violence that was employed. The action of the police once again had the effect of lending credence to the Arab belief that the government was with them in their struggle against the Jews. On August 22 the Arabic paper *Falastin* stated ominously: "In

Jerusalem there is great excitement. The atmosphere is tense, and it is apprehended that tomorrow [Friday, August 23] when many fellaheen [peasants] assemble for prayers in Jerusalem a substantial answer will be given to these incidents."[6] A delegation of representatives of the Yishuv urged Luke to order the police to remove the clubs and knives carried by the Arabs entering the city. Luke responded by stating that such a step could be dangerous, since it would antagonize the Arabs carrying such articles who had no malicious intentions. An eyewitness reporter perhaps best described what took place on August 23 in the Damascus paper *Alif Beh* of August 28:

El Charam el Sharif was filled Friday with thousands of fellaheen from the villages in the vicinity of Jerusalem and Hebron, in addition to the inhabitants of Jerusalem. The enlightened Arabs had felt the approaching danger. Some of the speakers called on them to be quiet, but who can calm the stormy sea? So the crowd went out of the gates of the Mosque, through the Nablus Gate near the Meah Shearim; the soldiers stood at this gate but they did not prevent anyone, and did not try to stop anyone.[7]

The pogrom that took place in Jerusalem on August 23 was triggered in part by a propaganda campaign launched during the preceding week that claimed the Jews were planning to attack and raze the mosques on the Temple Mount. Since the mobs of Arab peasants from the surrounding villages appeared at their services armed with knives and clubs, it was fully evident that the affair had been planned and coordinated. The collusion of British officials with the Arab rioters was blatant. In numerous incidents the Arab attackers fled when the British forces arrived on the scene or were driven off by those Jews, who had arms with which to defend themselves. In each instance, however, the British proceeded to disarm the Jews, rendering them defenseless against further attack. The attacks were by no means confined to Jerusalem.

On Thursday, August 22, Aref al-Aref, found guilty with Haj Amin al-Husseini in 1920 of helping foment the Nebi Musa riots in Jerusalem, visited Hebron and began inciting the Arabs to attack the Jews there, irrespective of the fact that they were not Zionists. Indeed, if anything, they were vehemently opposed to Zionism. On Friday morning the Jews of Hebron learned from an Arab source that the Arabs of the city were arming themselves. The traditional Orthodox community was defenseless. Rabbi Jacob Slonim, head of the Sephardi community, and Rabbi Frank, head of the Ashkenazi community, appealed to the

Arab governor of Hebron, Abdullah Kardos. He assured them that they had no need for concern: nothing was going to happen. Should there be an incident, there were sufficient soldiers in the streets, dressed in civilian clothes, to deal with any contingency. The next afternoon an Arab mob broke into the yeshiva (seminary) and killed the only student remaining in the vacated building. On Saturday morning, August 24, the rabbis appealed to the governor once again, and he gave them the same assurances. They then turned to Raymond Cafferata, the British officer in charge of the police. He, too, reassured them that there was no reason for concern. Then for the next two hours both the Arab governor and the British head of the police disappeared, after disarming the police, and a massacre of the defenseless Jews of Hebron took place: sixty-five were murdered and fifty-eight were wounded. After the two allocated hours were up, Cafferata reappeared, arms were returned to the police, and order was restored.

The pogroms in Jerusalem on August 23 and Hebron the next day were followed by an attack on the Jews of Safed on August 29, and by assaults on Jewish settlements throughout the country. The settlements in the Lower Galilee and the Jordan Valley were particularly vulnerable because, by order of the high commissioner on July 25, all their government-supplied arms were confiscated. The settlements of Motzah, Artuf, Hulda, and Beer Tuvia suffered heavily, although self-defense units in the newer settlements were successful in containing the Arab attacks. In total, 133 Jews, mostly defenseless anti-Zionist Orthodox, were killed and 339 wounded; 116 Arabs are known to have been killed and 232 wounded, almost all due to action by the police (except for six killed in a counterattack by Jews along the border between Tel Aviv and Jaffa). The high Arab death toll at the hands of the British authorities indicates that British complicity in the riots was sporadic and not well coordinated. It also suggests that while the British had no intention of helping the establishment of a Jewish state in Palestine, they also had no intention of turning the country over to the Arabs. Their actual policy appears to have been to divide and rule.

In the aftermath of this period of Arab massacre and British perfidy, the high commissioner apparently became increasingly determined to restore stability and confidence in the country. With a sense of evenhandedness that is rather mind-boggling, and fully reminiscent of the comparable evenhandedness of the military administration after the Nebi Musa riots of 1920, he proceeded to deal with the perpetrator and the defender as equals. In addition to larger numbers of Arabs, about forty Jews were arrested and held for weeks in Acre Prison, to await trial

for murder, on the basis of their being found with arms in their possession. Of these, twenty-five Arabs and one Jew (a police constable named
Hinkis, who killed an attacking Arab) were condemned to death. The
sentences of all, except for seven of the Arabs, were subsequently commuted to terms of imprisonment of eighteen months or less.

Once again, as in the riots of 1920 and 1921, in response to outcries
in England and other Western countries, the British government announced the appointment of a commission to investigate the causes of
the violence. It was widely expected that the Labour Party, which had
recently formed a coalition government, would see to it that the commission would be more objective than the heavily criticized Haycraft
Commission of 1921. Some of the leading members of the party, such
as Josiah Wedgwood and the new prime minister, Ramsey MacDonald,
had been consistent supporters of the Balfour Declaration and the idea
of a Jewish national home. Lord Passfield (Sidney Webb), the colonial
secretary, announced the appointment of the commission, to be headed
by Sir Walter Shaw, on September 3, 1929. He affirmed, "No inquiry is
contemplated which might alter the position of this country in regard
to the Mandate or the policy laid down in the Balfour Declaration of
1917 and embodied in the Mandate, of establishing in Palestine a national home for the Jews."[8]

For a brief moment it seemed as though the erosion of the Balfour
Declaration that had begun with Herbert Samuel had come to an end.
However, by the end of the month it was clear that the MacDonald
government would continue the policy of erosion. On September 29,
Jabotinsky wrote: "Everybody in England knows that the Commission
has been set up with the sole view to whitewashing the Palestine Administration, and they will whitewash it."[9]

The Shaw Commission arrived in Palestine in late October 1929,
and returned to Britain at the beginning of January 1930. As Jabotinsky predicted, the commission clearly exceeded its mandate as publicly
stated by the colonial secretary. It not only whitewashed the high commissioner and the Palestine administration; it also absolved the mufti
and the Arab Executive of any significant responsibility for the riots,
which it concluded were spontaneous and not planned. The commission then went on to recommend, in part: "That the British Government should issue a clear statement of policy defining the meaning it
attached to the passage in the Mandate concerning the safeguarding of
the rights of non-Jewish communities . . . and should review the machinery for its regulation and control with the object of preventing a
repetition of the 'excessive' Jewish immigration of 1925 and 1926."[10]

In brief, the Shaw Commission accepted the explanations given by the Arabs for the riots and rejected those offered by the Jews. The Palestine administration, itself being charged by the Jews with passive, if not active, complicity in the violence that occurred, understandably gave its support to the Arab version of what took place. The report, which was published on March 31, 1930, was celebrated loudly by the Arabs as a victory and was received with great disappointment and largely silent outrage by the Jews. The latter, although determined by the report to have been the victims of Arab aggression, were at the same time accused of having provoked the attack.

The Labour-led government discarded its earlier position with regard to its obligations under the Balfour Declaration somewhere along the line. It now adopted the idea suggested by the Shaw Commission that the Mandate and the Balfour Declaration really imposed upon Great Britain two separate but equal obligations to both Jews and Arabs. This notion was patently false, as was made abundantly clear by Balfour and Lloyd George on a number of occasions. Nonetheless, on April 3, Prime Minister MacDonald announced the new official policy of the British government with regard to its obligations under the Mandate: "A double undertaking is involved, to the Jewish people on the one hand, and to the non-Jewish population of Palestine on the other; and it is the firm resolve of His Majesty's Government to give effect, in equal measure, to both parts of the Declaration and to do equal justice to all sections of the population of Palestine."[11]

In the meanwhile the British government undertook to carry out some of the recommendations of the Shaw Commission report. In May 1930, Sir John Hope Simpson was appointed to look into the questions of land settlement, immigration, and development. While this was being done, the undistributed portion of the immigration certificates (3,300) allotted under the schedule for 1930 was suspended, an act that brought strong protests from Zionist circles. The Vaad Leumi called for a general strike, to be carried out on May 22.

The move by the Vaad Leumi pointed up the lack of cohesion within the Yishuv. The Vaad Leumi had never bothered to consult the Agudah about its participation prior to publicizing the decision to call a general strike. The members of the Vaad Leumi evidently preferred not to have to deal with the non- or anti-Zionist community. However, given the sizable non-Zionist Jewish community of Jerusalem, it was essential that the community as a whole participate in the strike if it were to be effective. The Agudah was ambivalent about participation for at least two reasons, aside from its pique at not having been consulted; first, it was generally opposed to political demonstrations directed against the British, and second, it was divided about the desirability of further immigration of secular Jews into the country. Many of its members viewed the stoppage of immigration as a punishment meted out by Heaven because of the violations of the Sabbath perpetrated by the Zionists. After some deliberation, the Agudah declined to participate. However, once the day of the strike arrived and the shops of the Agudah members remained opened, a number of clashes with Zionist activists took place that forced the Agudah to reconsider its position. Negotiations were quickly reopened, and the Agudah succeeded in extracting a price for its participation in the strike. The Vaad Leumi agreed to prohibit soccer games in Jerusalem on the Sabbath. They further agreed, out of a sense of fairness, to compensate the professional players for the financial losses they would incur as a consequence of stopping the games.

The participation of the Agudah in the general strike brought about a split within the conservative Orthodox community that reflected deep divisions over the question of cooperation with the Zionists. Some Orthodox leaders were genuinely concerned that cooperation, even when restricted to specific and special instances, conferred legitimacy on secularism. This concern was articulated in the Agudah paper *Kol Yisrael* on August 4, 1930:

Each instance of joint action is an independent event, however, many such events aggregate and create a pattern of love, brotherhood and friendship. . . . Soon we will begin "to understand" our friends and the terms "freethinkers" and "strict observers" will gain legitimacy among us, as though, Heaven forbid, there are two approaches to Judaism that are reflected in the different camps. . . . Before long we will no longer feel anguish when one of our brethren desecrates the Sabbath or revulsion over non-kosher food, etc.[12]

Notwithstanding such reservations, the Agudah, pressed by the overriding need for Jewish solidarity, altered its stance from one of anti-Zionist opposition to one of non-Zionist cooperation, thanks to the threat posed by Arab militancy and British complacency or occasional overt hostility during this troubled period. This approach established the basis for similar non-Zionist cooperation with the government of Israel after the state came into being.

On May 27, 1930, the British government released a preliminary statement of its new policy in the form of a speech to be delivered before the Permanent Mandates Commission. The government not only justified the suspension of Jewish immigration on primarily economic grounds, it also indicated its agreement with the basic economic arguments raised by the Arabs well in advance of the conclusion of the Hope Simpson study of the economic issues that the government itself had commissioned. This clearly suggested that the Hope Simpson study would be nothing but a charade.

In June the Permanent Mandates Commission convened an extraordinary session to review the 1929 disturbances. Along with the Shaw Commission report the British government submitted a White Paper setting forth its most recent reformulation of its Palestine policy. The Permanent Mandates Commission took strong exception to Britain's conduct as the Mandatory and rejected the contention of the Shaw Report that the outbreak was unexpected and unpremeditated. It held that with a little foresight the whole tragic affair could have been avoided, and that the inaction of the Palestine administration was the fundamental cause of the serious dimensions of the disturbances. It also charged Britain with having done too little to help the Arabs adapt to the reality of the new circumstances engendered by Jewish immigration. The commission further alleged that Britain had consciously ignored the warnings it had received that its forces in Palestine were inadequate to carry out its responsibility to secure "the essential condition for development of the Jewish National Home, security for persons and property."[13]

Not surprisingly, the Hope Simpson Report, which was published on October 20, 1930, turned out to be an essentially incompetent study. It provided fallacious underpinnings for the British government's policy of further retreat from the Balfour Declaration, and provoked a decade and a half of unrelenting controversy. Hope Simpson calculated the extent of cultivable land in the country on the basis of aerial surveys of only one-tenth of the total area of the Galilee, Samaria, and Judea. Making the totally unwarranted assumption that the ratio of cultivable to uncultivable land in the area surveyed held for the other nine-tenths, Hope Simpson estimated the cultivable area of Palestine to be only 6,544,000 dunams. This constituted a reduction of almost 40 percent from the estimate provided earlier in the year to the Shaw Commission by the commissioner of lands of the Palestine administration.

Starting from this false premise regarding the extent of cultivable land available, Hope Simpson reached some portentous conclusions. For one thing, he held that even if all the cultivable land not already occupied by Jews were to be divided equally among the Arabs, there would not be enough to support each Arab family at an acceptable standard of living. He had determined somehow that an Arab peasant family required 130 dunams of land, and that the 61,408 such families in Palestine averaged only 90 dunams per family. Consequently, he concluded that since the land was already overcrowded, there was no cultivable land available for agricultural settlement by new immigrants. (It is noteworthy that the September 1, 1938, issue of *Great Britain and the East* estimated that in nearby Cyprus, where the standard of living at the time was rather higher than in Palestine, "about 27 acres [108 dunams] of unirrigated land is needed to keep a man and family of four. . . . But less than six acres [24 dunams] of irrigated land is enough to keep a family.") Then, after presenting a number of recommendations regarding development in the country, Hope Simpson concluded: "It is my personal belief that with thorough development of the country there will be room not only for all the present agricultural population on a higher standard of life than it at present enjoys, but for not less than 20,000 families of settlers from outside."[14] The implication of this was that for the immediate future, no further agricultural immigration should be permitted. However, at some indeterminate point in the future a maximum of 20,000 families of agricultural immigrants might be accommodated.

The publication of the Hope Simpson Report was accompanied by the issuance of a government statement of policy, the Passfield White Paper. The latter set forth some principles that brought cries of indignation not only from Zionists but also from Conservative members of Parliament, who saw it as a gross betrayal of Britain's earlier commitments. It stipulated that "in estimating the absorptive capacity of Palestine at any time account should be taken of Arab as well as Jewish unemployment in determining the rate at which Jewish immigration should be permitted."[15] In other words, Zionist industry and agriculture would have to solve the endemic Arab unemployment problem before they could create labor vacancies to accommodate new Jewish immigration. The White Paper also omitted any reference to the Hope Simpson calculation of the possibility of future accommodation for as many as 20,000 families of new immigrants. Furthermore, it provided that any state lands which should become available were to be held in reserve for settlement not by Jews, as required by Article 6 of the Mandate, but by landless Arabs. It was clear from this that the Colonial Office contemplated a virtual cessation of all activities that might contribute to the building of a Jewish national home.

A few days after the White Paper was issued, General Jan Smuts, prime minister of South Africa, sent a cable to MacDonald, urging him to reconsider the action he had taken.

The Declaration was a definite promise to the Jewish world that the policy of the National Home would be actively prosecuted, and was intended to rally the powerful Jewish influence for the Allied cause at the darkest hour of the war. As such it was approved by the Government of the United States and the other Allies, and accepted by the Jews in good faith. It represents a debt of honour which must be discharged in full at all costs and in all circumstances. The original Declaration was far too solemn to permit of any wavering now.[16]

The policies articulated in the Passfield White Paper represented an unequivocal repudiation of the conciliatory policy that Weizmann had consistently pursued for more than a decade in the face of ever mounting internal opposition. Weizmann therefore felt it necessary to resign from the presidency of the Zionist Organization and the Jewish Agency simultaneously with the publication of the document. He then called for an emergency session of the Zionist Congress to determine how to respond to the British move. Two days later, the chairman of the administrative committee of the Jewish Agency, Felix Warburg, resigned with a bitter and outspoken attack on the honor and credibility of Passfield and the government he represented. At the same time, Lord Melchett resigned as chairman of the council of the Jewish Agency. He declared in a public letter: "The grotesque travesty of the purpose of the Mandate given in the Government Paper can only be described as an insult to the intelligence of Jewry and a deliberate affront to the Mandates Commission."[17] Weizmann complained to Lord Passfield on October 29, 1930, that the White Paper of October 1930 was inconsistent with the terms of the Mandate and marked the reversal of British policy in regard to the Jewish National Home.

The outcry, particularly from outraged British politicians, was such that it quickly became apparent to MacDonald that the furor could become an instrument for turning the Labour government out of power. To prevent this, he would be forced to retreat somewhat from the policies announced by the Passfield White Paper. At the same time, it would be necessary to prevent a test vote of confidence in the House of Commons that could bring the government down before it could come up with a formula for smoothing over the affair. To accomplish this, it would be necessary to get the Zionists to back off, and the vehicle for doing this was the international socialist movement, which did not want to see the collapse of a Labour government in Britain.

As it turned out, Weizmann's principal support in Palestine derived from the Labor bloc that had just recently been admitted to membership in the Second International. Accordingly, Leon Blum of France and George Lansbury of Britain, members of the International's Palestine Committee, appealed to the Labor movement in Palestine to intervene with Weizmann, in the name of solidarity, to prevent the Passfield White Paper from being put to a test vote in Parliament. MacDonald gave assurances that if he were allowed to save face, the issue would be resolved to Weizmann's satisfaction. The intervention was successful. On November 14, several days before the debate on the question in the House of Commons was to take place, it was announced that "doubts having been expressed as to the compatibility of some passages of the White Paper of October with certain articles of the Palestine Mandate, and other passages having proved liable to misunderstanding, His Majesty's Government . . . invited members of the Jewish Agency to confer with them on these matters."[18]

Weizmann, unaccountably, had backed off from his unprecedented attack on the government and reverted to his traditional policy of accommodation. He informed the Zionist Actions Committee that the emergency Zionist Congress, which was expected to be vehemently anti-British, was to be postponed. His rationale for the delay was that Zionist finances were in poor shape, and it would be best to concentrate on practical rather than political affairs. This brought the Mizrahi to resign from the Actions Committee in protest. However, between his loyalists and the support of the Labor bloc, Weizmann was able to prevail.

On November 17, as expected, the government came under attack in the House of Commons. Lloyd George insisted that the establishment of the Jewish national home was the dominant British obligation established by the Balfour Declaration, and demanded that the Mandate either be carried out as intended or be surrendered. During the debate R. Hopkin Morris, who had been a member of the Shaw Commission, admitted that "the Jews are perfectly right—what was promised to them meant a Jewish State."[19] Even Herbert Samuel, the original architect of the retreat from the clear pro-Zionist intentions of the Balfour Declaration, attacked the government for having gone too far. Nonetheless, the Passfield White Paper was never put to the test vote so feared by the cabinet.

The meetings between the Jewish Agency and the government began on November 18, 1930, and concluded on February 11, 1931. The results were contained not in another White Paper but in a public letter to Weizmann released two days later. The letter was supposed to be the authoritative interpretation of the Passfield White Paper. It recognized that the Palestine Mandate involved an obligation to the entire Jewish people, not only to those resident in Palestine. It explained that the restrictions on land transfers affected only lands that were needed for Arabs displaced by Jewish land purchases, and were not intended to prevent further acquisitions by Jews. It gave assurances that only economic considerations would be introduced in the determination of the absorptive capacity of the country for purposes of setting immigration limits, and indicated that the government was not opposed in principle to the Jewish Agency's policy of requiring Jewish labor on Jewish development projects. Upon its publication, Weizmann announced, "[T]his statement of policy . . . has, in my opinion, re-established the basis for that co-operation with the Mandatory Power on which our policy is founded."[20] However, as a British political analyst noted shortly afterward, the real

difference between the new document and its immediate predecessor lay, not in its statements of fact or in its pronouncements upon policy, but in its concentration upon those particular facts and those particular points of policy which were agreeable to Zionists, and in its replacement of the phraseology which had given offence to the Jews by a phraseology which was courteous and considerate in its tone towards them almost to the point of being ingratiating.[21]

In other words, there was really not much of any substance that was new in the MacDonald letter.

Weizmann's enthusiasm over the letter was criticized at the Zionist Congress later that year. There was a feeling that since the letter had not been released as a White Paper—that is, as an official statement of government policy—its value was more limited than Weizmann made it appear. Nonetheless, in his autobiography, Weizmann insisted that his acceptance of something less than an official White Paper was vindicated by subsequent events:

It was under MacDonald's letter to me that the change came about in the Government's attitude, and in the attitude of the Palestine Administration which enabled us to make the magnificent gains of the ensuing years. It was under MacDonald's letter that Jewish immigration into Palestine was permitted to reach figures like forty thousand for 1934 and sixty-two thousand for 1935, figures undreamed of in 1930.[22]

However, given the pattern of British government conduct in administering the Mandate, there was no way that Weizmann could have known at the time, other than as a matter of blind faith, that MacDonald's letter was worth the paper on which it was written.

The issuance of the Passfield White Paper and the MacDonald letter had a clearly unintended effect. It demonstrated conclusively to both the Arabs and the Jews that, notwithstanding the British government's posture of acting on high principle, it was inconstant in its policies and could be swayed one way or the other by sufficient pressure and agitation.

NOTES

1. Frederick H. Kisch, *Palestine Diary*, p. 201.
2. Christopher Sykes, *Crossroads to Israel*, p. 85.
3. Maurice Samuel, *On the Rim of the Wilderness*, p. 48.
4. Paul L. Hanna, *British Policy in Palestine*, p. 186, n. 36.
5. Maurice Samuel, *What Happened in Palestine*, pp. 51–52.
6. Ibid., p. 64.
7. Ibid., pp. 89–90.
8. *The Times*, September 4, 1929.
9. Joseph B. Schechtman, *Fighter and Prophet: The Last Years*, p. 122.
10. Royal Institute of International Affairs (RIIA), *Great Britain and Palestine 1915–1945*, pp. 46–47.
11. Hanna, *British Policy in Palestine*, p. 101.
12. Menachem Friedman, *Society and Religion*, pp. 329–330.
13. RIIA, *Great Britain and Palestine*, p. 49.
14. Ibid., p. 54.
15. Ibid., p. 56.
16. Lord Russell of Liverpool, *If I Forget Thee*, p. 103.
17. *The Times*, October 22, 1930.
18. Ibid., November 14, 1930.
19. William B. Ziff, *The Rape of Palestine*, p. 134.
20. RIIA, *Great Britain and Palestine*, p. 83.
21. Arnold J. Toynbee, *Survey of International Affairs, 1930*, p. 302.
22. Chaim Weizmann, *Trial and Error*, p. 335.

5

Prelude to Open Conflict

Notwithstanding Weizmann's evident euphoria over the MacDonald letter, other Zionist leaders did not generally view it with much enthusiasm. Weizmann's tenure as head of world Zionism had seen his initial achievement of the Balfour Declaration successively whittled down by the Churchill and Passfield White Papers, and he no longer commanded the authority or respect required to continue to dominate the Zionist movement. For some time the increasingly powerful American Zionists had targeted him as an impediment to a successful challenge of Britain's policy in Palestine. Stephen S. Wise stated in May 1928: "England will not do anything more until it is compelled to. The right kind of Zionist leadership is necessary and a stronger and more aggressive policy toward the mandatory power must be adopted if the Balfour Declaration is to be carried out. Until this change is brought about, England will do very little toward the creation of a Jewish National Home." Apparently irritated by a comment made by Weizmann that "a struggle with England would last five minutes and that will settle it," Wise asked:

How can a self-respecting Jew utter such words as those voiced by the leader of the World Zionist Organization? It means no change or improvement in Zionism until the Zionist leadership is deposed. As one who helped Brandeis to obtain President Wilson's endorsement of the Balfour Declaration, I will not cease to demand the maximum from England unless you want her promise to become a "scrap of paper."[1]

Since his resignation from the Zionist Executive in October 1930, Weizmann had remained interim head of the movement, pending elections to the Seventeenth Zionist Congress that began on June 30, 1931, in Basel. Even his close associates urged him not to run for the presidency again. His outspoken policy of collaboration with the British, regardless of their betrayals, made him the prime target of the opposition to continuation of such an approach. Joseph Klausner (1874–1958), one of the leaders of Russian Zionism and a former supporter, had published a virulent attack on Weizmann in Palestine the previous month. He accused him of degrading the Zionist movement by his compromise of Zionist principles and unnecessary concessions. A particular bone of contention was Weizmann's insistence on bringing non-Zionists into the Jewish Agency, on the assumption that such a marriage of convenience would produce large amounts of money for the work in Palestine. This expectation was not realized, while the non-Zionists such as the Agudat Israel were given a voice in determining the future of the Zionist enterprise. Even among the General Zionists, especially with the defection of Stephen Wise and many of the American Zionists, Weizmann's supporters at the Congress numbered no more than twenty-five out of eighty-four delegates.

Opposition to Weizmann also grew in Germany and, most especially, in Poland. It was in the latter country that the idea of *grosszionismus* (Maximalist Zionism) was being promoted. The program of the Maximalists called for full realization of the 1897 Basle Programme, calling for a Jewish national home in all of Palestine, including Trans-Jordan, concentrated efforts to increase the absorptive capacity of the country, and a vigorous new leadership to carry out the program. A group headed by Nahum Goldmann split from the General Zionists and formed a new party, the Union of Radical Zionists, that advocated an aggressive Zionist policy. The Radicals were opposed to Weizmann's reelection because it would preclude cooperation with the Revisionists and other Maximalist groups. However, since the main opposition to Weizmann and his policies came from Jabotinsky and the Revisionists, Weizmann was able to retain the support of the Labor movement in Palestine because of its vehement opposition to Jabotinsky.

Weizmann's approach to the Zionist Congress was to defend the policy of incrementalism as the only viable approach to building the Jewish homeland. He argued, in effect, that the approach of the old Hovevei Zion, and not that of Theodor Herzl, was the more appropriate policy: "If there is another way of building a country save dunam by dunam, man by man, and farmstead by farmstead—again I do not know it."[2]

But this argument was seen by many as no longer realistic, given the gains achieved by the Arabs as a result of British policy, which in itself was a reflection of Zionist complacency. Jabotinsky took the position that economic achievements alone would not provide the political basis for a Jewish state. While the Jews could justly take pride in having accomplished much toward bringing the country back to life, it was the Arabs who were gaining the upper hand politically, attaining a position that now allowed them to determine the pace of immigration and settlement. The vague idea that at some time in the indeterminate future there would be a sufficient mass of Jews in Palestine to make the Jewish homeland a reality was no longer acceptable.

Jabotinsky and his supporters were also very concerned about the loose talk that had become commonplace in Zionist circles about the need for parity in Palestine between Jews and Arabs, and perhaps most especially by the idea of a binational state that was being discussed by some. Indeed, Weizmann tried to get the idea of binational parity incorporated into official Zionist policy. To the Revisionists this kind of thinking was nothing less than a complete rejection of basic Zionist principles. They therefore felt that it was absolutely necessary to reorient the Zionist movement back to the principles of its founders. Jabotinsky demanded that the congress get back to fundamentals. It was unfair, in his view, to blame Britain for its retreat from the Balfour Declaration if the Zionist leadership had acquiesced in every step of that retreat. It was now essential to tell Britain and the world that Zionist aims had not changed since the Balfour Declaration, and that Zionism would not allow those aims to be modified by the White Papers of Churchill and Passfield.

Jabotinsky decried the stultifying effects of Weizmann's approach on the Zionist movement. "Zionism has lost its spell over the Jewish soul. . . . It has become a political necessity to clean the atmosphere, and this can be done by telling the truth. Why should we allow the term 'Jewish State' to be called extremism? The Albanians have their State, the Bulgarians have their State; a State is, after all, the normal condition of a people. If the Jewish State were in existence today, nobody would say that it is abnormal." Jabotinsky then called upon the Zionist Congress to declare unequivocally that "[t]he aim of Zionism, expressed in the terms 'Jewish State,' 'National Home,' or 'a Homestead guaranteed by public law,' is the creation of a Jewish majority in Palestine on both sides of the Jordan."[3] Although he refrained from attacking Weizmann personally, it was quite evident that Weizmann was one of those whom he considered to have wandered rather far from the original political conception of Zionism.

It is difficult to discern what Weizmann actually believed about these critical issues. In a letter to James Marshall of January 17, 1930, Weizmann wrote: "The declaration in favour of the Jewish National Home in Palestine was naturally coupled with a guarantee for the 'civil and religious rights' of the non-Jews in the country; there was to be absolute equality of individual rights between Jews and Arabs." However, insofar as "group rights" were concerned, he asserted that "there can be no doubt that the picture in the minds of those who drafted the Balfour Declaration and the Mandate was that of a Jewish Commonwealth in Palestine. Palestine was to be a Jewish State in which the Arabs would enjoy the fullest civil and cultural rights; but for the expression of their own national individuality in terms of statehood, they were to turn to the surrounding Arab countries."

Notwithstanding this cogently argued position, Weizmann was fully prepared to surrender the Jewish state for a binational state if only the Arabs would be seriously willing to cooperate in the endeavor. But, he complained, "while we accept the principle of equality between Jews and Arabs in the future Palestinian state, the Arabs press for having that state constituted immediately, because circumstances would enable them now to distort it into an Arab dominion from which no path would lead back to real equality."[4] A week later he wrote in the London Zionist Hebrew weekly, *Haolam* (January 24): "Palestine is not only an Arab country nor is it only a Jewish country. It is a country belonging to both of us together. The formula 'without a Jewish state there is no existence for the Jewish people' has a lot of assimilation in it. 'The State of the Jews,' 'A National State,' these are terms which do not suit our movement."[5]

In this same vein, at a meeting of the Zionist Actions Committee on August 27, 1930, Weizmann explicitly denied that "the Jewish State and Zionism are one and the same thing. That is not true. It is not correct that the Basle Programme [1897] and the Balfour Declaration contain the Jewish State." At the same time, he acknowledged, "Lord Balfour and Lord Robert Cecil originally probably envisaged a Jewish State. I did so too." Then, adopting a position clearly reminiscent of the views of Herbert Samuel, he argued, "Certainly we have a right over Palestine, but also the Arabs have a claim over the land. . . .We will certainly try to bring the maximum number of persons to Palestine and when we shall be the majority there, we will not dominate the Arabs, just as we will not allow ourselves to be dominated while we are the minority. That is the contents of the Balfour Declaration and the Palestine Mandate."[6]

Shortly before the Zionist Congress convened, Weizmann met with the leadership of *Mapai* (Israel Labor Party—a fusion of Ahdut Ha'avodah and Hapoel Hatzair). He came to solicit the support of the Labor movement in the impending struggle over the question of political parity that was expected to take place at the congress. Weizmann argued: "There is the question of parity, and—I believe—it will be possible, after preparations, to reach an agreement with the Arabs about this, which is a great compromise on our part. And the main thing—the mere fact that both sides will sit together means that compromises must be made. . . . The people must understand that we cannot follow the road of expelling the Arabs from the country for our settlement."[7]

Weizmann received the strong support of the Mapai for this approach. In its platform for the Zionist Congress, published on March 21, 1931, the Mapai called for the equal participation of Jews and Arabs in the management of the country. It should be noted that at this particular point in time, the primary concern of Ben-Gurion and Mapai was to prevent implementation of the British scheme for a legislative council based on proportional representation, a scheme that would have effectively made the Jews a permanent minority. Ben-Gurion and his associates were aware, however, that a successful call for parity would also preclude the country from ever becoming a Jewish state. Nevertheless, at this point in its history Mapai was an advocate of a binational state, which was defined by Katznelson as

a state whose two nationalities enjoy an equal measure of freedom, independence, participation in government, and rights of representation. Neither nationality encroaches upon the other . . . a bi-national political order does not recognize the population at large but takes cognizance of its two national segments to both of which the right to share in shaping the country's regime is secured in equal measure and both of which are equally entitled to guide its destinies.[8]

Weizmann had correctly anticipated that this approach would be strongly opposed by the Revisionists. However, Jabotinsky was by no means the only one who attacked Weizmann's position. Stephen Wise mounted an even sharper attack on Weizmann personally. Weizmann was taken to task for having sacrificed the integrity of the Zionist enterprise by his determination to broaden the Jewish Agency to include

non-Zionists. Wise also condemned Weizmann's failure to stand up for
the Yishuv before the British government. He told Weizmann from the
podium: "You have sat too long at English feasts. Only men who believe in their cause can talk to the British, but not a leadership which
says in effect, 'You are big and we are small, you are omnipotent and we
are nothing.' "[9] Wise's verbal assault finally caused Weizmann to storm
from the platform in protest when he characterized the Passfield White
Paper, which still constituted official British policy, notwithstanding
the MacDonald letter, as the "Passfield Pogrom."

Ben-Gurion and Chaim Arlosoroff, the rising star of the Labor
movement in Palestine, came to the defense of Weizmann with a vigorous attack on the opposition for sloganeering and a lack of realism.
Wise, in a separate discussion with the leaders of the Mapai, told Ben-
Gurion and Berl Katznelson that while he had nothing against their
movement in principle, he considered them as unprincipled as the rest
of the Zionist leadership. He charged the Labor movement with a willingness to barter its political ideals for the sake of maintaining its immediate political strength. "I cannot understand how you with your ideals
can stick through thick and thin to a man of the character and spirit of
Weizmann as you have done for ten years or more."[10]

By the end of the debate, the most acrimonious since the Uganda
controversy (the conflict over the 1903 proposal to settle the Jews in
East Africa), the congress was about evenly divided between supporters
and opponents of the Weizmann policy. Then, Weizmann chose the opportunity of an interview with the Jewish Telegraphic Agency to press
his position further. He told the interviewer: "I have no sympathy or
understanding for the demand of a Jewish majority [in Palestine]. . . .
The world will construe this demand only in one sense, that we want to
acquire a majority in order to drive out the Arabs." He then went on, in
another address to the delegates, to state:

I have said that a numerical majority in itself is no adequate guarantee for the
security of our National Home, for I am convinced that such security can be
created first and foremost through far reaching political guarantees and
friendly behaviour towards the non-Jewish world about us in Palestine. The attitude of our constantly growing, dynamically developing National Home towards the Palestine Arabs should be guided by the principle of complete parity
between both peoples irrespective of their numerical strength.[11]

Weizmann's candid statement of his views to the Jewish Telegraphic
Agency proved disastrous for his reelection, notwithstanding the con-

tinuing support of the Labor delegates. The opposition, with Nahum Goldmann leading the assault against Weizmann's continued leadership and Wise maneuvering behind the scenes, took Weizmann's statement as a virtual declaration of war against the Zionist movement. Goldmann demanded a vote of confidence, which Weizmann lost 123 to 106. At the same time, the Revisionist demand for an unequivocal declaration by the congress on the final aims of Zionism was defeated overwhelmingly. However, Weizmann also failed to get "parity" accepted as a principle of Zionist policy.

Although Weizmann himself was pushed out of office, the majority of the new Zionist Executive, headed by Nahum Sokolow, were Weizmann supporters who were elected over the strenuous opposition of the Revisionists. As a result, Weizmann's policies of incrementalism, compromise, and accommodation continued to dominate the movement even without his direct leadership. One immediate consequence of this lackluster approach to the achievement of Zionist aims was a failure to generate much enthusiasm or financial commitment for the Zionist cause among world Jewry.

To a large extent the entire acrimonious debate at the congress about parity was pointless, since the concept was anathema to the Arabs and generated little interest among the British. Passfield had already made his position on parity clear to MacDonald in a letter of July 24, 1931, in which he rejected the idea in principle:

I would remind you of the impossibility of accepting the new principle which the Zionists seem to be going to press, namely that of Parity. This is a word full of danger. The Jewish population of Palestine is still under 20% of the whole, and with the Arab birthrate of 55 per 1,000 there is little prospect of that proportion being much (if at all) increased for years to come. The application of parity to Land Development would be wholly impracticable.[12]

This view was maintained consistently by the Colonial Office in the years to come.

It was not long before some of the Labor leaders who rallied to Weizmann's defense during the Zionist Congress also began to acknowledge that the parity approach was unrealistic. Arlosoroff, who was elected to the Zionist Executive as director of the political department of the Jewish Agency, quickly became rather pessimistic about the possibilities of reaching an accommodation with the Arabs on the basis of communal parity. On February 11, 1932, he met with Auni Abdel Hadi to discuss an Arab-Zionist rapprochement. He noted in his diary: "Abdel Hadi said that he sees no use in a discussion between Jews and Arabs on fundamental problems. He understands very well Jewish National-ism, but there is a fundamental clash of interests which cannot be can-celed through talks. . . . I explained to him how we understood it [the term 'parity'] to differ from equality, which means in fact the despotic domination of numbers."[13]

Arlosoroff soon began to speak in terms of more drastic alternatives. Two of these appeared realistic to him. As he wrote in a private letter to Weizmann on June 30, 1932, the first was "to continue holding the ba-sic principles of Zionism, but narrowing down the geographical area in which it will materialize; instead of the whole of Palestine—only dis-tricts or certain parts of it." In other words, a viable solution might be to partition the country between the Jews and the Arabs. If this was not feasible, he was prepared to consider a second and more extreme alter-native, one that effectively negated the very notion of binationalism.

The alternative, Arlosoroff argued, was to take steps to assure that the Jews would become a majority in the country. This would require

a transition period of a national minority government that would take control of the state apparatus, the administration and the army—in order to forestall the danger of a take-over by the non-Jewish majority or of rebellion against us (which we could put down only if the state apparatus and the army were in our hands). During this transition period the systematic policy of development, immigration and settlement would be carried out.

He acknowledged that this position was "perhaps dangerously close to well-known forms of popular political thinking [i.e., Revisionism] from which we have always kept distant." But, he insisted, "I shall never ac-cept the defeat of Zionism before an attempt has been made equal in its seriousness to the difficulties we face in our struggle to renew our na-tional life."[14]

In the face of the futility of attempting to get the Arabs to agree to surrender their majority status in order that the Zionists might have parity, Weizmann appeared to be prepared to make a further conces-sion. That is, he was ready to modify the idea of parity to mean a 60–40 ratio in favor of the Arabs. Arlosoroff took issue with this and wrote to Weizmann on November 21, 1932: "Parity, as a constitutional princi-ple that aims at preventing the domination of one part of the popula-tion over the other, can mean nothing other than complete equality."[15]

Notwithstanding Arlosoroff's own reservations about the utility of continued cooperation with the British, once he and his Mapai colleagues took control of the Zionist Executive, they also adopted Weizmann's conciliatory approach. This was made clear at a meeting of the General Council of the Zionist Organization held in London from July 28 to August 8, 1932. Arlosoroff took the position that there was reason to believe that matters would take a turn for the better with the new high commissioner, who had assumed his post only half a year earlier. Meir Grossman of the Revisionists roundly attacked this tepid posture as being altogether unrealistic. What was needed, he argued, was a change of policy. A mere change of personnel meant little. Now that the Mapai had replaced the General Zionists as the dominant voice in world Zionism, it became the target of the Revisionist onslaught.

Relations between the Revisionists and Mapai became increasingly acrimonious as the two parties found themselves at loggerheads on virtually every issue of any consequence. This happened in part because their memberships derived in the main from different segments of the Jewish community. The Revisionists drew their membership primarily from the middle class. They had the support of the bourgeoisie and intellectuals of Polish Jewry, and were considered to be the only group that might ultimately contest Labor's domination of the Yishuv and the Zionist movement. The Union of Zionist Revisionists was founded in 1925 by followers of Jabotinsky, and it participated in the Fourteenth Zionist Congress with a delegation of four. In 1927 it was able to have ten delegates, the number doubling to twenty-one in 1929. At the 1931 congress the Revisionist delegate strength reached fifty-two, and they were able to play a decisive role in Weizmann's defeat.

With the rise of Adolf Hitler in Germany and the growing exodus of Polish Jews in 1933, there was every reason to believe that Revisionist delegate strength at future Zionist congresses would continue to increase. The Revisionists thus began to pose a serious threat to Mapai's preeminent position. As tension between the two groups mounted with the approach of the Eighteenth Zionist Congress that year, a tragic incident took place that was exploited most successfully by the Labor leadership to attack their political opposition.

On the night of June 16, 1933, as Arlosoroff was taking a stroll with his wife on the beach at Tel Aviv, he was attacked and shot by two assailants. He died several days later without having regained consciousness. Almost immediately, and before any serious investigation had taken place, it was decided that the crime had been committed by Revisionists, and the police did not search any further for suspects. At a memorial meeting held in Warsaw two days after the killing, Ben-Gurion, in an outburst of cynical and irresponsible partisanship, declared: "I have no doubt that this was an act of political terror."[16]

On June 19, Abraham Stavsky, a recent immigrant from Poland, was arrested and charged with the crime. According to a statement made by a Colonial Office representative in the House of Commons on June 22, Mrs. Arlosoroff "identified him as resembling the companion of the man who fired the shot."[17] This notwithstanding that prior to her mysterious change of testimony, Sima Arlosoroff was heard by several witnesses as indicating that her husband had been killed by Arabs. On July 22, another twenty Revisionists were arrested as suspects, and Mrs. Arlosoroff identified one of them, Zvi Rosenblatt, as the one who fired the shot. Abba Ahimeir, editor of the Revisionist weekly *Hazit Haam*, was accused of having instigated the murder. When two Arabs, Abdul Majid and Issa el-Abrass, confessed to having committed the crime, they were induced by the authorities to withdraw their confessions. It was evident that the police had no interest in prosecuting anyone other than Revisionists for the crime. In his memoirs, Joseph M. Broadhearst, a former commander of the British police in Tel Aviv, stated: "We did not have any incriminating evidence, not one real clue, but since the victim was a politically symbolic figure, we had to do something. Thus we decided to arrest a number of militant extremists whose ideas were opposed to those held by the victim. We knew for a fact that none of the accused had been involved in the murder. We were forced to pervert justice for reasons of state."[18]

The Labor movement discarded all restraints in characterizing the killing as a political assassination, irrespective of the fact that Mrs. Arlosoroff's testimony was completely uncorroborated by the results of the police investigation. In its report to the League of Nations in 1934, the British government stated: "Rightly or wrongly, the crime is ascribed to Revisionist preachings against what that Party is said to regard as the timorous methods of the Jewish Agency."[19]

A broad anti-Revisionist coalition, formed by Labor and the General Zionists, produced a statement calling for the outlawing of the entire Jabotinsky movement: "We declare that the moral responsibility for this brutal assassination falls upon the entire Revisionist Movement which has produced such a murderer. . . . Whoever is still concerned about the fate of Zionism must shake himself clear of the Revisionist past. No intercourse whatever with Revisionism! Let our motto be: 'Expel the Revisionist gangs from Jewish life!' "[20] The leaders of the Labor movement found in Arlosoroff's murder an opportunity to demolish their political opposition, and they sought to exploit the occasion to the fullest, irrespective of the fact that there was no evidence whatever that the Revisionists had any complicity in the crime.

Jabotinsky refused to take this blood libel passively, and lashed out at the Zionist leaders who had cynically exploited the tragic death of Arlosoroff for petty partisan purposes. He charged them with irresponsibility and a violation of civilized norms by condemning a person before his guilt was established by an impartial court of justice. He was particularly outraged at their ascribing guilt to the community to which an individual belonged, something to which history should have made Jews especially sensitive:

I accuse a large section of Jewry, in this case, of ignominiously violating both these principles. They see a young Jew in a Palestine prison swearing his innocence, fighting for his life and his honor; they have not yet heard any proof against him, yet they already proclaim him a murderer and push him to the gallows. Moreover, they are charging an entire movement, numbering tens of thousands of adherents, and ten times that number of sympathizers, with moral complicity in the hideous crime. And they do it for the glaringly obvious and ugly motives of party vendetta and vote-catching.[21]

(It is noteworthy that a similar politically motivated ascription of collective guilt to the political opposition was echoed by the Labor alliance in the wake of the assassination of Prime Minister Yitzhak Rabin some sixty years later, but with little practical avail.)

At the time, however, even the powerful and legendary oratory of Jabotinsky was not able to ameliorate the political damage done to the Revisionists by the sustained barrage of villification to which they were subjected. At the Eighteenth Zionist Congress, which convened later that summer, the Labor bloc succeeded in gaining approval, by 2 votes out of 300, of a motion to preclude Revisionist participation in the Zionist Presidium, notwithstanding the time-honored tradition that all parties were to be represented in its composition.

It took almost a full year for the Palestine administration to bring the accused to trial. In the interim, little by little the mood was shifting in favor of the innocence of the accused, notwithstanding the unrelenting anti-Revisionist propaganda campaign carried on by the Labor movement. A powerful voice raised in support of the accused was that of the venerated chief rabbi, Abraham I. Kook. On May 16, 1934, Abba Ahimeir was acquitted of the charge of conspiracy to murder. Then, surprisingly, on June 8, Zvi Rosenblatt, whom Mrs. Arlosoroff positively identified as having pulled the trigger, was found innocent, while

Abraham Stavsky, who was identified by Mrs. Arlosoroff as "resembling" the man who accompanied the one who fired the gun, was found guilty and sentenced to death by hanging. The very absurdity of what had taken place in the Palestine courtroom resonated throughout the Jewish world as a travesty that demanded rectification. The defense lodged an appeal, and tremendous pressure began to be applied to the Colonial Office, demanding guarantees of a fair trial. From the floor of the House of Commons, Colonel Josiah Wedgwood demanded that the colonial secretary see to it "that England shall not risk being found guilty of judicial murder."[22]

Stavsky Defense Committees were organized all over the world. Finally, on July 19, the Court of Appeal overturned Stavsky's conviction. Nonetheless, on July 22, the Histadrut newspaper, *Davar*, declared that Stavsky and Rosenblatt remained murderers. A Mapai manifesto stated that although the court had freed them, in the eyes of the party they remained guilty, and Arlosoroff's murder would be avenged.

The British police never discovered Arlosoroff's murderers. However, on July 16, 1955, at a twenty-second anniversary memorial meeting in honor of Arlosoroff held in Tel Aviv, Yehuda Tennenbaum-Arazi, a devoted member of Mapai, who as a police officer had been involved in the original investigation and trial, stated flatly: "Abraham Stavsky did not kill Arlosoroff; Arabs did."[23] Subsequently, demands by the Revisionists for a full investigation by a special commission of the Zionist Organization, and by the Herut Party for the appointment of a Knesset judicial committee to oversee such an effort, were overwhelmingly rejected by the Labor-dominated governing coalition. The question of why and by whom Arlosoroff was assassinated remains unresolved to this very day.

Nonetheless, the only plausible explanation so far—unacceptable to the traditional Zionist historiography, which is understandably reluctant to admit even the remotest connection between the Jewish Agency and the Nazi government of Germany—has been offered by a pair of investigative journalists. The assassination took place only several days after Arlosoroff, in his capacity as director of the political department of the Jewish Agency, returned from a two-month official stay in Germany, of which Hitler had just become chancellor. During his visit Arlosoroff looked up a number of friends and acquaintances from his student days. In this process he also sought to contact Magda Friedlander, who had been a close friend of his sister Lisa. Magda, whose parents were not Jewish, was the adopted daughter of Max Friedlander, a Jew, who married her divorced mother. Magda Friedlander had become Magda Quandt by her first marriage, and in 1931 became the spouse of Dr. Joseph Goebbels, then Berlin *Gauleiter* (district leader) of the Nazi Party, who was unaware of her Jewish connections. Then, shortly after Hitler came to power on January 31, 1933, a family squabble led Magda to reveal to Goebbels her adoption by a Jewish stepfather and other Jewish connections including that of an old friend who was now a senior official of the Jewish Agency. Almost immediately every one of Magda's Jewish connections, disappeared, including Max Friedlander, who was arrested by the Gestapo in March 1933.

The following month, Arlosoroff arrived in Berlin for the purpose of establishing contacts between the Jewish Agency and the new German government. While there, he attempted unsuccessfully to arrange a meeting with his old friend Magda Goebbels, evidently unaware that this might pose an extreme embarrassment to her husband and possibly a threat to his future in the Nazi regime. According to the investigative journalists, Goebbels was reluctant to take any action against Arlosoroff in Germany because he carried a British passport and was effectively on British government business; his disappearance might cause an international incident. Instead, two Gestapo agents, who arrived in Jerusalem at the beginning of April for an unrelated purpose, soon established contact with a Nazi Party cell in the German community of Sarona on the outskirts of Tel Aviv. There they arranged for the contracted assassination of Arlosoroff to eliminate a potential danger to the personal well-being of Joseph Goebbels.[24]

A truce was ultimately negotiated between Jabotinsky and Ben-Gurion on October 26, 1934. The agreement between the Revisionist World Union and the Zionist Executive stipulated that "without infringing upon the freedom of discussion and criticism within the Zionist movement, all parties undertake to refrain from means of party warfare which are outside the limits of political ideological discussion and are not in conformity with the moral principles of Zionism and of civilized conduct."[25] On November 11, a second agreement was signed that put in place an arrangement between the Histadrut and the Revisionist National Labor Organization designed to eliminate the growing fratricidal competition between the two. A third and final agreement, signed on December 14, provided for a suspension of the Revisionist boycott against the Zionist national funds, as well as the restoration of the right of members of the Revisionist Brit Trumpeldor to immigration certificates. However, the truce was short-lived.

Ben-Gurion, who was in London, where the negotiation with Jabotinsky took place, returned to Palestine to present the agreement to the
Histadrut Executive. However, before he returned, word of the agreement leaked out, creating a furor among the Histadrut's membership
who had taken the earlier total disparagement of the Revisionists by
their leaders at face value. Upon his arrival, Ben-Gurion encountered
an unexpected alliance between the extreme left and right wings of the
Labor movement, the latter still smarting at the loss of Arlosoroff,
whom they considered one of their own. The Histadrut Executive
stood its ground against Ben-Gurion and rejected the proposed agreement. Ben-Gurion would not accept this repudiation of his leadership,
and insisted on a referendum involving the entire organization. In
March 1935, a referendum was duly held on the Labor agreement negotiated with the Revisionists, and the proposed accord was rejected by
a margin of three to two. Under normal circumstances, such a defeat,
which was equivalent to a vote of no confidence, should have required
Ben-Gurion to resign as general secretary of the Histadrut and surrender his seat on the Jewish Agency Executive. However, Ben-Gurion did
no such thing. He insisted on remaining at the helm of the Labor movement, despite his repudiation by the membership.

With no little embarrassment to himself, Ben-Gurion had to inform
Jabotinsky that the Histadrut had rejected their agreement. At the
same time Jabotinsky accused the Zionist Executive of acting in bad
faith by effectively reneging on the other agreements that had been
concluded. Relations continued to worsen once again, and in response
to the results of an organizational referendum held in June 1935, the
Revisionists decided to secede from the World Zionist Organization.
They boycotted the Nineteenth Zionist Congress that year and established their own separate and parallel New Zionist Organization. It was
their aim and hope that other Zionist groups dissatisfied with Labor's
domination of the Zionist movement would join them. This did not
happen to any extent, and the New Zionist Organization became in effect just another name for the Revisionists.

Dissatisfaction with Labor's domination of the Zionist movement
was also reflected in Palestine with respect to the institutions of the
Yishuv, most especially the Haganah. Since the early 1920s the Haganah had been the responsibility of the Histadrut, which had treated it
for the most part with benign neglect. Without effective oversight the
Haganah became a world unto itself under the leadership of Joseph
Hecht, who ran the organization as he saw fit even though he nominally reported to the general secretary of the Histadrut, David Ben-

Gurion. While there was never any question about Hecht's commitment to the defense of the Yishuv, the Haganah's state of readiness had
eroded over the years of relative peace after the disturbances of 1921.
Thus, when the riots of 1929 broke out, the Haganah's unimpressive
performance in defending the Yishuv became a matter of broader concern, and the Histadrut began to pay more serious attention to its
long-standing but long neglected responsibilities for oversight of the
organization.

At the same time, concerns were raised outside the Labor movement
about the Haganah remaining under the exclusive control of the Histadrut. It was argued that defense of the Yishuv was a communitywide
responsibility to be shared in by all segments of the population, including those opposed to the views of the Labor movement. To avoid the
possibility of a demand for an alternative defense organization that was
not under Labor's control, an agreement was hammered out that provided for parity control of the Haganah. That is, the Histadrut would
have half of the seats in an overall directorate and the other half would
be held by other institutions such as the Vaad Leumi. This arrangement
was later to prove unsatisfactory to the Revisionists and others who
wished to reduce Labor's influence over the Yishuv. The problem, as
they saw it, was simply that the parity arrangement continued to ensure
Labor dominance. More than 80 percent of the Histadrut were also
members of the Mapai and its affiliate organizations. Since the Mapai
was also the major political party, it controlled a majority of the Vaad
Leumi. Thus, while the parity arrangement provided ostensibly nonpartisan control of the Haganah, it in fact perpetuated control by the
Mapai.

Among the officers of the Haganah there was a closely knit group of
friends who had immigrated from southern Russia during the early
1920s, and were known as the "Odessa contingent." They were a particularly militant group that was quite impatient with the passivity
which characterized the Yishuv in the aftermath of the 1929 riots. The
members of the group were concentrated primarily in Jerusalem, although an offshoot, the "Sharon contingent," settled in the western
Jezreel Valley. Eliahu Ben-Horin, one of those from Jerusalem, had
been in contact with Jabotinsky and became an active Revisionist. He
and another fellow officer, Abraham Tehomi, had met with Jabotinsky
during the late 1920s to discuss the possibility of organizing a new military organization to complement the Haganah. Tehomi argued that
the Haganah, by its constitution and orientation, was geared toward
static defense. That is, it saw its mission as repelling Arab attacks. What

was needed, in his view, was a new organization orientated toward offensive action that would bring the struggle to the enemy.

Although Jabotinsky declined to assist in creating such a force, being opposed in principle to nonlegal organizations, Tehomi continued to pursue the idea and began to gather a following among the Haganah commanders in Jerusalem. After the promulgation of the Passfield White Paper, Tehomi, who was at the time Haganah commander in Jerusalem, attacked the British Labour government as "Socialist Jesuits" in a speech to an assembly of Haganah officers. This remark was interpreted by some Histadrut loyalists as an assault on Histadrut's leadership of the Haganah, and they marked Tehomi as someone to be watched carefully.

Following this incident Ben-Horin left for the United States, on a mission for the Revisionist Party. Shortly afterward Tehomi announced that he was going to the United States for six months, to visit family. The Histadrut loyalists immediately construed this coincidence as a conspiracy, and rumors soon spread that Tehomi and Ben-Horin had gone to raise funds to establish an independent Haganah that would be linked with the Revisionists and the Brit Trumpeldor. Since Tehomi had taken six months' leave, the Haganah leadership decided to exploit the opportunity to replace him with a Histadrut loyalist.

Tehomi left Palestine in March 1931, but was soon back. Upon his arrival in Piraeus, Greece, he had run into a problem with the American consul. A medical team boarded the ship there to examine those destined for the United States and were disturbed by the condition of Tehomi's arm, which had been injured in an accident in 1928. Upon their recommendation the consul refused to give him a visa, and he was forced to return to Palestine. On his return he requested that his leave be canceled and that he return to his post in Jerusalem. He was informed that this was impossible because a new commander had already been appointed, and that the decision could not be revoked. This led to an immediate revolt against the Haganah leadership by Tehomi and a number of officers loyal to him. It quickly became known that Tehomi's conflict with the Haganah leadership was not a military issue but a political one, and many Haganah members who were not members of the Histadrut were prepared to defect with him. Shortly thereafter, Tehomi and his friends and supporters bolted from the Haganah and established the *Irgun haTzvai haLeumi* (National Military Organization) in Jerusalem, which was popularly known as Haganah "B."

Tehomi went to the Zionist Congress in 1931, hoping to garner support from the various groups that were opposed to the Weizmann-

Labor coalition. However, he was unsuccessful in generating any mean-
ingful assistance. Even Jabotinsky refused to help him. He returned to
Jerusalem empty-handed but not discouraged. He began recruiting
among non-Labor-oriented students. Two of these, David Raziel and
Abraham Stern, were to play very important roles in the later armed
struggle against the British. Tehomi established contact with the Brit
Trumpeldor defense group in Tel Aviv that, under the leadership of
Jeremiah Halpern, was already operating outside the Haganah frame-
work. It joined the Haganah "B" as a unit. Brit Trumpeldor groups in
Rosh Pina and Yesud haMaaleh also joined. In December 1932, the
Haganah branch in Safed, heavily influenced by the Revisionists, de-
fected en bloc and also joined the Haganah "B."

Despite these early gains, the Haganah "B" had no regular source of
funds and was severely limited in its actual operational capacity. Tehomi, who was not a Revisionist even though the bulk of his support
came from Revisionist circles, understood that under the circumstances
it made little sense to maintain a separate organization that was essentially duplicative of the Haganah. He therefore sought to use the Haganah "B" as a bargaining chip in negotiations to bring about unification
of the defense organizations. But the idea of unification did not sit well
with the staff of Haganah "B," among whom were many Revisionists with
little interest in subjecting themselves once again to indirect Histadrut
and Mapai control. Unification talks nonetheless took place early in the
spring of 1933, and an agreement was worked out. However, it came
apart after only two weeks when members of the Histadrut attempted
to disrupt a Brit Trumpeldor demonstration in Tel Aviv. The possibilities of unification seemed especially remote after the Arlosoroff affair.

A Haganah "B" delegation went to the Zionist Congress at Prague
in 1933, once again to seek support, and this time they were more successful. Tehomi proposed to the leadership of the Revisionists, Mizrahi,
and General Zionists that a public oversight council should be established. Jabotinsky reluctantly agreed to participate in the council,
which was joined by Rabbi Meir Berlin of Mizrahi, Emmanuel Neumann
of the General Zionists, and Meir Grossman. After this, the split in the
defense structure of the Yishuv along political lines seemed irreversible.

General Sir Arthur Wauchope arrived in Palestine in November
1931, to take up the post of high commissioner. Well-meaning, but seriously hampered by a lack of understanding of the country and its
problems, he was ill served by his aides, who failed to carry out the es-

sential task of keeping him out of trouble. Sir Arthur soon proceeded to stir up a hornet's nest.

The idea of a legislative council had originated with Herbert Samuel, who was forced to abandon it by 1923 as a result of the adamant opposition of the Arabs and the ambivalence of the Jews to such an institution. The Arabs were against it simply because it did not provide the self-rule they uncompromisingly demanded. The Jews looked askance at the proposal because, being a representative institution, it would place them in a powerless minority position, and that was not what the Balfour Declaration or the Palestine Mandate had intended. There was, however, a suggestion of such a representative body incorporated into the Passfield White Paper, and the new high commissioner decided to make his mark by establishing a legislative council that would serve to bring the Arabs and Jews together.

On November 10, 1932, Wauchope informed the Permanent Mandates Commission that the legislative council idea, although long dormant, was by no means dead, and that he intended to bring it to realization. As should have been expected, he was promptly denounced for his efforts by the Jewish leadership, who saw the imposition of such a council as a further betrayal not only of the Mandate but also of the 1931 MacDonald letter. At the same time, significant developments were taking place in the Arab community that were exacerbated by the ill-timed and ill-conceived initiative.

The beginning of the decade saw the transfer of leadership of the Palestine Arabs from the landowning Western-oriented politicians of the Muslim-Christian Associations and the Arab Congress, represented by Musa Kazim, to the Supreme Muslim Council and Haj Amin al-Husseini. There was a considerable difference between the two. Musa Kazim represented the old school of Arab nationalists in Palestine, who originally saw their future within a Greater Syria, and who remained somewhat disoriented after this notion was quashed by the French. The mufti, on the other hand, was primarily interested in power and religion. He wanted to become the caliph of Islam.

The caliphate, the most prominent institution in Islam, had been held for centuries by the Ottoman sultans. It was abolished by Kemal Ataturk in 1924 and was promptly arrogated by King Hussein of Hejaz, who as a Hashemite claimed lineal descent from the daughter of the Prophet. He held the position for only a very brief period because he was overthrown by Abdul Aziz Ibn Saud, king of Nejd, that same year. A Pan-Islamic Congress held at Mecca in 1926 failed to agree on a suitable candidate. The office of caliph thus remained vacant, and Haj

Amin began to campaign for the position. To bolster his claim, he supported steps to make Jerusalem an important Muslim center, something it had never really been. In January 1931, the body of Muhammad Ali, the former leader of the Indian Caliphate Committee, was interred in the Haram ash-Sharif precinct on the Temple Mount. A few months later, the former King Hussein of Hejaz was similarly buried there.

Haj Amin, together with Shawkat Ali, the new leader of the Indian Caliphate Committee, called for a world Islamic Congress to be held at Jerusalem in December 1931. One of the main purposes of the religious convocation was to establish a University of al-Aqsa in Jerusalem, making it a major center of Muslim learning and giving its mufti enhanced status in the Muslim world. The move was strongly opposed by the heads of Cairo's ancient al-Azhar University, which had long been the cultural and religious center of the Arab and Muslim world. The Islamic Congress failed to achieve the mufti's purposes, primarily because the rival Palestinian clan of the Nashishibis understood what Haj Amin was after, and did all they could to prevent him from obtaining it. They could not abide the notion of the Husseinis capturing the caliphate.

Nonetheless, Haj Amin succeeded in making himself the preeminent Arab leader in Palestine and in changing the intrinsic character of the Arab-Zionist confrontation. The earlier Arab leaders were vehemently anti-Zionist without holding any particularly strong feelings toward the Jews as such. The mufti changed all this. Under his leadership Arab nationalism became identical with anti-Semitism. His program for achieving the goals of Arab nationalism was simple—a holy war against the infidel.

Under this simplistic scheme no distinction could be drawn between Jewish and British infidels, all of whom were presumed to be in league against the Muslim Arabs. It was to take some time before his ideas spread throughout significant portions of the Arab population of Palestine. However, Haj Amin had already shown the extremes of which he was capable. Previous Arab outbreaks, such as that of 1920, were primarily anti-Zionist in character. The outbreak in 1929 was another matter. The pogroms of that year were distinctively anti-Jewish, drawing no distinctions between Zionists and non-Zionists. Hebron, for example, where one of the deadliest assaults took place, had an essentially anti-Zionist Jewish population.

As the mufti consolidated his control over the Arab community, the possibility of an accommodation between Zionism and Arab nationalism became increasingly remote. It took the somewhat naive Zionist leadership, which was still preoccupied with promoting the notion of communal parity as the solution to their problem with the Arabs, some time to digest that reality.

The new effort initiated by Wauchope to institute a legislative council was characterized by the mufti's followers as part of an elaborate British plot to dilute Arab control over the country in order to accommodate the Jews. This could not be tolerated. The Arab Executive Committee, with the encouragement of the mufti, held a rally in Jaffa on March 26, 1933, that called for a boycott of both Jewish and British goods and a policy of noncooperation with the British administration. Later, in August, reports of the demands of the Eighteenth Zionist Congress that was being held in Prague poured more fuel on the flames of Arab dissatisfaction with the course of events. In view of the distressing events taking place in Europe, the Zionist Congress demanded a revision of the existing Immigration Ordinance, which it saw as too restrictive and which the Arabs considered far too liberal. The congress protested the restriction of immigration at a time when the Jewish masses of the Diaspora found themselves in a serious economic and political crisis. It called upon the Executive of the Jewish Agency "to demand from the Government the transfer of responsibility for Jewish immigration into Eretz Israel, in accordance with the Mandate, to the Jewish Agency."[26]

The Arab Executive called for a general strike to take place on October 13. It then sponsored a protest march in Jerusalem, in defiance of a government ban, that was forcefully dispersed by the police. A similar event took place on October 27, in Jaffa, where the police also had to use their guns to restore order. This was followed by outbreaks in Haifa and Nablus, and by new disturbances in Jerusalem on October 28 and 29. To Wauchope's surprise, the outbreak of Arab violence in October 1933 was directed not at the Jews but exclusively at the British. The logic of the mufti's decision in favor of this approach was remarkably simplistic. In his view, without British support the Zionists would be powerless to stand in the way of Arab rule in Palestine. Consequently, the path to the defeat of Zionism led to a prior confrontation with its British backers.

The riots in Haifa, Jaffa, Jerusalem, and Nablus resulted in the death of 26 Arabs and 1 Englishman, and 178 Arabs and 56 British injured. There were no Jewish casualties. One of the Arabs who was injured was the venerable Musa Kazim, now in his eighties; he died several months later, in March 1934, leaving a fractionated Arab community that the mufti was easily able to dominate. The leaders of the outbreaks were offered suspended sentences in exchange for a commitment to stay out of politics for a period of three years. The mufti, who conveniently left the country to collect funds for his university project before the demonstrations actually began, was exonerated of any blame, although one of his aides, Sheikh Muzaffar, went to jail rather than accede to the terms insisted upon by the British for suspension of his sentence. Unaccountably, Arabist romanticism remained so deeply embedded in the Colonial Office that despite all the evidence to the contrary, the British continued to believe in the mufti's moderation throughout the decade.

At the same time, events in Europe were taking shape that would link the fate of the Jews of Europe with the progress toward achieving Zionist aims in Palestine. The fateful day occurred in January 1933, when Paul von Hindenburg, the German president, appointed Adolf Hitler as chancellor of Germany. One of Hitler's first acts as de facto ruler of Germany was to rectify the conspicuous absence of anti-Jewish legislation in the country. In April 1933, the new regime began the process of official anti-Semitism with the benign-sounding "Law for the Restoration of the Civil Service," which ended Jewish participation in the country's professional, cultural, and commercial life.

Jewish immigration into Palestine in 1931 totaled 4,075, few of whom came from Central Europe. The following year a small but significant number of Central European Jews correctly interpreted the signs of what was coming and joined the influx into Palestine, which more than doubled to 9,553. In 1933, Hitler's accession to power helped precipitate a tripling of immigration to 30,327. To their credit, the British understood the pressing need for the Jews to get out of Europe, and despite warnings about the dangers of allowing such large numbers into the country, they continued to allow the Jews to make maximum use of the flexibility afforded by the existing immigration regulations. Accordingly, in 1934 the figure rose to 42,359, the largest recorded up to that time. In 1935, the year that the infamous Nuremberg Laws were instituted, a total of 61,854 Jews from all over Europe entered Palestine.

As anti-Semitic pressures increased in Europe, the Zionist approach to the question of the Jewish national home began to become grounded in a new realism. It was no longer possible to debate whether it should be a cultural center for a far-flung Diaspora, or whether some accommodation could be reached with the Arabs that would satisfy them that they ran no risk of being dominated by a future Jewish majority in the country. It also was no longer possible to be concerned about whether the number of immigrants would exceed the theoretical economic absorptive capacity of the country, and thereby negatively affect

the standard of living. The Jews of Europe needed a refuge immediately, and at the rate of the 1935 immigration, the Jews might well be
the majority in Palestine within a year.

This unprecedented influx, seen through Arab eyes, confirmed their
worst fears about a Zionist conquest of Palestine. The Jews, on the
other hand, exhibited little satisfaction at the limited numbers of immigrants who were being permitted to enter the country, and they continued to flay the British administration in the press for not making larger
numbers of immigration certificates available. From the Arab viewpoint, the very composition of the immigrants attested to the fact that
the Jews were using the emergence of Nazism as an excuse for taking
over Palestine. After all, less than an eighth of those who entered the
country between 1932 and 1935 were from Germany, where the bulk
of the immigration should have come from, while approximately 43
percent came from Poland. The reasons for these skewed numbers were
complex, and no one even tried to explain them to the Arabs, who drew
the conclusions that best served their interests.

The facts were that the open persecution of the Jews by the Nazis,
which was met largely by silence and indifference in the Western world,
opened a floodgate of imitative persecutions in Eastern Europe, where
a vicious latent anti-Semitism lay just below the surface, ready to rise at
any moment. The German Jews, large numbers of whom were assimi-
lated, had no tradition of escape from persecution and continued to
hope that the Nazi threat would pass. The Jews of Poland and Eastern
Europe had no such illusions, and many found it much easier to uproot
themselves from their homes. It has also been suggested by some that
part of the reason for the vast disparity between the numbers of German and Polish Jews entering Palestine during the early 1930s lay with
the Jewish Agency's methods of allocating immigration certificates.
According to this thesis, since most of the Jews in Palestine were from
Eastern Europe, and they therefore had the greatest representation in
the Jewish Agency, certificates were allocated in a manner calculated to
maintain East European dominance in the Yishuv.[27] However, none of
this was of any interest to the Arabs. The pattern of immigration confirmed their suspicions, and that was sufficient.

The Nineteenth Zionist Congress, which saw the return of Weizmann to the presidency of the world movement, met in Lucerne, Swit-
zerland, in the fall of 1935, and passed a resolution against the
establishment of the proposed legislative council in Palestine. The high
commissioner was advised of the Zionist opposition to his plan and the

determination of the Yishuv to boycott participation in the council. In November the mufti made the Arab conditions for participation known to Wauchope. These included a sovereign Parliament that reflected the Arab majority in the country and a ban on all further Jewish immigration and land transfers to Jews. While the Arab demands were being considered in London, Wauchope formally presented the offer of a legislative council and home rule to both Arabs and Jews in December. The following month the British government responded to the Arab demands by rejecting the cessation of all immigration. But, at the same time, it indicated the possibility that legislation placing some restrictions on land transfers might be introduced.

On April 2, 1936, the Arabs were invited to send a delegation to London to discuss the matter. The invitation was accepted, but the Arab leadership was still divided over the question of whether to accept the British offer of a home rule constitution. Some of the Arab leaders had come to the realization that acceptance of the British offer would give them effective control of the country even if the Jews should elect to participate in the new political process. However, this would also mean an acknowledgment of the validity of the Balfour Declaration and the Palestine Mandate, something that was difficult for the ardent nationalists among them to accept after having categorically rejected the establishment of a legislative council, for that very reason, for more than a decade.

While the Arabs deliberated about what to do, a series of debates took place in Parliament that clearly indicated that the mood of the House of Commons was running against the government's proposals. The parliamentary opposition to the establishment of the legislative council was not simply a reflection of support for the Zionists. There were many who held that it would require a longer period of British tutelage than that provided for in the proposal to ensure that a genuinely democratic legislative system would be established. To forestall any domestic political embarrassment over a possible failure by the government to carry the day on the issue, the government effectively dropped the constitutional scheme for Palestine on April 8, 1936. It announced that it was delaying action on the proposal pending further discussions with the proposed participants. Within days, there was a new and major outbreak of Arab violence.

NOTES

1. Melvin I. Urofsky, *A Voice That Spoke for Justice*, p. 220.
2. Walter Laqueur, *A History of Zionism*, p. 495.

3. Joseph B. Schechtman, *Fighter and Prophet: The Last Years*, p. 149.

4. Chaim Weizmann, *The Letters and Papers of Chaim Weizmann*, series A, vol. XIV, pp. 206–209.

5. Susan L. Hattis, *The Bi-National Idea in Palestine During Mandatory Times*, p. 88.

6. Ibid., p. 89.

7. Ibid., pp. 90–91.

8. Ibid., p. 97.

9. Urofsky, *A Voice That Spoke for Justice*, p. 277.

10. Ibid., p. 278.

11. Hattis, *The Bi-National Idea in Palestine*, p. 92.

12. Ibid., p. 106.

13. Chaim Arlosoroff, *Jerusalem Diary*, p. 208.

14. Ibid., p. 341.

15. Ibid., p. 348.

16. Yitshaq Ben-Ami, *Years of Wrath, Days of Glory*, p. 315.

17. Schechtman, *Fighter and Prophet*, p. 185.

18. Jacques Derogy and Hesi Carmel, *The Untold History of Israel*, pp. 44–45.

19. Ibid.

20. Ibid.

21. Ibid., pp. 186–187.

22. Ibid., p. 202.

23. Ibid., p. 203, n.

24. Ibid., ch. 2.

25. *The Jewish Daily News Bulletin*, October 29, 1934.

26. *Palestine: A Study of Jewish, Arab, and British Policies*, vol. 2, pp. 769–770.

27. Albert M. Hyamson, *Palestine Under the Mandate 1920–1948*, pp. 68–69.

6

The Arab Revolt, 1936–1939

In the early spring of 1936, British domination of the eastern Mediterranean came under serious challenge for the first time since 1918. The Italian-Ethiopian war was drawing to a close with a troublesome loss of prestige for Britain, which adamantly opposed, but was unable to prevent, Italian adventurism in Africa. To make things worse, Italian agents were busy spreading anti-British propaganda throughout the region in an effort to enhance their own position at Britain's expense. A real threat of a war between Italy and Britain seemed to be emerging. During April, negotiations were being concluded for the Anglo-Egyptian treaty (signed August 21) and the Anglo-Iraqi treaty (ratified June 30), agreements that moved these Arab countries toward independence. These developments, along with the highly divisive issue of the legislative council that the high commissioner had reintroduced, contributed to a state of tension in Palestine. Many Arab leaders came to believe that the hour was at hand to force Britain to make some major concessions to Arab nationalism and the demand for Arab self-determination in Palestine.

It was not long before a flagrant outrage perpetrated against the Jews of Palestine set in motion a series of events that rocked the country for a good part of the year. On the night of April 15, ten automobiles traveling the Tulkharm-Nablus road were stopped and their occupants robbed by Arab bandits. Three of the travelers who were Jews were separated from the rest, and shot. Because the three were selected for execution only because they were Jewish, anti-Arab feeling rose dramatically in the Yishuv. The following night two Arabs were found murdered near Petah Tikva, presumably in retaliation for the outrage. On April 17, the burial of one of the Jewish victims of the Tulkharm road shootings, an immigrant from Greece, provided the spark for a disorderly anti-Arab demonstration in Tel Aviv that spilled over into a number of assaults on Arabs in the area. Two days later, spurred on by false reports that the Jews were murdering Arabs, mobs in the Manshieh quarter of Jaffa attacked the Jews there and murdered three before the police, reinforced by troops, were able to restore order.

On April 20, an Arab National Committee was set up at Nablus to advocate and organize a general strike that would force the British authorities to accede to the Arab demands for self-rule that had been presented to the high commissioner the previous November. Within days similar committees sprang up throughout the country, and the general strike began on April 22, with an almost complete cessation of Arab business activity and labor. Three days later, a new organization composed of Palestinian Arab notables, the Arab Higher Committee, was established to assume leadership of the strike and subsequent negotiations with the British authorities. The mufti, Haj Amin al-Husseini, headed the committee, which included Auni Abdel Hadi and Ahmad Hilmi Pasha of the Istiqlal Party, and local Arab Muslim leaders Ragheb Bey Nashishibi, Jamal Bey al-Husseini, Abdul Latif Bey Salah, and Hussein E. Khalidi. In addition, Yacoub Ghussein and Yacoub Faraj represented the Greek Orthodox Arabs, and Alfred Rock represented the Roman Catholics.

The Arab Higher Committee submitted its demands to the high commissioner in a letter that called for the prohibition of Jewish immigration, the prohibition of the transfer of Arab lands to Jews, and the establishment of a national government responsible to a representative council. In the absence of a conciliatory gesture from the Palestine administration, it resolved to continue the general strike until the British government changed its current policy, beginning with an immediate cessation of all Jewish immigration. At this point, sensitive to criticism of its stewardship of the Mandate by the League of Nations, the British government was unwilling to make such a concession under obvious Arab pressure. Instead, Wauchope continued to urge the Arabs to send a delegation to London to discuss the legislative council proposal, as they had agreed earlier. The Arab Higher Committee's refusal to comply with this request brought the matter to an impasse.

A general congress of local Arab committees convened in Jerusalem on May 8. It unanimously adopted a resolution calling not only for a continuation of the strike but also for civil disobedience in the form of a refusal to pay taxes after May 15, unless the government prohibited any further Jewish immigration. Wauchope continued to believe that it was still possible to reconcile Jewish and Arab aspirations, and on May 13, he informed the Arab Higher Committee that Britain would establish a royal commission to investigate the causes of their grievances as soon as order was reestablished. The colonial secretary announced the formation of the commission in the House of Commons on May 18, with the proviso that the commission would not proceed to Palestine until order was restored. Moreover, to avoid giving the public the impression that the government was caving in to Arab demands, the high commissioner published a reduced Labor Schedule that same day. It permitted the issuance of a total of only 4,500 immigration certificates for the period from April to September 1936, about 40 percent of the 11,200 certificates requested by the Jewish Agency.

The general strike spread from Jaffa and Jerusalem to other towns, and was accompanied by sporadic physical assaults on Jews. In the countryside guerrilla warfare was waged from the hills with hit-and-run attacks on the police and Jewish settlements. Jewish crops were destroyed and telephone lines were cut. One of the unintended outcomes of the strike in Jaffa was that the Jewish Agency was presented with an appropriate occasion to press its long-standing demand for a Jewish port in Tel Aviv. The British administration had consistently refused to sanction a rival port within two miles of the facilities at Jaffa. Now, the strike at the port in Jaffa bolstered the argument that the Jews required the ability to import goods directly. On May 13, the political representative of the Jewish Agency wrote to the government, cautioning that the "Government's refusal to take immediate action in this matter will inevitably strengthen the impression, widespread among both Jews and Arabs, that Government is not interested in hastening the end of the strike. From such an impression to the pernicious thought that the strike serves some useful purpose for the Government is but one step, and it is my painful duty to state that I find many people taking this step without hesitation."[1] This assessment struck home, since there was in fact a great deal of evident sympathy for Arab aspirations among government officials. As a result, the administration granted the long-sought permission for the port two days later.

The security situation took a sharp turn for the worse on May 16 with the shooting of several Jews as they left a Jerusalem cinema. The high commissioner imposed a curfew and collective fines on the Arab community, but was reluctant to make use of the reinforcements that had arrived earlier in the month to quell the nascent rebellion. On May 23, some sixty Arab agitators were taken into custody and placed in concentration camps, as were some of the prominent leaders of the strike, such as Auni Abdel Hadi and Ibrahim Shanti, the following month. On June 19, to facilitate police operations, the British ordered the destruction of 237 houses in Jaffa. On June 30, 137 Arab government officials, including all the senior members of the administration and the judiciary, presented a memorandum to the high commissioner that blamed the disturbances on the government's breach of faith in carrying out the promises made to the Arabs by the British authorities. Several weeks later some 1,200 junior-level Arab officials signed a similar memorandum. The following month a similar but more extreme and abusive letter was presented by the judges of the Muslim courts, which operated under the jurisdiction of the mufti's Supreme Muslim Council. It warned the British authorities of the dire consequences of a failure to change their policies.

However, despite the official British position condemning the strike, the evidence of complicity on the part of the Palestine government bureaucracy was unmistakable. Three American senators, Warren Austin, Royal Copeland, and Daniel Hastings, who visited Palestine in 1936, took the British administration to task. Senator Copeland stated bluntly,

[T]here are really two strikes going on in Palestine. One is conducted by Arab terrorists, who throw bombs and snipe at passersby in the streets and highways. The other is conducted silently by the Mandatory Government of Palestine against the proper administration of justice. The prolongation of the terror in the Holy Land is due . . . to a manifest sympathy for the vandals and assassins displayed by many officers who are sworn to uphold the law . . . creating a condition which could not but shock any American observer.[2]

In their response to the outbreaks of Arab violence, the official institutions of the Yishuv—the Jewish Agency, the Vaad Leumi and the Histadrut—followed the dual and sometimes conflicting policies of *haganah* (self-defense) and *havlagah* (self-restraint). The first meant that the Jews would defend themselves and their settlements against attack through the use of arms if necessary. The second policy called for restraint on the part of the Yishuv with respect to counterattacking or retaliating against the Arabs. This latter policy, in effect, knowingly ceded the initiative to the Arabs. The Zionist leadership was primarily concerned that if the Jews should undertake active measures against the Arabs, it would provide the British with an excuse to declare that the country was in a state of civil war. They might then cut off all immigration, as they had done in 1921 and 1929. What the Zionist leadership failed to see was that what they feared so much was going to happen anyway, because that was clearly the direction of British policy.

The dual policies of haganah and havlagah were maintained firmly by the leadership of the Yishuv, notwithstanding systematic provocations by the Arabs and the sharp denunciation of havlagah by the Revisionists, who nonetheless observed the policy in practice. The policy of havlagah remained a thorny issue throughout the period of the Arab riots, and provoked a sometimes acrimonious debate within the Yishuv and the Zionist world.

Ben-Gurion, a staunch advocate of havlagah, took the position that the Arab and Zionist aims were intrinsically different, and that they therefore could not be achieved by similar tactics. He was concerned that if the Jews retaliated in kind against the Arabs, a permanent state of war between the two peoples would result. Such a situation, he feared, would inhibit the inflow of Jewish immigration and capital even if the British were to allow unrestricted entry. He also was worried that reprisals against the nationalistically oriented Arabs would only serve to unite them further.

Opponents of the policy, and these included more than just the Revisionists, were primarily concerned about the differing psychological impacts of havlagah on the several parties involved: the Jews, the Arabs, and the British. In Palestine, the ideal of a new type of Jew, one who would no longer stand by passively in the face of attack, had been assiduously cultivated for a generation. It was feared that havlagah would undermine that ideal, generating instead a sense of helplessness and defeatism in the Yishuv. Insofar as the Arabs were concerned, havlagah would only encourage them to continue and intensify their attacks, in the hope that the Zionists would be forced to abandon their aim of a Jewish state in Palestine. Finally, notwithstanding British respect and possibly even admiration for Jewish forbearance, havlagah would strengthen the British belief that the Jews were not sufficiently warlike to be a critical political factor in any determination of the future of the country.

Jabotinsky, whose position on havlagah seemed somewhat ambivalent, since he supported it both publicly and privately notwithstanding his usual militancy, had a rather different concern that led him to back the policy. He wrote: "The Jews would have defended themselves from the first moment, were it not clear that in that eventuality the [British] police and soldiers would be turned against them, against the defenders, and the situation would assume an entirely different aspect. . . . We are confronted with the dilemma either to fight with British military forces or to be content with the role of cowards and to suffer the consequences."[3] At the time, even Jabotinsky agreed that it made little sense to engage in a military struggle with the British, since the Zionists wanted British help in bringing more Jews into the country.

During the summer of 1936 the armed revolt became more serious. Within a few weeks of its onset, the general strike achieved its intended effect of drawing the attention of the neighboring Arab states to the Palestinian Arab cause. Committees for the defense of Palestine were set up in Amman, Baghdad, Beirut, and Damascus. The guerrilla bands operating in the countryside were soon augmented, and supplied with additional arms and trained leaders from Syria and Iraq. One of the more prominent of the latter was Fawzi ad-Din al-Qawkaji, a Syrian who had once been a military adviser to King Ibn Saud and was more recently an officer in the Iraqi army who resigned his commission to participate in the Palestine disorders. He appointed himself generalissimo of the rebel forces.

At the same time, the British attempted to make use of the good offices of the Arab rulers in British-dominated territories in resolving the mounting crisis. On June 16 and again on August 4, Emir Abdullah of Transjordan met with members of the Arab Higher Committee in Amman and tried unsuccessfully to get them to end the strike and to accept the offer of a royal commission to study their grievances. A similar intervention was then attempted by Nuri as-Said, foreign minister of Iraq, acting on behalf of King Ghazi. There was a widespread rumor that Nuri had a proposal to offer that included the suspension of Jewish immigration, and that the British administration had agreed to accept it. He assured the Arabs of Palestine that "the Palestine Government would not only announce stoppage of Jewish entry into Palestine but would also declare an amnesty for individual Arabs participating in the outbreaks, as *quid pro quo* concessions for Arab cessation of the strike."[4] When this turned out to be untrue, the Arabs were more frustrated than ever.

In the meanwhile, on July 29, a royal commission was appointed under the chairmanship of Earl Peel. Its purpose was "To ascertain the underlying causes of the disturbances which broke out in Palestine in the middle of April; to inquire into the manner in which the Mandate for Palestine is being implemented in relation to the obligations of the Mandatory towards the Arabs and the Jews respectively; and to ascertain whether . . . the Arabs or the Jews have any legitimate grievances upon account of the way in which the Mandate has been, or is being, implemented."[5]

The announcement of the formation of the Peel Commission had no discernible effect on events in the country, and British passivity with regard to Arab mischief making finally came to an end in September 1936. The seriousness of the disturbances and their possible repercussions in other Arab countries forced the British cabinet to devote its attention to the problem on September 2. Two days later the War Office announced plans for a further bolstering of the Palestine garrison. This was followed on September 7, with a Colonial Office statement of policy that reaffirmed the determination of the government to uphold the Mandate and to carry out its coequal obligations to both Arabs and Jews.

The Arabs now found themselves in a difficult position. The strike had already gone on for about six months, and the enthusiasm of Arab businessmen for its continuation was waning. Although the strike had never been total, the Arab community had endured enormous financial losses and was near economic exhaustion. There was particular concern among growers over the possibility of forfeiting the coming citrus season. On September 12, Wauchope informed the Arab Higher Committee that the British, whose forces in Palestine had now grown to 20,000, were prepared to take serious military steps to suppress the disturbances. Confronted by this challenge, the Arab leaders decided to retreat. They found a face-saving device in the appeal by King Ibn Saud, King Ghazi, and Emir Abdullah, which stated: "We have been deeply pained by the present state of affairs in Palestine. For this reason we have agreed . . . to call upon you to resolve for peace in order to save further shedding of blood. In doing this, we rely on the good intentions of our friend Great Britain, who has declared that she will do justice. You must be confident that we will continue our efforts to assist you."[6]

Simultaneously with the publication of this appeal on October 11, the Arab Higher Committee announced that it was acceding to the wishes of the Arab potentates and calling an end to the general strike and the accompanying disorders, to take effect on the following day. The British, presumably as part of the deal, allowed al-Qawkaji to slip across the Jordan and made no move to disarm the guerrilla bands that remained in the hills. The latter viewed the end of the strike as a respite that provided an opportunity for some rest and the leisure to recruit additional volunteers before renewing the armed struggle. As one writer observed: "By putting an end to the strike the Arabs had relinquished

their non-violent, and retained their violent, weapons."[7] The protracted violence had produced 1,351 casualties, including 187 Muslims, 10 Christian Arabs, 80 Jews, and 28 British dead.

With peace restored, the Peel Commission set sail for Palestine on
November 5, 1936. That same day the government announced its rejection of the Arab demand that Jewish immigration be halted. However, it added that "His Majesty's Government have thought it right, in
the present circumstances obtaining in Palestine, to ask the High Commissioner to take a conservative view of the economic absorptive capacity of the country."[8] Accordingly, the Labor Schedule established for
the next six months allowed for only 1,850 immigration certificates, a
60 percent reduction from that approved the previous April, and a far
cry from the 10,695 that had been requested by the Jewish Agency.

The British were clearly sending a signal to the Arabs that while they
would not be pressured into prohibiting immigration, they were prepared to accommodate them by reducing the inflow of Jews to a trickle.
The Arab Higher Committee, however, obstinately unwilling to accept
anything short of an abject surrender to its demands, failed to recognize that the British were in the process of capitulating to them. It refused to have any representation before the Peel Commission until
Jewish immigration was banned totally. In discussing these events, one
student of the period observed:

The restrained policy of the government would have been justified had there
been any basis for hope that an Arab-Jewish compromise might result from the
activities of the Royal Commission. However, in view of Arab intransigence,
neglect to crush the revolt held nothing but danger for the future by encouraging the nationalists to think they could defy Great Britain with impunity.
The government's activities, nevertheless, had the temporary effect of restor-
ing order and opening the way for the investigation of the Peel Commission.[9]

The immediate consequences of the Arab general strike and the accompanying violence were not viewed as all bad in Zionist circles. It was
believed by many that one of the chief causes of the disturbances was
the perceived weakness of the Yishuv. The implication drawn from this
perception was that if the Yishuv had been stronger, an accommodation
with the Arabs could have been reached. The Arab strike thus served to
reinforce the conclusion that it was essential to the success of the Zionist enterprise to increase the growth of the Yishuv, to enhance its defense capabilities, and to free it from any dependence on Arab markets
and services. Achievement of the latter was facilitated considerably by

the virtual disappearance of all Arab workers from the Jewish settle-ments and their subsequent replacement by Jews. As the Yishuv's lead-ership assessed it at the time, the Arabs' net gain from their protracted and costly strike and accompanying violence was inconsequential, since they failed to attain any of their primary aims: self-government, suspen-sion of Jewish immigration, and a prohibition of further land purchases by Jews.

On the other hand, the Zionists were confronted by the reality of the Arabs' readiness to make considerable sacrifices in pursuit of their aims, which they expressed unequivocally—something the Zionists them-selves were loath to do. The debate over aims thus emerged to the fore once again. It was clear that the Revisionists, at the right end of the po-litical spectrum, wanted a Jewish state with a Jewish majority, while the leftist Hashomer Hatzair (Young guard) declared for a binational so-cialist society in Palestine as a prelude to a socialist Middle East. Al-though most tended to agree with the Revisionist position, the Zionist movement as a whole continued to be unwilling, or perhaps unable, to define its ultimate aims. As a result, the continuing equivocation about specific aims helped prevent further divisions within the Zionist Or-ganization and the Jewish Agency.

In May 1936, Ben-Gurion presented the Jewish Agency Executive with the argument that an accommodation with the Arabs might be achievable if the Zionists seriously addressed Arab fears of Jewish politi-cal and economic domination. He proposed an agreement that would provide for laws to protect small Arab landowners from encroachment, and would satisfy Arab political demands by establishing Arab-Jewish parity in a Palestine executive body. To assuage Arab concerns about eventually becoming a minority in the country, Ben-Gurion proposed the establishment of a regional federation of the Middle East states that were within the British sphere of influence and control, which the Jew-ish state would join. Presumably, Palestinian Arabs' nationalist aspira-tions would be satisfied by their becoming part of an Arab-dominated federation, notwithstanding the fact that the Palestinian Arabs would be citizens of an essentially Jewish state.

These ideas were rejected by Moshe Sharett and other Zionist lead-ers as being quite unrealistic—they actually offered the Arabs nothing of any consequence with respect to their goals. Furthermore, as Sharett pointed out, the idea of parity in a Palestinian executive body would hardly have any appeal to the Arabs, since they surely would not con-sider that a Jewish concession. By granting the numerically fewer Jews parity with the much larger number of Arabs, Ben-Gurion's scheme actually proposed extracting a major concession from the Arabs rather than offering one from the Jews. Nonetheless, the proposal was raised repeatedly in subsequent discussions with Arabs as an example of Zionist good intentions. Needless to say, it made little impression on the Arabs.

The one area in which there was a reasonable chance for agreement with the Arabs concerned immigration, an issue over which there was strong disagreement in Zionist circles. Those who supported a compromise on immigration took the position that the high commissioner would never allow immigration totals to exceed the limits of 1935. Indeed, they believed that it was more likely that the British would place further arbitrary curbs on Jewish entry to placate the Arabs, who were demanding an absolute ban on immigration. Sharett argued that a Zionist initiative in this regard would forestall a British move and would be of greater benefit to the Yishuv. The opponents of this position argued that at a time when the situation for Jews in Europe was deteriorating rapidly, it was unconscionable to consider voluntarily reducing Jewish immigration into Palestine. Indeed, they held that it was now more imperative than ever to push for mass immigration in order to assure the quick emergence of a Jewish majority in the country. In their view, any agreement to curtail immigration would only serve as a spur to even greater Arab demands. The Arabs would then be sorely tempted to repeat the process once more—that is, a renewal of the disturbances, to be followed by further Jewish concessions.

The view favoring concessions on immigration ultimately prevailed, and the Jewish Agency decided to develop a proposal on curtailment. It concluded that it would use the 1935 immigration figure as the bottom limit for the expected negotiations with the Arabs. The notion that this concession would be acceptable to the Arabs was of course quite unrealistic, since it was the level of the 1935 immigration that played a major role in precipitating the Arab disturbances in the first place. Jabotinsky offered a far more realistic appraisal of the Arab position. He maintained that even if one could convince the Arab leaders outside Palestine that the country in itself was unimportant and would in any case become part of an Arab federation, the Arabs of Palestine would never agree to such a compromise. Moreover, he doubted that the Arabs would ever willingly accept a non-Arab state in their midst. This meant, in effect, that the Zionists had but two options: either to sacrifice the Zionist enterprise in its entirety or to go on with it full force, regardless of Arab opposition.

However, as Jabotinsky pointed out, pursuit of the latter course would require that the Yishuv develop a very substantial military capability. Unless the Yishuv was perceived as undefeatable, the Arabs would never relent in their efforts to put an end to the Zionist dream. He argued that the Arabs would have to be completely disabused of the idea that they could prevent the emergence of a powerful Jewish state before a viable compromise could be negotiated with them. Jabotinsky also firmly rejected the position suggesting that it was immoral for Jews to settle in Palestine over the objections of the Arabs, particularly since the Arabs preferred to speak in pan-Arab terms. In the latter context, the Arab homeland stretched from Morocco to Iraq. As far as he was concerned, there was no reason for the Jews to have any qualms about controlling a tiny fraction of that vast territory.

Among the bevy of proposals for compromise that the Jewish Agency kept producing during this period, one in particular captured the interest of the British. This was a scheme for the cantonization of the country into a number of small distinct territories linked together in a federation within Palestine. Shortly before the violence of 1936, a former official of the Palestine administration, Arthur Cust, had proposed just such a plan, calling for the division of Palestine into a Jewish and an Arab canton, with British-controlled enclaves at the port of Haifa and the holy places. The Jewish canton would include the coastal plain and other areas of heavy Jewish settlement. The Arab canton would be united with Transjordan. Each was eventually to become independent and would have a large measure of autonomy in the interim. Cust's plan was published in February 1936, but it received little attention until he presented it at a meeting of the Royal Asian Society at which Chaim Weizmann was present. His scheme envisioned the ultimate partition of Palestine, an idea that Mordechai Nemirovsky (Namir), a leader of Mapai, was also proposing. At the time, the proposal failed to generate any serious interest in Zionist circles, presumably because it implied a cessation of Jewish settlement in the areas designated as Arab territory.

Zionist leaders continued to attempt to reach a compromise with the Arabs through a variety of unpublicized channels and discussions, all to no avail. In most instances, the moderate Arabs they dealt with, like Musa Alami, were quite unrepresentative of the Arab leadership, and their proposed comprises led nowhere. In the last analysis, they always came up against the mufti, without whose cooperation no compromise settlement was possible. No proposal was agreeable to him unless it ensured a permanent powerless minority status for the Jews in Palestine, something that clearly was not acceptable to any Zionist.

There simply was no basis for the negotiation of such irreconcilable aims and purposes.

The Peel Commission began its work on November 12, 1936, and held sixty-six meetings, thirty-one of which were open to the public. Since the Arab Higher Committee refused to participate in the proceedings, the bulk of the testimony received by the commission was from British officials and Zionist representatives. The Arab boycott, having failed to achieve anything other than to deny the Arabs the opportunity to present their own case before the commission, was finally called off on January 6, 1937, a week before the commission was scheduled to depart from Palestine. To accommodate the Arabs, the commission remained in the country for an additional week to take their testimony.

The Peel Commission's report, which was issued in July 1937, made it clear that notwithstanding the government's commitment to the policy of equal obligation in carrying out the Mandate, "[T]he primary purpose of the Mandate, as expressed in its preamble and its articles, is to promote the establishment of the Jewish National Home." However, it went on to argue, the mandate did not

contemplate, however remotely, the forcible conversion of Palestine into a Jewish State against the will of the Arabs. For that would clearly violate the spirit and intention of the Mandate System. It would mean that national self-determination had been withheld when the Arabs were a majority in Palestine and only conceded when the Jews were a majority. . . . The international recognition of the right of the Jews to return to their old homeland did not involve the recognition of the right of the Jews to govern the Arabs in it against their will.[10]

With the absence of any evidence that the Arabs were prepared to accept Jewish domination in Palestine, the commission concluded that the Mandate had become unworkable and should be abrogated. The commission acknowledged that it was unrealistic to believe that both Arab and Jewish nationalist aims could be fulfilled within a common state. It also held that it was equally unrealistic to attempt to sacrifice the claims of one to those of the other. Accordingly, the only practicable solution appeared to be some arrangement that would permit and facilitate the simultaneous but separate development of the Jewish and Arab communities.

The advocates of this general approach fell roughly into three groups. The first, which was made up primarily of the established Zionist leadership, proposed a general plan whereby the Jews and Arabs would be constituted as separate autonomous communities within a federal framework in which both would be represented equally, regardless of the size of the relative populations. This was in essence a rehash of the long-standing Zionist parity proposal that had been rejected repeatedly by the Arabs. A second group advocated cantonization along the lines of the Cust plan. The third group favored outright partition of Palestine into separate Arab and Jewish states, the frontiers to run generally along lines similar to those proposed under the cantonization plan.

The commission dismissed the parity proposal out of hand as unrealistic and certain to be rejected once again by the Arabs. Faced with the choice between cantonization and partition, the latter seemed to them to make better sense. Under a cantonization scheme, neither the Jews nor the Arabs would have the independence of the other that they really wanted. Accordingly, the commission recommended the division of Palestine and Transjordan into three entities. A sovereign Jewish state would include all of Palestine north of Beit Shean and all of the coastal area north of a point midway between Gaza and Jaffa. An Arab state would be composed of the rest of Palestine and Transjordan. A third area, which would remain under a permanent British mandate, would include Jerusalem, Bethlehem, Lydda, Ramle, and a corridor to the sea at Jaffa. Jaffa itself, notwithstanding the fact that it would be totally surrounded by Jewish territory, would become part of the Arab state. The commission further proposed that Nazareth, the Sea of Galilee, and an area near the head of the Gulf of Aqaba should be permanently attached to the district of Jerusalem under a British mandate. Then, without blushing, the commission proposed that since the new Arab state would incorporate impoverished Transjordan while losing Jewish revenues, the Jewish state should provide an annual subsidy for its operation.

Simultaneously with the publication of the commission's report on July 7, the government issued another White Paper on the subject.

In the light of experience and of the arguments adduced by the Commission they are driven to the conclusion that there is an irreconcilable conflict between the aspirations of the Arabs and Jews in Palestine, that these aspirations cannot be satisfied under the terms of the present Mandate, and that a scheme of partition on the general lines recommended by the Commission represents the best and most hopeful solution of the deadlock.[11]

The White Paper went on to state that pending the completion of a detailed partition scheme, steps would be taken to prevent Jewish land purchases that might be prejudicial to the probable terms of the scheme. It also announced the decision to restrict total Jewish immigration into Palestine for the period from August 1937 to March 1938 to a maximum of 8,000.

It appears that the partition idea was originated by Professor Reginald Coupland of Oxford, one of the dominant personalities on the Peel Commission, who received quiet encouragement for the proposal from Chaim Weizmann, who was enamored with the idea. Weizmann observed to his private secretary that "the long toil of his life was at last crowned with success. The Jewish state was at hand."[12] Toward the end of January 1937, Weizmann and Coupland met privately at Nahalal to conclude their discussions of the partition proposal. When Weizmann emerged from the hut where his meeting with Coupland took place, he announced to the puzzled farmers who had gathered outside, "Today, in this place, we have laid the foundations of the Jewish State!"[13]

Coupland, of course, had no way of knowing that Weizmann was quite out of touch with his own Zionist constituency on the question. Indeed, before the report was even issued, the Zionist Executive effectively rejected its conclusions. At the end of April, it issued a statement announcing that the Zionist Organization would oppose any attempt to curtail Jewish rights, to impede the development of the national home, or to reduce its territory by cantonization or partition. The general Zionist mood of defiance was reflected in the stance taken on the matter by the *Jewish Chronicle*: "Partition is completely and irrevocably out of the question. . . . No Zionist, who *is* a Zionist, will look at or touch it. It is an evil and intolerable thing which revolts alike our dearest sentiments and our common sense . . . and the sooner it is buried and out of sight forever the better for all concerned."[14]

When the Peel Commission report and the White Paper were published, the Jewish Agency protested that the commission's recommendations were contrary to the Mandate. Moreover, it argued that the partition scheme was a blatant breach of Britain's commitment to the Jews in the Balfour Declaration, which had promised a national home in all of Palestine. When Ben-Gurion learned of the limit on immigration announced by the White Paper, he was furious. For a moment, he advocated a complete break with the British. He told his colleagues: "If this was the method by which the Jewish State was to be established, he had no faith whatsoever that the Government would carry out that policy. This British Government was not going to get Haifa and Jerusalem by dirty tricks of this kind; they could return the Mandate to the League, or else they would have to fight for it."[15] However, his colleagues quickly convinced him to back down and accept the superior wisdom of Weizmann in the matter of Anglo-Zionist relations.

At the Twentieth Zionist Congress, which opened in Zurich on August 3, 1937, a strange assortment of unlikely allies joined forces to oppose acceptance of the Peel Commission's recommendations. Ussishkin and his following, the Mizrahi, Stephen Wise and the American Zionists, Meir Grossman's Jewish State Party, and the left-wing Hashomer Hatzair, joined by Berl Katznelson and Golda Meir of the Mapai, all attacked the proposals both in principle and as a practical matter, albeit for very different reasons.

Mizrahi rejected them because the Jewish claim to Palestine was based on the biblical covenant, something that could not be negotiated away as a matter of expediency. Rabbi Yaacov M. Harlap, one of the leading rabbis of Jerusalem, stated this position in a responsum on August 18.

It is clearly forbidden for Jews to surrender any part of the Holy Land, for such a surrender of a small or a large part of what is holy in the holiness of the Land is tantamount to "not acknowledging one's country," and there is no difference between not acknowledging the whole country and acknowledging only part of it . . . and by inference surrendering any part of the country, which is much more than non-acknowledgement, is a denial of country and is certainly a very great sin.[16]

Hashomer Hatzair, by extreme contrast, was opposed to the scheme because the organization still harbored illusions about the viability of a binational state that it was unwilling to abandon.

Outside the official Zionist framework, almost simultaneously, the Revisionists called on Jews throughout the world to remain "faithful to [the] ideal of a Jewish State on both sides of the Jordan," and the Rabbinical Council of the non-Zionist Agudat Israel World Organization declared that "the frontiers of our holy land have been defined by the creator of the world. . . . It is therefore impossible for the Jewish people to renounce these frontiers."[17] (It is noteworthy that the arguments made by the Mizrahi and Agudat Israel are still being made today with regard to negotiations over the future of the territories of Judea, Samaria, and Gaza.)

Weizmann found himself in the awkward position of defending the concept of partition in the abstract while rejecting the specific terms of the partition proposal in the commission report. He began with an emotional attack on the government:

I say to the mandatory power: you shall not play fast and loose with the Jewish people. Say to us frankly that the National Home is closed, and we shall know where we stand. But this trifling with a nation bleeding from a thousand wounds must not be done by the British whose Empire is built on moral principles—that mighty Empire must not commit this sin against the people of the Book. Tell us the truth. This at least we have deserved.

Weizmann then followed with a defense of the principle of partition. The critical issue, he argued, was whether any particular proposal met two fundamental criteria.

Does it offer a basis for a genuine growth of Jewish life? . . . for creating a Jewish agriculture, industry, literature, etc.?—in short all that the idea of Zionism comprises. . . . Does the proposal contribute to the solution of the Jewish problem. . . . If the proposal opens a way, then I, who for some forty years have done all that in me lies, who have given my all to the movement, then I shall say Yes, and I trust that you will do likewise.[18]

In the heat of the sometimes highly emotional debate, Weizmann was charged by some with treason to the Zionist cause by having committed himself to partition in advance of the convening of the congress. This was substantiated to some extent when Meir Grossman published a verbatim report of a July 19 conversation on the subject between Weizmann and Colonial Secretary William Ormsby-Gore in *The Jewish Chronicle* on August 13. The issue of partition was extremely divisive. Even the leadership of the Haganah in Palestine was divided: Eliahu Golomb favoring partition and Shaul Meirov (Avigur) opposed to it.

Nonetheless, an alliance between Weizmann and Ben-Gurion, driven by the fear that the partition scheme might be the best that could ever be gotten from the British, managed to gain majority approval of the concept of partition by a vote of almost two to one. But this approval did not extend to the boundaries proposed in the Peel Commission report. The resolution merely empowered the Zionist Executive "to enter into negotiations with a view to ascertaining the precise terms of His Majesty's Government for the proposed establishment of a Jewish State."[19] After the vote Ben-Gurion explained to the press: "The debate has not been for or against the indivisibility of the Land of Israel. No Zionist can forego [*sic*] the smallest portion of the Land of Israel. The debate concerned which of two routes would lead quicker to the common goal."[20] In other words, acceptance of partition by the Zionist movement did not nullify its claim to all of Palestine. It was merely a first step in a longer process.

Weizmann had earlier responded similarly to criticism that he should have demanded the inclusion of the Negev in the proposed Jewish state with the comment that "it would not run away."[21] Yet, even for Weizmann, it was a hollow victory. He noted bitterly,

I have borne most things in silence; I have defended the British administration before my own people, from public platforms, at congresses, in all parts of the world, often against my own better knowledge, and almost invariably to my own detriment. Why did I do so? Because to me close cooperation with Great Britain was the cornerstone of our policy in Palestine. But this cooperation remained unilateral—it was unrequited love.[22]

The reception given the Peel Commission proposals was no warmer in Arab circles. Notwithstanding the split that began to emerge in the Arab ranks once again, between the Husseinis and Nashishibis, on July 11, the Nashishibi-dominated National Defense Party rejected partition as incompatible with Arab aspirations. The Arab Higher Committee followed suit on July 23. The Iraqi government expressed its displeasure with the proposal, and issued a warning to Abdullah of Transjordan, the only Arab leader who might have expected to gain something from the partition scheme. He was cautioned that the wrath of the Arab world would come down on the head of anyone who agreed to serve as the leader of the Arab state proposed under the partition plan.

In early September, Nabih Bey Azmey, the president of the Palestine Assistance Committee, convened a Pan-Arab Congress at Bludan, Syria. Attended by some 500 delegates from Syria and the neighboring countries, and presided over by the former Iraqi Prime Minister, Tawfiq as-Suwaidi, the congress resolved: "[W]e must make Great Britain understand that it must choose between our friendship and the Jews. Britain must change her policy in Palestine or we shall be at liberty to side with other European Powers whose policies are inimical to Great Britain."[23] This barely veiled threat to throw Arab support to Italy could not but be taken into serious consideration by the British government, given the prevailing international political climate.

The year 1936 had been a particularly disturbing one for Britain's far-flung interests. Italy had completed the conquest of Ethiopia, Hitler had marched into the Rhineland, and an alliance between Hitler and Mussolini was in the process of formation. In Spain, there was a civil war raging, the consequences of which were uncertain should the fascists prevail. The outbreak of a general war in Europe seemed quite conceivable, even if not deemed very probable. In the event of such a war, Britain would have to be concerned about the security of its lines of communication to its imperial holdings in India and Southeast Asia, as well as to its bases and fuel supplies in the Middle East. With regard to the latter, Britain would find it necessary to maintain relative stability in the region, and the situation in Palestine threatened that stability. It was clear that the primary destabilizing element in Palestine was the seemingly unbounded ambition of the mufti. The British perception appears to have been that although the Jews were a nuisance, they could be expected to behave responsibly in a crisis, whereas the Arabs could not be relied on in this regard.

Accordingly, it was decided that it would best serve Britain's broader interests to reach an accommodation with the Arabs outside of Palestine at the expense of the Jews in Palestine. In return, it was expected that the Arab leaders would put pressure on the Arab Higher Committee to be more accommodating in assuring the desired degree of stability. The government therefore accepted the Peel Commission proposals under the assumption that they would satisfy Arab national opinion outside Palestine. However, once it became clear that the partition plan was unacceptable to general Arab opinion, the scheme was quietly abandoned as new restraints on Jewish immigration and land purchase were implemented. Little if any significance was attributed to the increasingly precarious situation of the Jews in Europe, who desperately needed refuge.

As it turned out, the British assessment of the Palestine situation was quite astute. The Jews, notwithstanding their betrayal by the British, cooperated with them in the war against Germany, and the Arabs, placated to some degree by the Jewish losses, remained generally passive throughout the period of crisis.

The incremental abandonment of the partition scheme during the year following the Peel Commission report was accompanied by an upsurge in Arab violence in Palestine and Arab hostility outside the country. On September 27, 1937, the murder of the district commissioner of Galilee, Lewis Yelland Andrews, in Nazareth forced the British to take action. The Arab Higher Committee was declared illegal and the mufti was removed from his position as president of the Supreme Muslim Council. The following day arrest orders were issued for Jamal Husseini and five other members of the committee, who were held morally responsible for the recent outbreak of violence. Jamal escaped to Syria. The mufti, fearing arrest as well, fled secretly to Lebanon on October 15 and set up residence in the coastal village of al-Zuq, north of Beirut.

The Arab Higher Committee soon reconstituted itself in Damascus and continued to direct the violence in Palestine from there. More than a rebellion against the British, the violence became a struggle for control of the Arab community itself and for the consolidation of Husseini dominance in Arab Palestine. Political opponents of the mufti were terrorized and murdered, and wealthy Arabs were subjected to extortion while others were forced to contribute to the struggle in other ways.

One unanticipated consequence of Arab violence in 1936 was the growth of the Jewish constabulary, recruited primarily from the villages, which increased in size from some 3,500 at the end of 1936 to about 5,000 a year later. The combined defensive capabilities of the legal Jewish constabulary and the illicit Haganah were sufficient to assure that no isolated Jewish villages or settlements would have to be abandoned. In fact, at the outbreak of Arab attacks, new Jewish settlements were being established at the rate of about one a month. Many of these were located in areas where settlements had not previously existed or were few in number, both in anticipation of a curtailment of future land transfers and out of a desire to expand the areas of Jewish settlement in the event of a partition of the country.

The conclusion of the Peel Commission's work in Palestine gave the clear impression to many of the official Zionist leaders that partition would take place sooner or later, and that it was necessary to prepare for the defense of the fledgling Jewish state that would emerge. There was now a call for the merger of the dissident Haganah "B" with the main body. At this point, all the parties represented on the governing board of Haganah "B" were in favor of the merger, for which Tehomi had been working for some time. However, it was clear that the merger could not take place without Jabotinsky's personal approval. Indeed, Tehomi was told as much by Moshe Rosenberg, one of his closest collaborators and a member of Brit Trumpeldor. "As long as Jabotinsky does not give us the 'green light' for such a merger, we will not move; and should you, as our local commander, order us to do so, we will revolt."[24]

Considerable pressure was brought to bear on Jabotinsky to approve the merger by a number of leaders of the Yishuv. However, he was reluctant to agree to it for partisan political reasons. In his view, it was essential to mount an effective campaign opposing the partition plan, and the Haganah "B" was prepared, albeit with some reluctance on the part of a number of its members, to support him and the Revisionist movement in such an effort. Since it was clear to Jabotinsky that, notwithstanding its ambivalent public statements on the question, the Jewish Agency would ultimately back partition, the proposed merger with the

Histadrut-controlled Haganah would eliminate any independent armed force that could be used to help foil the partition scheme. Moreover, although Jabotinsky had previously supported the policy of havlagah, or self-restraint, he had done so as a matter of expediency rather than out of principle. He anticipated that at some point in the not too distant future, it might become necessary to reject havlagah and take the necessary countermeasures against the Arabs, and perhaps also the British. A merger of Haganah "B" with the Haganah would preclude this from happening. Consequently, Jabotinsky refused to give his consent to the merger.

In the meantime, Tehomi, who had been using the Haganah "B" as a means of enhancing his bargaining position for a reconciliation with the Haganah leadership, went ahead with the merger, thereby precipitating the revolt within the organization about which he had been forewarned. On April 10, 1937, Tehomi and his followers were expelled from the organization, which now reasserted its independent existence as the *Irgun Zvai Leumi*. The overwhelming majority of the Haganah "B" members remained in the new Irgun and declared their allegiance to Jabotinsky's political leadership. In Ramat Gan, out of 350 members, only one sided with Tehomi. All in all, only a few hundred out of the approximately 3,000 members of the Haganah "B" followed Tehomi into the Haganah.

Jabotinsky held no official position in the Irgun, but he was nonetheless considered the organization's supreme commander with regard to matters of policy. He was thus asked to confirm the nomination of Robert Bitker as the Irgun's first military commander. It was understood, however, that since Jabotinsky resided outside Palestine, he would not interfere in any operational or personnel matters. The organization went through some initial growing pains that resulted in Bitker's removal in October 1937, to be replaced by Moshe Rosenberg, who was replaced later that same year by David Raziel.

The Irgun first broke with the havlagah policy in early September 1937, when three Jews were murdered by Arab terrorists. The Irgun's retaliatory attack cost thirteen Arab lives. At a meeting of the Vaad Leumi in October, Eliahu Golomb demanded of Arye Altman, the head of the Revisionist New Zionist Organization in Palestine, that the Irgun merge with the Haganah and accept the discipline of the existing Jewish national institutions. This meant in effect coming under the direction of Ben-Gurion and the Histadrut. Golomb suggested that if the Irgun should refuse, the Haganah might have to take other measures to ensure compliance with the demand, thereby effectively raising the specter of civil war. This threat was to be repeated a number of times over the course of the following year.

In the meanwhile, continued Arab provocations directed at Jews praying at the Western Wall in Jerusalem culminated in a spectacular retaliatory attack by the Irgun that took place in and around Jerusalem on November 14. The Arab village of Lyftah, the source of numerous assaults against Jews, was hit particularly hard. The severity of the reprisals by the Irgun brought the Jewish Agency to denounce the action as besmirching the moral record of Palestinian Jewry. Jabotinsky, however, took a rather different view of the matter. After twenty Revisionists, including his son Eri, were arrested by the British and interned at Acre, Jabotinsky stated: "The tendency of the Jews to hit back cannot be stopped by arrests and imprisonments; I personally feel very proud that my son is among the arrested."[25] The London *Times*, with greater detachment, observed that "since the Jews began reprisals, the attacks on them have decreased."[26]

On March 3, 1938, Sir Harold MacMichael arrived in Palestine to replace Wauchope as high commissioner. MacMichael came bearing a reputation as one highly sympathetic to the Arab cause. Although he pledged to eliminate lawlessness in the country, his regime was soon characterized by precisely the opposite. Arab violence increased significantly in both frequency and severity. Shortly after his arrival, Arab marauders from the village of Jaouni attacked a bus on the Safed-Rosh Pina road, killing fourteen Jews and raping four Jewish women. On April 21, three members of Brit Trumpeldor from Rosh Pina attempted to retaliate against an Arab bus traveling on the road to Jaouni. The assault misfired, and none of the Arab passengers were hurt. The three young men, however, were apprehended. On June 3, the British military court in Haifa condemned two of them, Abraham Shein and Shlomo Ben Yosef (Tabacznik), to be hanged, and the third, Shalom Zurabin, to be placed under medical observation.

The severity of the sentences was clearly outrageous, given that no one was injured in the attack. Ben Yosef was to be executed because he had been found with arms in his possession. It was clear that the British were determined to teach a lesson to the supporters of Jabotinsky. Appeals to the colonial secretary were of no avail. He told Jabotinsky that the "unruly elements must be taught a lesson which would be severe enough to intimidate them and keep them quiet."[27] Shein's sentence was subsequently commuted to life imprisonment, but Ben Yosef was executed on June 29, 1938.

The execution clearly constituted judicial murder for political purposes. It had enormous impact on Jabotinsky's attitude toward the
British and contributed greatly to his later decision to mount an armed
rebellion against British authority in Palestine. Until the execution of
Ben Yosef, Jewish blood had been spilled in Palestine only as a consequence of the Arab-Jewish conflict. Now, in the view of Jabotinsky and
others, including some prominent Englishmen, Britain had made itself
a belligerent on the side of the Arabs in that struggle. Expressing his
outrage at the British government's complicity in the Arab violence
that was racking Palestine, Josiah Wedgwood stated in the press on July
21: "For two years murder and destruction of Jewish property have
gone unpunished under British rule. The Administration continues to
be strictly impartial between the murderers and the murdered. I have
not known of such a black page of incompetence and hypocrisy in British history."28

The British used the independent military activity of the Irgun as a
case in point to demonstrate that the Jewish Agency was not really in
control of the Yishuv, at least insofar as the policy of havlagah was concerned. This in turn raised the pressure on the Irgun to adhere to the
same policies that governed the activities of the Haganah. The question
of the possibility of the Haganah's employing violence to force the Irgun to comply with the policy of self-restraint was discussed frankly by
Jabotinsky and Golomb in London on July 10, 1938. While Golomb
denied that the Haganah was prepared to undertake a civil war against
the Irgun, he clearly implied that an agreement between the two organizations, along the lines he proposed, was the only means of precluding the possibility of civil strife.

Several weeks later, while speaking to representatives of the Jewish,
Polish, European, and American press in Warsaw, Jabotinsky made reference to a recent dispatch by the Jerusalem correspondent of the *New
York Times*, who reported an impending armed pogrom by the leftist
parties in Palestine against the Revisionists. He noted,

[T]his danger is unfortunately real. Already at the beginning of July I heard
the same threat from a man [Golomb] who is very close to the security service
of the Jewish Agency; he made it perfectly clear to me that, should they not
succeed in achieving unity on the havlagah question, the elements who are under the influence of the Agency would use their arms against the Revisionists.
At about the same time the same threat was repeated in Tel Aviv by another
authoritative personality to a representative of the New Zionist Organization.

Jabotinsky then went on to stress that "the tradition of physical violence against ideological opponents is of long standing in Leftist circles." He gave warning that "such an attempt at an internal Jewish pogrom will result in an internal Jewish self-defense," which would not be limited to Palestine alone, but could, "in a very serious form, be transplanted to the Diaspora countries."[29]

Jabotinsky's counterthreat proved to be hollow. The Irgun and its supporting organizations were far too weak to take on the leftist establishment, and could do little but stand by helplessly as hundreds of their members and supporters were identified by the Haganah, arrested, and interned by the British. The Irgun, weakened by the arrests, needed a respite, and soon agreed to negotiate a peace with the Haganah. The negotiations lasted through the summer and were concluded on September 20, 1938, in a tentative agreement reached at the home of Israel Rokah, the mayor of Tel Aviv. The essence of the agreement was that any reprisals against the Arabs planned by the Irgun would have to be agreed upon by a joint Haganah-Irgun commission of four, in which each organization would be equally represented. The Irgun was to retain its distinctive identity and could be represented by autonomous units in all local self-defense structures. In some places, self-defense responsibilities were to be assigned entirely to the Irgun.

When he initialed the draft agreement, Golomb stressed that his side would consider the agreement as valid only after Jabotinsky and the Executive Committee of the Histadrut gave their formal approval. Jabotinsky promptly agreed, but expressed concern that the agreement might well be rejected by the Left, as had been the case in 1935 when he had reached an agreement with Ben-Gurion regarding political cooperation. Jabotinsky's concerns were well founded. Ben-Gurion was adamantly opposed to the pact.

Although the key problem was alleged to be the Irgun's breach of the policy of havlagah, this seems to have been an excuse rather than the real reason. The fact was that since the renewal of Arab attacks in the summer of 1937, there had been a small section of the Haganah known as "field squads" that pursued a policy of selective counterattacks. These assaults were euphemistically characterized as aggressive defense. The "field squads" were inspired and led by Yitzhak Sadeh, a respected Haganah officer, with the quiet encouragement of the Haganah's governing body. Consequently, the issue was less over the observance of havlagah than over who should decide when a breach of the policy was appropriate. In other words, it was a matter of partisan politics.

Ben-Gurion was interested in reaching an understanding with Jabot-insky that would bring the Revisionists back into the World Zionist Organization, where they would be subject to the discipline of the Labor-dominated majority. He wanted any agreement between the Haganah and the Irgun to achieve the same end. He was therefore upset that the proposed Haganah-Irgun agreement did not repudiate reprisals by the Irgun, but only restrained them by the requirement for joint prior approval. He saw this as giving unacceptable legitimacy to the Irgun and its less restrained approach to dealing with the problem of defense of the Yishuv's interests. Accordingly, Ben-Gurion did everything he could to scuttle the agreement. As early as September 13, while the negotiations were under way, he wired Golomb from London: "Absolutely opposed negotiations and proposals of agreements." On September 20, when the Jewish Telegraphic Agency announced that the agreement had been signed, Ben-Gurion wired that he saw this act on Golomb's part as a "grave breach of discipline." Three days later he wired an order to Golomb: "If not signed, don't; if signed, annul signature."[30] Ben-Gurion's refusal to approve the agreement effectively wrecked the opportunity for practical cooperation between the Haganah and Irgun. The Haganah's campaign of attrition against the Irgun, through its active collaboration with the British authorities, was resumed and intensified.

During the first six months of 1938, the Arab campaign against partition took on the aspect of an organized guerrilla war, with bands operating from bases in the hills of Samaria and Galilee. Attacks were mounted against Jewish settlements and British military patrols. Roads and railway tracks were mined, and attempts were made to sabotage the oil pipeline from Iraq that terminated at the refineries in Haifa. Unsympathetic Arab village mayors and police were assassinated, and new recruits were forcibly enlisted in the mufti's gangs. The two principal leaders of the rebellion were Abdul Rahim Haj Ibrahim and Aref Abdul Razzik, both of whom were in constant communication with the mufti and the Arab Higher Committee, which operated from exile in Syria. By the character of some of the arms discovered on captured and killed guerrillas, it appeared that they were receiving some help from Axis sources. At the same time, the Germans and the Italians kept up a barrage of radio propaganda accusing the British of atrocities against the Arab population.

By the summer of 1938, it was quite obvious to the British that the idea of partition had fully run its course. The Arabs simply would not accept it, even though the Jews were prepared to be far more accommodating. The colonial secretary, Malcolm MacDonald, had advised Weizmann in early July that continued pursuit of the partition scheme would destabilize the entire Arab and Muslim world. In September, John Shuckburgh, undersecretary for the colonies, spoke with Weizmann about two possible alternatives to partition; one called for a five-year limitation of Jewish immigration, while the second reintroduced the notion of establishing several Jewish-controlled cantons. In November, the Woodhead Commission, appointed in January 1938 to look into the details of implementing partition, effectively buried the partition proposal in its report, which concluded that it was simply impracticable.

It took a year and a half for the British to formally kill the partition idea even though it was apparent to everyone that it was dead before the ink was dry on the Peel Commission's report. The intriguing question is why there was such a delay. It surely was not on account of any continuing British allegiance to the commitments of the Balfour Declaration, which they had consistently violated for two decades. On the contrary, it was abundantly evident to all but those who insisted on clinging to long-cherished illusions, that the British government was fully committed to sacrificing Jewish interests in Palestine to the Arabs. They had already abandoned their responsibilities under the Mandate, and would soon scuttle any hope of a Jewish homeland. The reason for the delay, as suggested by one student of the period, was a matter of domestic political tactics. The disfranchisement of the Jews in Central and Eastern Europe had strengthened the moral position of the Zionists.

Britain's delay in abandoning the National Home was rooted in her reluctance to outrage public opinion at a time of great distress for the Jews. The event was delayed further by the exercise of whatever political influence the Zionists still wielded in Britain. Through astute diplomacy and propaganda and close contacts with British policymakers, the Zionists had been able to gain time until the pressure to kill the partition plan became too strong.[31]

In October 1938, the colonial secretary proposed a roundtable conference, to be attended by both Jews and Arabs, as a vehicle for arriving at an alternative solution to the Palestine dilemma. While the initial Zionist reaction was not unfavorable, it soon became apparent that the purpose of the conference was to obtain Jewish acceptance of British capitulation to Arab demands, the foremost of which was a cessation of immigration to Palestine. Following the "Crystal Night" of November 1938 and the pogroms that were directed against the Jews of Germany, which greatly exacerbated the Jewish refugee problem, opposition to the conference began to mount significantly. Nonetheless, the Zionist leaders reluctantly agreed to participate, out of the fear that if they refused, the conference would take place without them. At least if they were present, they reasoned, they might be able to limit the damage to the Jewish cause.

To the chagrin of the Zionist leadership, Britain also invited the participation of the Arab states, thereby implicitly giving them a direct voice in the future of Palestine and the future of Jewish settlement there. Officially, the Zionists refused to attend if the Arab states were present. However, it was clear that they would in fact attend rather than forgo the opportunity, no matter how inconsequential, to present their case once again. The Zionist opposition took a rather different view of the matter. They pointed out that the Zionist presence at the conference would make little difference, since the Arabs refused to sit with the Jews. They would each meet separately with the British, and there would be no dialogue whatever between Arab and Jew. Moreover, in their view, since the British had decided to sell out the Jews, nonparticipation would at least serve as a form of protest against the travesty that was about to take place.

As things turned out, the Zionist opposition's concerns about the conference were prescient. MacDonald signaled the stance that the British government would adopt at the talks in a January 18, 1939, memorandum submitted to the cabinet committee on Palestine. His position was: "Our main aim during the London discussions should be to reach agreement, . . . expressed or tacit, with the Arab delegations . . . and to make concessions to them, perhaps considerable concessions." He rationalized his conclusion by suggesting that "in the long run it is the wisest policy from the point of view of the Jews themselves."[32]

Some, particularly the Revisionists, refused to accept the rationale that the participation of the Arab states in the conference was essential because of Britain's overriding concern for security in the Middle East. In their view, the Arabs never posed a significant threat to the British. The Arab scare was simply being exploited by the anti-Zionists in the Foreign Office as an excuse to facilitate Britain's further betrayal of its longstanding commitments to the Jews. By late January 1939, it seemed clear that the majority of the Yishuv was opposed to Jewish participation in the London Conference, while the majority in the Jewish Agency favored attending. The latter prevailed.

The London Conference opened on February 7, 1939. The Jewish delegation consisted of a permanent nucleus of five members chosen by the Jewish Agency from its Executive, and some thirty-two representatives of Palestinian organizations, Zionist and non-Zionist bodies in Great Britain, and delegates from Belgium, Eastern Europe, France, Germany, Poland, South Africa, and the United States. Weizmann, Ben-Gurion, and Sharett headed the delegation. The Arabs were represented by two delegations from Palestine, representing the mufti and the Nashishibis, respectively, as well as by official delegations from Egypt, Iraq, Saudi Arabia, Transjordan, and Yemen.

The first phase of the British-Jewish talks consisted of five meetings that concluded on February 14. During these discussions MacDonald assumed the role of spokesman for the Arab position. He essentially reiterated the view already expressed by the Peel Commission: that Britain could not impose a Jewish homeland on an unwilling Arab population. The talks covered no new ground and were more in the nature of a ritual recitation of known positions. The Arab position left no room for compromise at all, since it refused to recognize any Jewish claim to Palestine. The Arab side was totally and unalterably opposed to any further Jewish immigration or settlement, and was prepared to accept a Jewish presence only as a permanent minority in the country.

MacDonald's proposals were officially rejected by the Jewish delegation on February 17. The following day MacDonald met with Ben-Gurion and told him that it looked like the meeting was going to break up, in which case Britain would impose its own solution to the problem. He pointed out that "the Palestine Arabs are insisting on the immediate establishment of an Arab State and they are not going to budge from that position. I do not see any chance of an agreement with the Arabs. In these circumstances, it would perhaps be better not to have an agreement with you. Without an Arab agreement, an agreement with the Jews might only increase the opposition of the Palestine Arabs."[33]

The second and final phase of the talks began almost immediately thereafter. On February 20, MacDonald presented three different immigration proposals. The one that he favored would allow the entry of between 15,000 and 30,000 Jews per year for the next ten years. At the end of this period, the Jews would constitute between 35 and 40 percent of the total population. The Arabs would then be given veto power over any subsequent immigration. A second plan would have eliminated the ultimate Arab veto in exchange for a lower immigration rate for the following decade. The third option, which MacDonald clearly did not favor, involved a cantonization plan.

The final British proposal that was presented to the Jewish and Arab delegations on March 15 was a revision of the one initially suggested by MacDonald, and was designed to be more favorable to the Arabs. It would permit the entry of 15,000 immigrants a year for five years, after which all immigration would be subject to an Arab veto. In addition, the proposal contained restrictions on land transfers as well as other features that were deemed unacceptable by the Zionists. The proposals were formally rejected by the Jewish delegation two days later. As anticipated, they were also unacceptable to the Arabs, notwithstanding the wide-ranging British concessions that would effectively have precluded the emergence of a Jewish state. This helped give some credence to the suggestion that the British proposals were deliberately designed to be unacceptable to both parties. According to this theory, an Arab-Zionist deadlock would necessitate the continuation of British rule in Palestine for an indefinite period, which is what some British strategists wanted. The final British proposals underwent some additional fine-tuning at a meeting with the Arab states that took place in Cairo, and were subsequently published as an official government White Paper on May 17, 1939.

The MacDonald White Paper echoed what had become the standard British line. It announced that the government would regard a Jewish state as contrary to its obligations to the Arabs under the Mandate, as well as to past assurances that the Arab population of Palestine would not be made the subjects of a Jewish state against their will. It simply reiterated the standard revisionist position of the government that the framers of the Mandate "could not have intended that Palestine should be converted into a Jewish State against the will of the Arab population of the country."[34] It then finally made explicit what had long been British policy in practice: "His Majesty's Government, therefore, now declare unequivocally that it is not part of their policy that Palestine should become a Jewish State."[35] What the British government did desire to see was the emergence of an independent state "in which the two peoples in Palestine, Arabs and Jews, share authority in government in such a way that the essential interests of each are secured."[36]

Accordingly, the White Paper declared: "The objective of His Majesty's Government is the establishment within ten years of an independent Palestine State in such treaty relations with the United Kingdom as will provide satisfactorily for the commercial and strategic requirements of both countries in the future." It also assured that during the transition period "both sections of the population will have an opportunity to participate in the machinery of government, and the process will be carried on whether or not they both avail themselves of it."[37]

The policy statement warned, however, that British relinquishment of the Mandate was dependent on the creation of conditions in the country that would allow the independent Palestine state to come into being. The absence of such conditions might necessitate a continuation of the Mandate past the ten-year period estimated in the document. The White Paper further indicated that the government no longer considered it advisable to adhere to the policy laid down in Ramsey MacDonald's 1931 letter to Weizmann, which stipulated the economic absorptive capacity of Palestine as the sole criterion for limiting Jewish immigration into the country. It noted that the earlier policy was predicated on the unfulfilled assumption that the Arabs would recognize the benefits to be derived for the economic development of the country resulting from continued Jewish immigration, and would therefore agree to the desirability of such immigration in appropriate numbers. Since it was now clear that such was not the case, the White Paper asserted that it was in the interest of Jews and Arabs alike that the country be allowed to develop peacefully, a condition that precluded the expansion of the Jewish community against the wishes of the Arabs.

Moreover, the White Paper asserted that the British government could not find anything in the Mandate or in other policy statements to support the argument that continued immigration for an indeterminate period was an indispensable requirement for the establishment of the Jewish national home. The White Paper all but took the position that the obligation to foster the creation of a Jewish national home, in accordance with the undertaking of the Balfour Declaration and the Mandate, had been fulfilled. Palestine was now to be treated like the other mandated territories and prepared for self-government, that is, to become an Arab state.

Notwithstanding the extent of Britain's capitulation to Arab demands, the MacDonald White Paper was roundly condemned and rejected by the Arabs. This was probably the greatest blunder in modern Arab history. Had they accepted its terms and cooperated with the British in its implementation, the future Jewish state might have been stillborn. Instead, they refused to budge from their position of total intransigence. On May 30, the Arab Higher Committee issued a statement that declared: "The ultimate decision as to the fate of a virile people depends on its own will, not on White or Black Papers. Palestine will be independent within the Arab union and will remain Arab forever."[38]

The blatant betrayal of Britain's commitments to the Jews reflected in the White Paper shocked the Jewish community of Palestine. On May 18, the day after its publication, protest demonstrations were held throughout the country. Weizmann and his policies were condemned in Tel Aviv, and not only by Revisionists. In Jerusalem, British police

were stoned, and one was shot to death. An oath was read in the synagogues and at public meetings that denounced the White Paper. The
oath directed an appeal to the British people against the decision of
their government. It declared, in part:

The Jewish population proclaims before the world that this treacherous policy
will not be tolerated. The Jewish population will fight it to the uttermost, and
will spare no sacrifice to frustrate and defeat it. No member of the Yishuv will
have a hand in the creating of any administrative organs based on this Policy,
nor will anyone co-operate with it. The Yishuv will neither recognize nor admit any callous restriction of Jewish immigration into its land. No power in the
world can destroy the natural right of our brethren to enter the ancestral land
for the purpose of rebuilding and living within it.[39]

Ben-Gurion sent a letter to the administration deploring and condemning the fatal shooting of the British constable in Jerusalem. He
warned them, however, "[T]he Jewish demonstration of yesterday
marked the beginning of Jewish resistance to the disastrous policy now
proposed by His Majesty's Government. The Jews will not be intimi-
dated into surrender even if their blood be shed."[40] After the promulgation of the White Paper, the Irgun reoriented its focus from the Arabs
to the British, now seeing the latter as the more dangerous enemy.

The government's Palestine policy was also attacked in both houses
of Parliament in rather harsh terms. The Labour Party attempted to
move an amendment that would have declared the White Paper to be
contrary to the Mandate, and received the backing of Winston Churchill and other members of the ruling party. In June 1939, the Permanent Mandates Commission met to consider the White Paper and
rejected the arguments that were made by the colonial secretary in its
defense. The commission reported to the League of Nations that "the
policy set out in the White Paper was not in accordance with the interpretation which, in agreement with the Mandatory Power and the
Council, the Commission had placed upon the Palestine Mandate."[41]

It was at last painfully obvious to most Zionist leaders that the long-
standing policy of reliance on Britain had proven a failure, although few
were prepared to admit as much publicly. The question before them
now was how the anti-Zionist British policy could be sufficiently undermined to force London to reverse it. This was the focus of the Twenty-
first Zionist Congress, which met in Geneva on August 16, 1939.

Only the Jewish State Party, headed by Meir Grossman, called for absolute noncooperation with the British government and a campaign of

civil disobedience. The main body of the delegates fell into three groups. One maintained that the time had come to abandon or at least overhaul Weizmann's policy of collaboration with the British administration. Ben-Gurion became the dominant spokesman for this viewpoint. He argued, in effect, that the White Paper was the logical consequence of a policy that led the Jews to support Britain even when it was sacrificing Jewish interests to appease the more militant Arabs. It seemed obvious that the only way Britain could be forced to reverse its policy would be for the Jews to impede implementation of the White Paper to such an extent that the British would find it necessary to appease them instead of the Arabs. He declared: "The White Paper had created a vacuum which must be filled by the Jews themselves. The Jews should act as though they were the State in Palestine and should so act until there would be a Jewish State there. In those matters in which there were infringements by the Government, the Jews should act as though they were the State."[42]

A second group expressed the opinion that continued cooperation with Britain was both unavoidable and desirable. This group reflected Weizmann's position, which was that the support of a major power was essential to the fulfillment of the Zionist program, and that only Britain, notwithstanding its appeasement of the Arabs, had thus far indicated any tangible support for Zionism. Rabbi Abba Hillel Silver of the United States warmly defended Weizmann's policy approach. He had concluded that the Zionist movement and Great Britain had not yet reached a parting of the ways, and that nothing should be done to precipitate such a final conflict between them. In opposing Ben-Gurion's position, Silver argued: "The White Paper was a temporary document only; while they should oppose it with all energy, there were good prospects of its being nullified, and therefore no extremist measures should be adopted. . . . It was dangerous to act as though they were the State, when they were not. . . . In their desperation they should not put weapons into the hands of their enemies."[43]

The third and largest group sought to find a middle position between these two alternatives. Berl Katznelson, the preeminent intellectual leader of the Zionist Labor movement, represented the views of this majority faction. He advocated support of illegal immigration and was supportive of the idea that Jews in Palestine should begin to carry weapons, with the understanding that such were to be employed exclusively for defensive purposes. It was this third group that ultimately determined the response of the Zionist movement to the challenge presented by the White Paper. Among other matters, the final resolutions of the Zionist Congress declared that "the Jewish people will not acquiesce in the reduction of its status in Palestine to that of a minority, nor in the subjection of the Jewish National Home to Arab rule."[44] At the same time, the congress also proclaimed its unwavering support of Britain in its defense of democracy in the Western world.

The official Zionist leadership had now become a proponent of illegal immigration into Palestine, a measure long demanded and sometimes implemented unilaterally by the Revisionists. At the same time, the Irgun took it upon itself to make it clear to the British that Palestine could not be pacified without Jewish cooperation. Its message was in the form of a series of reprisal raids against the Arabs that took place in February 1939. The implicit message to the British was twofold and unmistakable: the pro-Arab British policy would have to be implemented by force; and once the Jews took up arms, they would prove to be far more dangerous to British interests than the Arabs.

That summer, Jabotinsky concluded that there was no practical alternative other than an open rebellion against the British. He conceived and transmitted a detailed plan for the revolt to the Irgun commanders in Palestine. The plan was simple and bold. Jabotinsky, of course, had no illusions about the ability of the Irgun to defeat the British forces in Palestine militarily. His plan was primarily political in nature.

In October 1939, Jabotinsky would be among a boatload of illegal immigrants that would land in the heart of the country, preferably at Tel Aviv. The landing was to be assured by the Irgun, using force if necessary. At the same time, an armed uprising was to take place with as many official buildings as possible being occupied—particularly Government House in Jerusalem—above which the Zionist flag was to be raised. These positions were to be held at all costs for twenty-four hours. The Irgun was also to prevent Jabotinsky's arrest by the British for the same period. During the short-lived occupation of the key government positions, a provisional government of the Jewish state would be proclaimed simultaneously in the capitals of the United States and Western Europe. The provisional government would then begin to function as a government-in-exile, as the embodiment of Jewish sovereignty over Palestine. Presumably, the Zionist establishment, having failed in its policies for two decades, would then have no choice but to follow Jabotinsky's lead, bringing the entire Yishuv in Palestine and the entire Zionist movement outside into the struggle. Jabotinsky had clearly reached a point where he was prepared to take a desperate gamble in the hope of forcing the Zionist movement into an aggressive posture.

The feasibility of the plan became a matter of contention within the Irgun. Notwithstanding the objections of some of the commanders on a number of grounds, the overwhelming majority of them were prepared to implement it. However, one highly influential dissenter was Abraham Stern, who had long harbored a fundamental antipathy to Jabotinsky. Because of his objections, the matter was submitted for adjudication to the commander of the Irgun, David Raziel, who was being held by the British at that time in the detention camp at Sarafend. However, before the dispute could be resolved, World War II broke out, bringing about a dramatic change in the general situation.

The outbreak of hostilities had immediate repercussions in Palestine. As the threat of Italian intervention in the Middle East increased, the country was placed on a war footing and measures were taken, in conjunction with the French authorities, for the defense of Egypt, Palestine, and Syria. Arab terrorism and Jewish counterterrorism soon came to an end. There was little incentive for the Arabs to do anything further to weaken the British regime since they had little to gain from an Axis victory. The Libyan Arab experience with the Italians, who had just invaded Muslim Albania, had left a negative impression on the Arabs of Palestine, who were already weary of the long and only moderately successful struggle against Britain and the Jews. As for the Jews, as the British understood very well, they had little alternative but to throw their weight behind the British struggle against the hated Nazis. Finally, the new concentration of British forces in Palestine, coupled with the placement of the country on a war footing, simply made continued terrorism extremely difficult and dangerous for the perpetrators.

The Arab rebellion that began in 1936 had come to an end. During its course nearly 10,000 incidents of violence had taken place, including 1,325 attacks on British troops and police, 1,400 acts of sabotage against rail and telegraph lines, 153 acts of sabotage against pipelines, and 930 attacks on the Jewish population and settlements. The cost of the rebellion to the Arabs included some 2,850 dead, many thousands wounded, and more than 9,000 interned. It also resulted in nearly 1,200 Jewish and 700 British dead and wounded.

NOTES

1. Nevill Barbour, *Nisi Dominus*, p. 168.
2. William B. Ziff, *The Rape of Palestine*, p. 415.
3. Joseph B. Schechtman, *Fighter and Prophet: The Last Years*, p. 447.
4. *New York Evening Post*, August 28, 1936.

5. *The Times*, July 30, 1936.

6. Ibid., October 12, 1936.

7. John Marlowe, *The Seat of Pilate*, p. 141.

8. Barbour, *Nisi Dominus*, p. 173.

9. Paul L. Hanna, *British Policy in Palestine*, p. 126.

10. Palestine Royal Commission, *Report*, pp. 39–42.

11. Hanna, *British Policy in Palestine*, p. 131.

12. Christopher Sykes, *Crossroads to Israel*, p. 165.

13. Ibid., p. 166.

14. *The Jewish Chronicle*, April 30, 1937.

15. Chaim Weizmann, *The Letters and Papers of Chaim Weizmann*, series B: *Papers*, vol. II, p. 29.

16. Shmuel Dothan, "Religious Polemics Surrounding the 1937 Partition Plan," in Lee I. Levine, ed., *The Jerusalem Cathedra*, vol. 2, pp. 240–241.

17. J. C. Hurewitz, *The Struggle for Palestine*, p. 78.

18. Norman A. Rose, *The Gentile Zionists*, pp. 140–141.

19. *Manchester Guardian*, August 11, 1937.

20. Barbour, *Nisi Dominus*, p. 184.

21. *The Jewish Chronicle*, July 13, 1937.

22. Chaim Weizmann, *Trial and Error*, p. 393.

23. Marlowe, *The Seat of Pilate*, pp. 145–146.

24. Schechtman, *Fighter and Prophet*, p. 446.

25. Ibid., p. 452.

26. J. Borisov, *Palestine Underground*, p. 11.

27. Schechtman, *Fighter and Prophet*, p. 470.

28. *London Times*, July 21, 1938.

29. Schechtman, *Fighter and Prophet*, p. 462.

30. Ibid., p. 464. According to Schechtman, Ben-Gurion's wire messages were intercepted by the Irgun and later published in *The Jewish Call*, December 22, 1938.

31. Yehoyada Haim, *Abandonment of Illusions*, p. 135.

32. Rose, *The Gentile Zionists*, p. 182.

33. Michael J. Cohen, *Palestine: Retreat from the Mandate*, p. 76.

34. Great Britain, *Palestine, Statement of Policy*, Cmd. 6019 (1939), p. 3.

35. Ibid., p. 4.

36. Ibid., pp. 5–6.

37. Ibid., p. 6.

38. *Palestine: A Study of Jewish, Arab, and British Policies*, vol. 2, p. 908.

39. *Jewish Frontier*, October 1943, p. 14.

40. Ibid.

41. *Palestine: A Study of Jewish, Arab, and British Policies*, vol. 2, p. 927.

42. Ibid., p. 929.

43. Ibid.

44. Hanna, *British Policy in Palestine*, p. 149.

7

Palestine During World War II

The British declaration of war against Germany on September 3, 1939, was greeted by the Jewish Agency with an immediate proclamation of support, notwithstanding continuing disagreement over the MacDonald White Paper. "The war which has now been forced upon Great Britain by Nazi Germany is our war, and all the assistance that we shall be able and permitted to give to the British Army and to the British People we shall render wholeheartedly."[1]

That same day, the Executive of the Jewish Agency and the Vaad Leumi decided jointly to register volunteers to serve the needs of the Jewish community and to provide whatever services might be required by the British military. A total of 136,043 men and women volunteered by the end of the month. The Jewish Agency proposed that these volunteers serve in Palestine in distinct Jewish units. However, the Palestine administration was adamantly opposed to the idea, since it would strengthen the position of the Yishuv and further antagonize the Arabs, whose support of Britain in the war was tepid at best.

In October 1939, the mufti left French-occupied Syria for nominally nonbelligerent Iraq, which was coming under the control of the pro-Axis Rashid Ali al-Gailani. At the same time, the British announced that because of the level of illegal Jewish immigration into Palestine, no new immigration certificates would be issued for the following six months. This restriction was subsequently extended until June 1941, notwithstanding the increasingly precarious situation of the Jews of Europe who desperately needed a place of sanctuary.

Undeterred by the readiness of the Yishuv to mobilize in support of the war effort, the Palestine administration remained determined to prevent the enhancement of its self-defense capability. In October 1939, forty-three members of the Haganah, who had served as volunteers in Orde Wingate's Night Squads at the beginning of the war, were arrested for possession of arms while on a routine training exercise. When they were subsequently given long prison sentences—one a life term and the remainder ten years each—orderly protest demonstrations and a two-hour general strike were held on November 28. In January 1940, the police raided the agricultural boarding school at Ben Shemen, which had been subject to repeated attacks by Arab gangs, and unearthed a small arms cache that had been stored there in the event of further Arab assaults. On April 22, a British military court sentenced eight members of the staff of the school to prison terms of between three and seven years, even though the prosecution acknowledged that the arms were not intended to be used against the British.

As the Jews were pondering how to overcome the British opposition to their fuller participation in the war effort, the Palestine administration was preoccupied with implementing the restrictive measures of the MacDonald White Paper. The issuance of the Land Transfer Regulations on February 28, 1940, came as a shock to the Yishuv. The Jewish Agency had been notified of their impending promulgation only on the previous day, and was therefore not in a position to prepare the public. There was a sudden upsurge of anti-British feeling, as though this were the first time that the British had violated Jewish trust. The government responded with curfews, prohibition of public meetings, and repression by troops and police that further inflamed the situation. Mass demonstrations took place during the first week of March in Haifa, Jerusalem, Petah Tikva, and Tel Aviv. They soon became disorderly, and resulted in a number of scuffles with British troops and police. Seventy-four Jews were seriously injured, two subsequently dying, and 323 others were hurt. Twenty-five British were injured, five seriously.

Press censorship allowed neither reportage of the violence nor publication of the Vaad Leumi's protest, which was subsequently broadcast by the Haganah over its clandestine radio station, Voice of Israel. The Vaad Leumi statement declared:

The Land Transfer Regulations constitute a hostile attack. . . . The Jewish people are loyal to Great Britain in its war against the rule of aggression and wickedness in international relations. . . . But they will not agree . . . to be sacrificed in their National Home for the sake of appeasing the forces of aggression and

evil. . . . [The Vaad Leumi] protests in the name of the Yishuv against this de-
cree, which wantonly violates the clauses of the Mandate and nullifies the very
purpose for which the Mandate was entrusted to the British Government.[2]

The British Labour Party introduced a motion of censure against the
government on account of the regulations on March 6, but it was easily
defeated when it came to a vote.

The question of a Jewish military force first came up for discussion in
Parliament that same month. Prime Minister MacDonald, reluctantly
and only in response to prodding, reported that 1,709 Jews, as against
only 393 Arabs, had enlisted in Palestine for overseas service since the
beginning of the war. A Palestine Auxiliary Military Pioneer Corps,
consisting of 742 Jews and 306 Arabs, had served with the British
Army in France. Given the vast disparity between the sizes of the Jewish
and Arab populations in Palestine, these figures were rather embarrass-
ing for the government in view of its pro-Arab policy. Subsequently, the
government adopted a policy of balancing enlistments and limited the
number of Jewish volunteers accepted to the number of Arabs. When
later challenged to explain whether the enlistments in Palestine were
being deliberately restricted along communal lines, the undersecretary
of state for colonies, Henry George, insisted that the parity in enlistments was a consequence of equipment shortages. This lame excuse
was hardly credible, and under the pressure of public opinion in Britain
as the military situation continued to deteriorate, the government was
forced to abandon the limits on recruitment.

Expectations of a change in British policy were high when Winston
Churchill, an avowed and outspoken opponent of the White Paper,
took over the reins of government in May 1940. These hopes were
soon to be dashed. Churchill and his war cabinet refused to take any
steps or make any statements that deviated from the policies laid down
in the White Paper.

Two days after he took office, Churchill received a new offer to raise
a Jewish army, this time from Jabotinsky, acting on behalf of the Revisionists. Churchill passed the idea on to the new colonial secretary Lord
George Lloyd, who indicated his strong opposition to any such scheme.
He stated, quite accurately, "[I]t is clear that proposals of this kind,
whether emanating from the New Zionists or from the Zionists, have as
their prime object the recognition of the Jewish people as a nation, with
a standing in the War Councils of the Allies and ultimately in the discussions of terms of peace. In both cases the conversion of Palestine into a
Jewish State as a reward for Jewish military assistance is the objective."[3]

Colonel Josiah Wedgwood raised the matter of authorizing the creation of Jewish military units once again on May 23, on the heels of the
German invasion of Norway and the Low Countries. In response, Anthony Eden, the secretary of state for war, stated: "In the opinion of His
Majesty's Government, the raising of separate Jewish formations would
present great difficulties and it would be of much more advantage if the
Jews who are anxious to serve enlist in His Majesty's Forces in the ordinary way."[4]

When Italy entered the war on June 10, Weizmann appealed unsuccessfully to the British authorities once again. He pointed out that
Mussolini had actively supported the Arab rebellion since 1935, and
might attempt an attack on Palestine. (Italian aircraft bombed Haifa in
July, August, and September, and Tel Aviv in September, 1940.) He
urged that the Jews be organized for home defense, and that they be allowed, "under the direction of the Jewish Agency and the Jewish National Council [Vaad Leumi], and under control of the British Military
Authorities, to organise as many military units as they could, and to
train and drill their men, as far as possible with the help of the British
forces in the country."[5]

While Lord Lloyd tried to pass the blame for the failure to accept the
Jewish offer to objections raised by the War Office, it was in fact Lloyd
himself who was most adamantly opposed to the idea. He wrote to
Churchill on June 27, in a note endorsed by Viscount Halifax and Anthony Eden:

I need hardly emphasize the objections to this Zionist plan for arming the Palestine Jews . . . the political and military consequences would be so grave that
any disadvantages would count as nothing in the scale . . . the arming of the
Jewish community in Palestine under British auspices would undoubtedly be
interpreted by Arab and Moslem opinion, not only in the Middle East but in
India, as a step toward the subjection of Palestine to Jewish domination.[6]

Churchill did not accept the arguments of his colleagues, but he did
nothing to counteract them. There wasn't an iota of evidence that India's Muslims had any significant interest in Palestine. They had not reacted when the sultan declared a holy war against the British in 1917,
and there was no reason to believe that they would do so now on behalf
of the Arabs of Palestine. Churchill advocated arming the Jews of Palestine in order to allow the return of some eight battalions of men that he
felt were sorely needed in England for home defense. However, the
military disagreed with this appraisal, and argued that the troops in Pal-

estine were needed there more as a reserve force to protect the Suez Canal. Weizmann tried once again to make the case for a Jewish military force in August with a letter to Churchill, in which he laid bare his deepest concerns for the Yishuv. He raised the specter that should a British withdrawal from the country become necessary, "the Jews of Palestine would be exposed to wholesale massacre at the hands of the Arabs encouraged and directed by the Nazis and Fascists. . . . If Palestine be invaded and the Jewish community be destroyed for lack of the means of self-defence, a grave responsibility will attach to the British Government which refused them."[7]

This latest appeal to Churchill seemed to have some effect, not because of the merit of the argument, but because he had already decided on August 16 to move most of the Commonwealth forces in Palestine to Egypt. This would leave a security gap that could be filled reliably by the Jews. Negotiations soon began over the formation of a Jewish force. On September 13, 1940, Eden officially notified Weizmann that "the Government have decided to proceed with the organisation of a Jewish army, on the same basis as the Czech and Polish armies. Its size to begin with, would be 10,000 including 4,000 from Palestine. They would be trained and organised in England and then dispatched to the Middle East."[8] The officers were to be selected by the Jewish Agency with the approval of the War Office. However, the units were to be used wherever in the region the War Office considered them needed, and not necessarily in Palestine. Although everything appeared to have been settled, nothing further was heard about the matter because of the overwhelming opposition to the scheme in the war cabinet, particularly by Lord Moyne, who took Lloyd's place as colonial secretary.

Notwithstanding the anger generated among Jews by the callousness of British policy with respect to the immigration of Jews who managed to flee Europe, the Zionist leadership persisted in attempting to bring about the formation of an all-Jewish force to fight under British command. After repeated inquiries regarding the government-approved scheme of September 1940, which still remained to be implemented, Lord Moyne informed Weizmann on March 4, 1941: "I am very sorry that I have to tell you that the raising of the Jewish contingent has to be postponed. . . . The Prime Minister has decided that owing to lack of equipment the project must for the present be put off for six months, but may be considered again in four months." Moyne added, "I can assure you that this postponement is in no sense a reversal of the previous decision in favor of your proposal."[9] A month later Moyne advised Weizmann that despite his earlier assurances, the Jewish

Agency proposal had been rejected. Although it was justified on the basis of equipment shortages, there was little question that the real reason was political. Movement toward creation of a Jewish fighting force within the British Army had apparently run into an impenetrable barrier.

It was not until 1944, notwithstanding the continuing agitation for such a unit during the intervening period, that the British relented. On September 29, 1944, referring to a government decision earlier in the month to form a Jewish Brigade Group, Churchill stated before the House of Commons: "I know there is a vast number of Jews serving with our forces and the American forces throughout all the armies, but it seems to me indeed appropriate that a special Jewish unit of that race which has suffered indescribable torment from the Nazi should be represented as a distinct formation among the forces gathered for their final overthrow."[10] The brigade was subsequently formed and trained, and on March 15, 1945, entered into active combat on the Italian front as an element of the British Eighth Army.

The announcement of the formation of the Jewish Brigade was received in Palestine with mixed emotions. There was resentment that the British had deliberately delayed its establishment until the war was nearly over. Some were concerned about the removal of the cream of the Yishuv's military potential from the country to serve primarily as occupation forces in Europe, at a time when critical decisions about the future of Palestine appeared to be on the horizon. Indeed, it was suspected that this had much to do with the decision to set up the unit at such a late date. Nonetheless, the brigade served a role in Europe that no one could have anticipated. Its members became instrumental in organizing the illegal immigration of the Jewish survivors of the holocaust into Palestine, an act of inestimable value for the achievement of Zionist aims.

While the Yishuv essentially cooperated fully with the British throughout the war, except with regard to the matter of illegal immigration, there was nonetheless one voice that categorically opposed such cooperation as long as the administration continued to implement the restrictive provisions of the White Paper. Abraham Stern, one of the leaders of the Irgun who had been interned by the British in August 1939 and released in June 1940, split with David Raziel on this issue while the two were still in the Sarafend detention camp. In Stern's view, as long as the British prevented Jewish victims of Nazism from reaching Palestine, they were no better than the Nazis, and had to be fought as Hitler's accomplices. He urged that the struggle against Britain continue unabated in order to compel it to make critical concessions.

Upon Stern's release from detention, he had a serious confrontation with Raziel, who had been let out several months earlier, a fact that Stern attributed to Raziel's willingness to cooperate with the British. Infuriated by the charge, Raziel resigned as commander of the Irgun and Stern took over. An appeal was made to Jabotinsky, who was in the United States trying to get support for a Jewish army, to intervene in the dispute. In August 1940, Jabotinsky sent a cable to Raziel telling him to reassume command of the Irgun, and another to Stern, asking him to step down and cooperate. Stern, a committed Anglophobe at this point, refused to comply. A week later, when Jabotinsky suddenly died of a heart attack in New York, there was no longer anyone to heal the breach.

Because many of the Irgun commanders refused to accept his arguments, Stern left the organization with some fifty others and set up the independent *Irgun Zvai Leumi be-Yisrael* (National Military Organization in Israel), which later became known as the Fighters for the Freedom of Israel (*Lehi*). Impoverished and without arms, in September 1940 the Sternists robbed a branch of the Anglo-Palestine Bank in Tel Aviv of about $20,000 and began to build a cadre of former colleagues in the Irgun who became increasingly angry at the British as the situation in Europe worsened. The Lehi subsequently drew much of its strength from among the disenchanted youth of the Sephardi community, which was largely ignored by the official Zionist bodies, and later from among some of the Jewish troops of the Polish army that began to arrive in Palestine in 1941.

When the threat of a German-Italian invasion of Palestine seemed increasingly probable during the winter of 1940–1941, the British military command began preparing plans for the evacuation of British forces that would have left the Jews in Palestine completely at Hitler's mercy. Representatives of the British military approached Stern with the proposal that he organize his men in special detachments to wage guerrilla warfare in the event of an Axis invasion. The British offered to supply the necessary food and war matériel for a protracted effort. Stern's response was: "The Fighters for the Freedom of Israel who are with me will fight against any invader within the boundaries of our national territory. Should the invader be Germany, we shall probably fight with greater zeal." However, he made acceptance of the British offer conditional upon their recognition of Jewish sovereign rights in Palestine. He wanted the anticipated British withdrawal to be permanent. "If after the war when victory is achieved you shall return to occupy this country, we shall turn our arms against you and fight you without respite. Our chief aim is complete independence in our own homeland. We shall not acquiesce to British rule, just as we shall not acquiesce to a German one."[11]

Stern was an enigma to the Yishuv and the Jewish world as a whole, and as a consequence was poorly understood. There was, however, a cold logic to his views that was so stark it was difficult to cope with. He fully recognized the Nazis for what they were, but at the same time saw the British for what they were as well. In his view, given the state of knowledge at the time (he knew as little about the impending holocaust as did the official Zionist leadership), there was little to choose between them. Thus, he was adamantly opposed to Jews from Palestine joining the British Army to fight the Germans, and condemned any effort to recruit for that purpose. His position is made quite clear in the following condensation of an illegal broadcast that he wrote during this period:

There is a difference between a persecutor [*tzorer*] and an enemy [*oyev*]. Persecutors have risen against Israel in all generations and in all periods of our Diaspora, starting with Haman and ending with Hitler. They have attempted to obliterate us both physically and spiritually. As long as we remain in the Diaspora, such oppression will continue. The source of all our woes is our remaining in exile, and the absence of a homeland and statehood. Therefore, our enemy is the foreigner, the ruler of our land who blocks the return of the people to it. The enemy are the British who conquered the land with our help and who remain here by our leave, and who have betrayed us and placed our brethren in Europe in the hands of the persecutor. The millions in Europe, who cried for emigration to and settlement on the land of the homeland, were not permitted to come by the foreign conqueror who thus precluded their rescue in full knowledge of the horrors of Hitler's mass exterminations. Thus, one should not confuse issues. Mobilization into the British army is a crime because it supports the foreign overlord. First and foremost, we must fight the enemy, the thief of our independence and impeder of our renaissance. How can we fight our persecutors in the world? Who among the peoples of Europe is not a persecutor of Israel? Who among the peoples of the world has not been, or is not, our oppressor? Therefore, mobilization is a crime. It is wrong to permit our youth to leave the country, because: (a) they are needed for the struggle against the foreign overlords; (b) they are needed to guard our brethren here from the Arab terrorists that are awaiting Hitler's victory, as well as the persecutor himself should he invade and set up an oppressive regime.[12]

Stern also ridiculed the notion that if there were a Jewish army fighting under the British flag, this would somehow translate into important gains at the postwar peace conference. He thought that the experience of World War I and the Jewish Legion should have been sufficient to demonstrate the absurdity of such an idea.

Stern was determined to do what he could to alleviate the plight of the Jews in Europe at all costs, even if it meant dealing with the hated Germans. There had been rumors that the Nazis planned to exile the Jews to Madagascar (nothing was known at the time of the "final solution"). Why not induce the Germans to redirect them to Palestine instead? In late 1941, Stern sent his second in command, Nathan Friedman-Yellin, to the Balkans for the purpose of trying to persuade the Axis authorities there to allow fleeing Jews to pass through the Balkans en route to Palestine. In response to arguments that his motives would be misunderstood by the Jewish public, Stern declared:

The British are fighting for British independence, the French for French independence, the Czechs for Czech independence, the Poles, the Yugoslavs—all for their own freedom. But the Jews are fighting for British freedom. When they fight for their own independence, they find Germany and Britain arrayed against them—the one crushing them where they are, the other preventing them from reaching refuge. Why should we not turn for help where we can get it? Why should we cooperate in our own enslavement? Is it I who am insane, or the others?[13]

In the meantime, illegal immigration into Palestine continued, and the Palestine administration decided to begin the deportation of illegals, something that had been envisioned in the White Paper as a means of combating such immigration. On November 11, 1940, two broken-down ships, the *Pacific* and the *Milos*, were intercepted by the British Navy off the Palestinian coast and brought to Haifa. The refugees on board were refused permission to land. The Jewish Agency tried to put the British in a corner by calling a general strike. This had the effect of forcing the government to take a public position on the issue. The high commissioner broadcast an announcement that the 1,771 passengers on the two intercepted ships would not be allowed to remain in Palestine. The official statement declared: "His Majesty's Government are not lacking in sympathy for refugees from territories under German control, but . . . they can only regard a revival of illegal Jewish immigration at the present juncture as likely to affect the local situation most adversely, and to prove a serious menace to British interests in the Middle East." They therefore decided to deport the refugees to a British colony where they would in effect be interned for the duration of the war. When the war was over, a decision would have to be made about where to send them, "but it is not proposed that they shall remain in the colony to which they are sent or that they shall go to Palestine."[14]

The refugees were transferred to the larger *Patria* for deportation to the island of Mauritius. On the morning of November 25, as passengers from yet another refugee ship, the *Atlantic*, were about to be transferred to the *Patria* as well, an alarm was sounded on the ship and the passengers were told to jump into the water. A few minutes later the ship was rocked by an explosion and began to sink. Some 240 refugees and about a dozen police were killed by the explosion or by drowning in this dramatic protest against British policy. Arthur Koestler was to write of this incident:

The passengers blew up their ship. They had reached their journey's end. They were not even threatened with deportation back to Europe; only to a tropical island without hope of return. But these people had become allergic to barbed wire. When a person reaches that stage he is past listening to the reasonable voice of officialdom which explains to him that he should never have escaped, or saved his wife and children, as "a revival of illegal Jewish immigration at the present juncture" was "likely to affect the local situation most adversely [in the words of the official government statement of November 20]."[15]

The survivors were permitted to remain in Palestine as an exceptional act of clemency, a sentiment that was not to be applied to subsequent boatloads of desperate refugees. On December 8, 1940, 1,584 refugees without valid visas were deported from Palestine to Mauritius. On December 19, in their first serious act of retaliation against the British, the Sternists bombed the government's immigration offices in Haifa to protest the deportations.

The impact of events in Europe also began to bring about a change in the political outlook of the leadership of the Zionist movement. It was beginning to dawn on them that it would be necessary to adopt the statist views of the much maligned Revisionists if the Zionist aims in Palestine were ever to be realized. Acknowledging that the Zionist leadership had "discouraged the demands for immediate Jewish statehood in the past," in the summer of 1941 Berl Katznelson argued: "If it were possible to have a regime that assures free mass immigration and colonization in Palestine, the existence of a Jewish state as such would become of secondary importance. But our experience in recent years should have taught us that in the present period of world history there is only one type of regime that can guarantee these conditions, and that is a Jewish state."[16] A few months later, even Weizmann, swallowing his antistatist declarations at the Twentieth Zionist Congress in 1937, wrote in a prestigious international journal: "The Arabs must . . . be clearly told that the Jews will be encouraged to settle in Palestine, and will control their own immigration; that here Jews who so desire will be able to achieve their freedom and self-government by establishing a state of their own, and ceasing to be a minority dependent on the will and pleasure of other nations."[17]

At about the same time, in December 1941, a barely seaworthy cattle ship, the *Struma*, reached Istanbul with a cargo of 769 Jewish refugees en route to Palestine. The Turks would not permit the passengers to disembark. The Palestine government refused to grant entry visas, and eventually, after two months of fruitless negotiations, the Turkish government ordered the ship out of its territorial waters. Although the British later relented and agreed to allow entry of the children who were under sixteen years of age, it was too late. On February 23, 1942, after being towed out of Istanbul, the *Struma* sank in the Black Sea, probably after hitting a mine. There was only one survivor. Disgust with the conduct of the British government was widespread, including many among the British public. On June 9, Lord Wedgwood opened the debate in the House of Lords by urging that the mandate over Palestine be transferred to the United States, since Britain had reneged on its commitments. He stated with bitterness: "I hope yet to live to see those who sent the 'Struma' cargo back to the Nazis hung as high as Haman cheek by jowl with their prototype and Fuhrer, Adolf Hitler."[18]

Britain's implementation of the White Paper, which was supplemented by a policy of restricting immigration from territories under German occupation, on the specious theory that German agents might thereby infiltrate into the country, had a devastating effect on the number of Jews who were able to find refuge in Palestine. The White Paper had provided for a quota of 75,000 immigrants for the five-year period ending March 31, 1944. However, by the end of 1942 only 52 percent of the total, or 38,930, more than half of whom were illegal, managed to enter the country. Requests for visas for Jews in countries about to be invaded by the Germans were almost invariably denied. The high commissioner rejected an appeal from the Jewish Agency on behalf of the Balkan Jews in October 1940. He allegedly did this with the comment that it would be wiser "to save up these permits for postwar use when they might be allotted to Jews of a 'better type' than those from the Balkans."[19] Similarly, in April 1941 an application for 100 permits to allow entry of prominent members of the Jewish community of Greece, who were then in grave danger, was rejected on the ground that saving 100 individuals would not benefit Greek Jewry, which numbered some 75,000 at the time.

It was against the background of this deteriorating situation, and the growing recognition that dramatic steps had to be taken to insure the Jewish future in Palestine, that the Zionist leadership turned for assistance to the American Jewish community, now the largest and most influential in the world. The American Emergency Committee for Zionist Affairs called an extraordinary political conference at the Biltmore Hotel in New York City in May 1942. Ben-Gurion and others made a strong appeal for support of a reorientation of Zionist activity to openly promote the idea of Jewish statehood. The statist approach won the approval of the majority of the 600 delegates in attendance. As a result, the conference produced a new declaration of Zionist aims, subsequently known as the Biltmore Program. It concluded:

The Conference urges that the gates of Palestine be opened; that the Jewish Agency be vested with control of immigration into Palestine and with the necessary authority for upbuilding the country, including the development of its unoccupied and uncultivated lands; and that Palestine be established as a Jewish Commonwealth integrated in the structure of the new democratic world.[20]

Ben-Gurion, chairman of the Jewish Agency Executive and a former staunch advocate of binationalism, had once again become a fiery proponent of the Jewish state idea. He returned to Palestine that summer to advocate the idea and seek the approval of the Zionist Actions Committee, which was now composed almost exclusively of members of the Yishuv. He quickly won support from the General Zionists and the Mizrahi. It goes without saying that the Jewish State Party, whose program was being adopted, was also most supportive, as the Revisionists would have been, were they still members of the World Zionist Organization. The main opposition to the Biltmore Program came from Ben-Gurion's Mapai Party, whose left-wing factions opposed an open declaration of the demand for a Jewish state. They understood that it would inevitably lead to the partition of the country, and they remained firmly committed to the idea of binationalism. Accordingly, they preferred to see an indefinite continuation of the British Mandate. The Zionist Actions Committee in Jerusalem finally adopted the Biltmore Program in November 1942, by a vote of 21 to 4. The negative ballots were cast by members of a new political bloc made up of the Hashomer Hatzair, the Left Poalei Zion, and others on the Left who would not accept Ben-Gurion's position on the issue.

Although he did not actively oppose it at the time, Weizmann thought that Ben-Gurion had gone too far in formulating and promoting the Biltmore Program. From Weizmann's standpoint, the whole thing was nothing more than a bid by Ben-Gurion to achieve dominance over the world Zionist movement. He wrote, in a letter dated January 8, 1943,

Ben-Gurion, after his stay here of 8 or 9 months, had absolutely nothing to show by way of achievement, and so he stuck to the Biltmore Resolution, more or less conveying the idea that it is the triumph of his policy as against my moderate formulation of the same aims, and he injected into it all his own extreme views, such as: an immigration of two million people in three years, or something to that effect; and the building up of a great defence force to fight either the Arabs or the British or both or goodness knows whom.[21]

As soon as the Biltmore Conference ended, Ben-Gurion sought to force Weizmann to resign for a variety of alleged sins, particularly his Anglophilia. Shortly thereafter, Weizmann drafted a strong letter to the Zionist Executive in Jerusalem that he never sent, but that reflected his candid opinion of Ben-Gurion.

I have watched Mr. Ben-Gurion carefully during his stay here. His conduct and deportment were painfully reminiscent of the petty dictator, a type one meets with so often in public life now. They are all shaped on a definite pattern: they are humorless, thin-lipped, morally stunted, fanatical and stubborn, apparently frustrated in some ambition, and nothing is more dangerous than a small man nursing his grievances introspectively.[22]

On other occasions Weizmann remarked, "It is perfectly useless to try and argue with him as I think the man suffers from some mental aberrations," and "I'm quite certain that he is developing fascist tendencies and megalomania coupled with political hysteria."[23] Although the extent to which the mutual animosities of Ben-Gurion and Weizmann negatively affected the Zionist cause is unclear, they certainly did not contribute to policy coherence.

The Allied victories at Stalingrad and in North Africa during the winter of 1942–1943 brought significant changes in the political environment in the Middle East. As soon the defeat of Germany and Italy could be even dimly perceived on the horizon, Britain began considering how best to restructure the region to serve its longer-term national interests. As early as May 1941, Anthony Eden had indicated the British government's interest in the emerging movement that sought to bring about some unity, or at least cooperation, among the several Arab states. Consequently, when Nahas Pasha of Egypt and Nuri Said of Iraq began to explore the question of Arab unity that same winter of 1942–1943, Britain demonstrated sympathetic interest in the direction of their thinking. From London's perspective, it would serve Britain's residual interests in the Middle East very nicely if it were perceived to be the sponsor of Arab independence and political development.

The idea of a possible Arab federation of states had important implications for the Zionist enterprise, since it was evident that there would be no place in such a political configuration for a Jewish homeland. Britain's support of the federation proposal therefore would ultimately lead it to resurrect the idea of partition, ceding to the Jews only those parts of Palestine where they already constituted the majority.

In July 1943, a special cabinet committee to consider the question of Palestine was established. At the same time feelers were extended to the Zionist leadership to determine if there was any latent interest in a reexamination of partition as a means of resolving the Arab-Zionist standoff in Palestine. In August, Sharett met in Cairo with Lord Moyne, who sought to convince him to accept partition as the basis for new negotiations over the future of the country. Sharett, who was actually delighted that partition was under active consideration once again, adamantly rejected the suggestion. But this was merely a bargaining tactic. He wrote to Nahum Goldmann on August 30 with regard to the renewed British offer of partition:

The line we should take is not to rush to its welcome but to keep coldly aloof and go on pressing for the "whole loaf." It will be disastrous, externally as well as internally, if at this stage partition became, or if the impression were created that it had become, our slogan. Internally, because a very violent controversy would then be revived—the last thing we need today. Externally, because the chances of any further political headway would thereby be destroyed.[24]

The question of partition was raised again in October 1943, at a meeting between Churchill and Weizmann. Churchill indicated that in a partition arrangement the Jews might receive the Negev as well as parts of Transjordan in addition to other areas, but Weizmann objected strenuously to the very notion of partition. However, it seems that Churchill was unimpressed by Weizmann's rejection of the idea and did not take it seriously. Weizmann had long been an outspoken advocate of partition, and everyone knew it. Indeed, it was Weizmann's support of partition that had served as the rationale for a serious split in the official Zionist leadership that took place in the summer of that same year.

Because of Weizmann's views on partition, Ben-Gurion displayed concern that Weizmann might abandon the ostensibly maximalist Biltmore Program. In June, Ben-Gurion accused Weizmann of being uncooperative and acting on his own in the name of the Zionist movement, which he failed to consult or heed. He therefore announced his intention to resign as chairman of the Jewish Agency Executive unless Weizmann ceased his unauthorized negotiations with the British government. Weizmann and his close associates reciprocated by charging Ben-Gurion with a lack of cooperation and responsibility, coupled with a tendency to occasional extremism that was dangerous to the Zionist cause. The crisis smoldered until October 26, when Ben-Gurion suddenly submitted his resignation at a meeting of the Smaller Zionist Actions Committee. Efforts to dissuade him failed, and on November 3, Ben-Gurion submitted his formal resignation to the Jewish Agency.

What was really at issue was dominance over the Zionist movement. It was simply a long-festering power struggle between Ben-Gurion and Weizmann, with neither prepared to give way, notwithstanding the efforts of the other Zionist leaders to bring about a reconciliation. However, when it became clear that neither Weizmann nor Ben-Gurion had the strength to dislodge the other, Ben-Gurion apparently concluded that Weizmann was no longer a danger to the Biltmore Program and decided that it made no sense to continue with the struggle. A peace commission of three went to London to negotiate terms with Weizmann for Ben-Gurion to return to the Jewish Agency Executive, which he did on February 27, 1944. Ben-Gurion now compensated for Weizmann's unilateral actions in London by taking actions in Palestine without informing Weizmann, who was equally helpless in affecting decisions there.

However, before Ben-Gurion resumed his leadership of the Jewish Agency, he precipitated a major political crisis in the Labor movement. Mapai's own left-wing faction refused to endorse the Biltmore Program and joined the binationalist opposition within the Histadrut, soon bolting from the party. After three months of constant bickering within both his own party and the Mapai-dominated Histadrut, Ben-Gurion insisted on new elections for the latter body. He apparently hoped to win a popular mandate by appealing directly to the approximately 75 percent of the Histadrut members who were unaffiliated with any political party.

By coincidence, the Yishuv was at that time engaged in a campaign for the fourth general election to the Jewish community's Elected Assembly. The Elected Assembly was constitutionally limited to a term of four years. However, as a consequence of the highly unsettled conditions in the country over the preceding decade, the third Elected Assembly had remained in office for more than thirteen years. In the intervening period, the Jewish population had tripled from some 170,000 to 550,000, with the electorate increasing from fewer than 90,000 in 1931, when the last Elected Assembly took office, to over 300,000 in 1944.

In the spring of 1944, the campaign for election of delegates to an expanded Elected Assembly of 171 members (in place of the existing 71-member body) got under way. Here, too, the fact that the overwhelming majority of the electorate was politically unaffiliated, while the electoral system was based on communitywide party tickets, worked to the advantage of the tightly organized political parties that dominated the Vaad Leumi, which was elected by the Assembly. In effect, the system was such that the overwhelming majority of the voters had no effective political voice.

The Mapai had been able to take advantage of this situation to dominate the Elected Assembly and the Vaad Leumi. It claimed that it spoke for the majority of the Yishuv, which in fact went unrepresented, and it was therefore extremely reluctant to heed calls by the Sephardim, some General Zionists, and the Revisionists to democratize the system. These groups advocated adoption of the Anglo-American system of electoral districts that would make the elected delegates more responsible to the electorate than to the central party headquarters. These disenchanted groups therefore boycotted the elections, which, originally set for May 24, were deferred to August 1, just five days before the scheduled Histadrut election.

Since the stand of the different political parties on the Biltmore Program was the critical factor in the Histadrut election, it became the dominating concern in the general election as well. This was a new departure, since issues of Zionist policy were usually dealt with in elections for the Zionist congresses rather than in the community elections. This change forced all parties across the political spectrum to take a position on the Biltmore Program. As a consequence, the nonparty voters who constituted the majority of the electorate were confronted by no fewer than twenty-four electoral tickets, some representing traditionally nonpolitical or semipolitical groups, amounting to a total of 1,694 candidates. With 67 percent of the electorate participating, Mapai retained its leading position in the new 171-member Elected Assembly with 63 seats. Of particular significance for the future was the surprising gain by the Poalei Mizrahi Party, which received seventeen seats. Together with the ten seats received by its parent organization, the Mizrahi religious bloc became the second largest contingent in the Assembly and a force to be reckoned with in coalition politics.

As a result of the controversy over the Biltmore Program, Mapai forfeited its majority in the Vaad Leumi, obtaining only five of the eleven seats, which forced it into forming a coalition to maintain its dominant position. In the Histadrut elections, because of defections resulting from disagreement over the Biltmore Program, Mapai's relative strength declined from 69.3 to 53.5 percent, giving it only a slight margin of control over what had become the most important institution in Yishuv politics. The net outcome of the entire process was a formal endorsement by the Yishuv of what became known as the Jerusalem-Biltmore Program. With Ben-Gurion once again assuming the position of chairman of the Jewish Agency Executive, he could claim the backing of the majority of the Yishuv for the demand for a Jewish state.

Another effect of the improving war situation was a further deterioration in relations between the Yishuv and the Palestine administration. Once again, as in 1940, the British attempted to weaken the defense capabilities of the Yishuv. The primary target was the Haganah's arms cache, and all centers of Jewish settlement became subject to searches. Those found in possessions of arms, even a single unauthorized bullet, received stiff prison terms. British aggressiveness in this regard put great pressure on the Haganah leadership, which was divided on how to respond. Moshe Sneh, the head of the Haganah's national command structure, had characterized Britain not as an enemy but merely as a bad partner. This meant that the Zionist future remained linked to the position of Britain in the Middle East, and that it did not serve Zionist interests to act toward it in a way that might transform it into an open enemy. However, British actions were making it ever more difficult to maintain this benign view. There was increasing concern that an open conflict with Britain might become unavoidable, notwithstanding the fact that the Haganah was in a rather poor state of readiness for such a confrontation.

A considerably less benign view of the British was held by the Irgun, which came under the political leadership of Menachem Begin soon after his arrival in Palestine with the Polish army in April 1942. Late in 1943, the Irgun attempted to set up a Yishuv-wide anti-British coalition comprising members of all three military organizations: the Haganah, the Irgun, and the Sternists or Lehi. The latter refused to participate in the *Am Lohem* (Fighting Nation), as the new structure was called. Numerous members of Haganah, primarily from its elite strike force Palmah, supported the idea, seeing it as an opportunity to bring activists from across the political spectrum into a common effort to establish the Jewish state. It was proposed, among other things, to organize Jews serving in the British Army into a future Jewish army. The ultimate aim of the movement was to force the British to recognize a Jewish state that encompassed, at a minimum, all of Cis-Jordan, the Hauran in Trans-Jordan, and the Sinai.

Am Lohem announced its existence on November 1, 1943, in a publication bearing its name, and stressed its broad-based composition. As its first major action, it planned to abduct the high commissioner. However, before the plan could be carried through, word of it leaked out. The Haganah national command became quite upset by this development because the proposed action did not have the policy approval of the Histadrut. On December 7, 1943, Sneh ordered the Haganah members to cease all participation in the Am Lohem within seventy-two hours, threatening severe sanctions for those who refused to comply. The Haganah command was shocked to discover the extent of sympathy for Am Lohem within its ranks, and was forced to undertake an extensive internal propaganda campaign to discredit it. An internal purge of Irgun sympathizers took place, accompanied by trials and expulsions, which succeeded in crippling the broad-based group.

Shortly after the collapse of Am Lohem, the Irgun terminated its almost four-year-old truce with the British. In January 1944, Begin proclaimed a revolt against Britain:

There is no longer any armistice between the Jewish people and the British Administration in Eretz Israel which hands our brothers over to Hitler. Our people is at war with this regime—war to the end. This war will demand many and heavy sacrifices, but we enter on it in the consciousness that we are being faithful to the children of our people who have been and are being slaughtered. It is for their sake that we fight, to their dying testimony that we remain loyal.[25]

The Irgun began its campaign with attacks on British institutions that had great symbolic as well as practical import for the Yishuv. On February 12, 1944, the government's immigration offices were blown up in order to destroy the records that enabled the British to determine which Jews were legal or illegal immigrants. This was followed on February 27 by the bombing of the Income Tax Building. On March 23, there were simultaneous attacks on the headquarters of the hated Criminal Investigation Division in Haifa, Jaffa, and Jerusalem. These attacks were accompanied by an intensive propaganda campaign that sought to rouse the Yishuv to a general revolt against British rule. Begin tried to encourage the establishment of a provisional coalition government that would incorporate the Irgun on the basis of full equality with the other elements of the Yishuv, and that would proclaim the creation of a Jewish state in all of Palestine. Although he had declared a revolt, Begin, like his mentor Jabotinsky, was not anti-British in the sense that he wished to see the British driven out of the Middle East. His overriding concern was with the achievement of Jewish independence, and to the extent that the British stood in the way of reaching that goal, they had to be fought.

Attempts were made at this time to form a common front between the Irgun and the Lehi, but they were only partially successful. Abraham Stern was murdered by the British in February 1942, and the organization was now led by a central committee composed of future prime minister Yitzhak Shamir, Israel Scheib (Eldad), and Nathan Friedman-Yellin. The Lehi, however, remained intrinsically anti-British and did not believe that political concessions could be gained from them through pressure. In its view, the British would have to be forced to leave Palestine, and this would happen only by making it too costly for them to remain there. Begin and the Irgun would soon come to share this belief. However, at the time, as a consequence of the fundamental differences in the purpose and objective of each group's revolt against the British, attempts to unite the two in the summer of 1944 were unsuccessful. The Lehi mounted a campaign of vengeance against the British police for the murder of Stern. Up to November 1944, the Lehi killed fifteen British policemen in retaliation, including the assistant superintendent of police, whom they held personally responsible for the killing, after stalking him for thirty-one months.

The Irgun's campaign aroused great concern in the Jewish Agency on several counts. First, it challenged the authority of the official representative institutions of the Yishuv and the Zionist movement. Second, its purposive activism generated a degree of support, and a larger amount of sympathy, among the general Jewish public that threatened the political position of the official bodies, which were seen as passive by contrast. Third, it was beginning to make inroads into the Haganah, many of whose members were inclined toward cooperation with the Irgun in the struggle against the British. Finally, the members of the Jewish Agency Executive were concerned that outsiders might obtain sufficient support to supplant its leadership. Of course, the Jewish Agency's concerns were not expressed in such bald terms. Instead, they were articulated as an issue of the Irgun's challenge to the democratically elected institutions of the Yishuv, a challenge that allegedly was being financed through extortion of an unwilling public.

The political department of the Jewish Agency, under Sharett, became the instrument for combating the challenges presented by both the Irgun and the Lehi. Sharett perceived the latter, in particular, simply as a terrorist group that could legitimately be fought by any means available. Accordingly, the Jewish Agency people had little hesitation in cooperating with the British against the Lehi. A secretive organization, calling itself *Mishmar haYishuv* (Patrol of the Yishuv), was established for the express purpose of fighting Jewish terrorism. However, the mainstream Haganah organization participated in the campaign as well. Thus, as a result of information provided by the Haganah's intelligence service to the British, after the killing of a policeman in Haifa, two Lehi members named Drucker and Luntz were trapped at Yavniel in April 1944. When they discovered that there was no way to escape, the two men chose to commit suicide rather be captured.

The problem in dealing with the Irgun was more complex. Most of the nonsocialists in the official bodies of the Yishuv, such as the General Zionists and the Mizrahi, were opposed both to cooperation with the British and to strong, independent action against the Irgun. For the most part, they were unwilling to go beyond verbal pronouncements and propaganda in either respect. Even elements of the Histadrut were opposed to collaboration with the British, although they generally favored direct action against the Irgun, should such become necessary. The most on which the leadership could gain a consensus, at the time, was the isolation of known Irgun members or supporters within the community, and the education of the public with regard to the dangers that could result from the actions of the separatists. The impact of these measures was, as might be expected, negligible.

The Irgun attacked the British central radio broadcasting station at Ramallah on May 17, 1944, and the Tel Aviv-Jaffa district police headquarters on August 22. Police installations at Beit Dagon, Haifa, Katara, and Qalqilya were raided on September 27, and government warehouses on October 6. At the same time the Lehi made an unsuccessful attempt to assassinate High Commissioner MacMichael on August 8, shortly before he was to be replaced by Field Marshall Lord Gort. However, they succeeded in a major act of political terrorism on

November 5 in Cairo. Lehi members Eliahu Hakim and Eliahu Bet Zouri assassinated the British secretary of state for the Middle East, Lord Moyne.

In the fall of 1944, the British began to apply increasing pressure on the official institutions of the Yishuv to take action against the Irgun and Lehi. On October 11, a joint statement by John V. Shaw, chief secretary of the administration, and the commander in chief of British Middle East forces, insisted that the actions of the underground groups were impeding the war effort. The statement called on "the Jewish community as a whole to do their utmost to assist the forces of law and order in eradicating this evil from their midst. Verbal condemnation of the outrages from the platform and in the press may have an effect, but it is not enough, what is required is actual collaboration with the forces of law and order, especially in giving information leading to the apprehension of the assassins and their accomplices."[26]

Although the Jewish Agency and the Vaad Leumi sought means by which to appease British anger, it was clear that there was substantial disagreement with their approach in the Yishuv. There was a stream of moderate opinion in the country that rejected both the British statement and its implications. This was demonstrated in the rebuttal published by Peretz Bernstein, a leader of the General Zionists, in the Hebrew daily *Haboker* on October 16:

It would be wrong to denounce terrorist activities as crimes while the democratic world praises similar underground activities in Europe, and if in other places such acts are not only permissible but ordered as part of warfare; it follows that this is not so much an ethical but a political question. . . . But how did these young people come to harbour such ideas? They had a precedent. It must be said quite plainly: the Arabs did benefit by acts of terrorism (facilitated with financial help from Germany and Italy), while the Jews were penalised for helping to maintain law and order.[27]

Initially, the political department of the Jewish Agency rejected the idea of collaborating with the British to suppress the Irgun and Lehi for practical reasons. First, there was a concern that the Irgun might retaliate by betraying Haganah people to the police, and second, there was a fear of precipitating a civil war. However, the Jewish Agency soon recanted and decided to attempt to break up the underground organizations by direct action. To prevent the Irgun and Lehi from forming a united front against the Haganah, they decided to concentrate on the Irgun first. It has been suggested by one historian of the period that this decision was predicated on internal political considerations. One of the Lehi leaders, Friedman-Yellin, was in close communication with Eliahu Golomb, and there was hope that "the tendency they then sensed in the Sternists to employ socialistic slogans and terms would lead to a rapprochement of the Stern group with the Hagana."[28]

The decision to act against the Irgun was taken in October 1944, and a special body to carry out this mission was created by the Haganah general staff. Special training for the group began on October 20. The "Season," as the anti-Irgun operation was called, was to be carried out by volunteers from the Palmah and the Haganah's intelligence service, organized as the *Mishmar ha'Ummah* (Patrol of the Nation). The initial plan was to cripple the Irgun by capturing 300–400 of its men, including the top echelon of leaders, and imprisoning them in Haganah jails. They were then to be released slowly and kept under continual surveillance. This plan proved to be overly ambitious, and a smaller-scale operation was actually undertaken. The "Season" was generally successful in interrupting Irgun activity from October 1944 until early May 1945, when the Irgun was able to resume its activities. However, the "Season" took on a more ominous and disturbing character in the period immediately following the assassination of Lord Moyne at the beginning of November 1944.

Lord Moyne, who was colonial secretary at the time of the *Struma* and the *Patria* incidents, had a fairly clear record of strenuous opposition to Jewish immigration into Palestine throughout the war years. Churchill, for his own political reasons, nonetheless portrayed Moyne as a friend of the Jews. He then made the Jewish community as a whole collectively responsible for the assassination. On November 17, he stated in the House of Commons:

If our dreams for Zionism are to end in the smoke of assassins' pistols and our labours for its future are to produce a new set of gangsters worthy of Nazi Germany, many like myself will have to reconsider the position we have maintained so consistently and so long in the past. If there is to be any hope of a peaceful and successful future for Zionism these wicked activities must cease and those responsible for them must be destroyed, root and branch.

Then, acknowledging the public condemnation of the terrorists and the Jewish Agency Executive's commitment to their eradication, Churchill added, "These are strong words but we must wait for these words to be translated into deeds. We must wait to see that not only the leaders but every man, woman and child of the Jewish community does his or her best to bring this terrorism to a speedy end."[29]

Churchill was demanding nothing less than that the Yishuv as a whole should serve as collaborators with the regime against their own people. Nonetheless, his ploy worked. It was forgotten that Churchill himself had initiated the retreat from the Balfour Declaration with the White Paper of 1922, and that his alleged Zionism found effective expression only when he was in the opposition, but never when in office. It was after all Churchill's regime that turned away the *Struma* and the *Patria*, and was enforcing the restrictions on immigration at a time when the Jews of Europe were undergoing the holocaust. Nonetheless, the Jewish Agency Executive became very disturbed by the seemingly fundamental change in Churchill's attitude in the wake of the Moyne assassination. They appeared panic-stricken over the possibility of British retaliation. It was decided to collaborate actively with the British authorities in wiping out the Irgun.

There is no little irony in the fact that Ben-Gurion was cynical enough to use the occasion to press the struggle against the Irgun, which expressly dissociated itself from the assassination, rather than simply focus on the Lehi, which had actually carried out the act. However, Ben-Gurion would not forgo the opportunity to exploit the angry mood of the Zionist leadership to attack what he correctly saw as a potential political challenge to Mapai dominance of the Yishuv and the Zionist movement.

The very idea of active collaboration with the hated British Criminal Investigation Department (C.I.D.) stirred up a serious controversy within the Yishuv generally, and most particularly within the Palmah. The latter split on the issue along party lines. The Ahdut Avodah (the former "B" faction of the Mapai) and the Left Poalei Zion were adamantly opposed to collaboration with the British. The Ahdut Avodah considered Britain to be the primary enemy and had moral qualms about turning over Jews to them. The whole issue became a matter of public debate at the Sixth Histadrut Convention held on November 20, 1944. Ben-Gurion took the rather bizarre position that it was wrong to cooperate with alien police against fellow Jews in the Diaspora, but that in Palestine there was no reason why the Yishuv should not cooperate with the British in a common cause. He argued:

We have blundered in overdoing the healthy Jewish instinct not to appeal to alien governors for help. It is an instinct that our history in dispersion proved right. . . . But it is a strange paradox that those in rebellion against our civic responsibility . . . should be shielded because of Jewish reluctance to accept aid from the constituted forces of law and order . . . it would be foolish, suicidal, to withhold cooperation or reject aid where our interests are the same.[30]

The Histadrut ultimately approved Ben-Gurion's proposal, which contained four draconian antiseparatist provisions. The first of these, as Ben-Gurion stated it, was:

Whosoever traffics with the gangs or aids in any way, handing out their prints and billposting their placards, though he press no trigger and throw no bomb, must incontinently be dismissed from his place of work . . . and struck off the rolls of the labor exchange. And not otherwise at school or college. If any student be known to take part in murder or marauding, or only distributes the poisonous effusions of the terrorists among his fellows—tear the wretched leaflets from his grasp and burn them! Expel him, so that he may feel, and his parents and companions, how we abhor his traitorous felony.[31]

Members of the Irgun and Lehi were also to be denied shelter and protection. Threats that actions against them might lead to civil war were to be ignored (Ben-Gurion alleged that there already was a civil war going on, although he surely knew it was unlikely that the underground groups would take any significant steps against persecution by the Yishuv). Moreover, there was to be collaboration with the British insofar as they were prepared to take steps to crush the terrorists. Ahdut Avodah and Left Poalei Zion dissociated themselves from the last provision. A new special organization, the *Neemanei haMoledet* (Faithful of the Motherland), composed of Histadrut members committed to combating the terrorists, was established. In practice, however, the Neemanei haMoledet confined its activities mostly to putting up anti-Irgun posters.

In the Jewish Agency Executive, Rabbi Judah L. Maimon (Fishman) of the Mizrahi and Itzhak Gruenbaum of the General Zionists objected strenuously to collaboration with the British, and resigned in protest. Weizmann, however, who had just returned to Palestine after a five-year absence, fully endorsed complete cooperation with the British. He went so far as to provoke widespread disgust when he told the Smaller Actions Committee on November 19: "I suffered a severe personal tragedy in the war with the loss of my pilot son, but the shock with which I heard from the Colonial Office about the murder of Lord Moyne by Jewish terrorists was far more severe and numbing."[32] The rest of the factions in the Jewish Agency Executive toed the majority line.

The "Season" actually accomplished very little beyond causing a temporary cessation of Irgun activity. As a consequence of the collaboration with the British, about 100 members of the Irgun were arrested and interned. However, it did serve the purpose of convincing the British that the Jewish Agency was really trying to cooperate. On February 1, 1945, Colonial Secretary Oliver Stanley was able to comment favorably before the House of Commons regarding the improvement in cooperation in stamping out the terrorists in Palestine. This was the reprieve that the Jewish Agency Executive sought. On the other hand, the collaboration created deep resentments among many against what came to be seen as partisan irresponsibility on the part of Ben-Gurion and his colleagues. Jabotinsky had once warned that socialists had a tendency to use violence against those who disagreed with them, and this seemed to be borne out in the case at hand, as it would be again in the years to come. The chief rabbis Isaac Herzog and Ben-Zion Uziel roundly and publicly condemned the kidnapping of Irgun members by Haganah volunteers as a desecration of the name of the Jewish people. By January 1945, newspapers such as *Ha'aretz* and *Hatzofeh*, which usually supported official Zionist policy, were condemning the practice.

The Irgun, for its part, took no reprisal actions against the betrayers—not that there was not a strong sentiment among many to do just that. Begin observed:

It cannot be denied that there were among us many who pressed for the adoption of this policy. They adduced legal, moral and practical arguments. A fighting underground has its own laws, one of which is that the informer must pay with his life. Was it moral, argued the comrades, that we, who were prepared to give our lives for our people should be persecuted by our kinsmen and without any attempt to retaliate on our tormentors?[33]

Nonetheless, Begin's influence prevailed, and he would not take action that could trigger civil strife among Jews. "We decided to strike out along a road which no underground had ever chosen in similar circumstances. We decided not to suspend, nor to promise to suspend, our struggle against British rule; yet at the same time we declined to retaliate for the kidnappings, the denunciations and the handing-over of our men."[34]

On the whole, the Irgun emerged from the "Season" with an enhanced image of national responsibility, compared with the Haganah and its political leadership, even in the eyes of many who disagreed with the Irgun's program and purpose. It was the official Zionist leadership that appeared to many as vindictive and somewhat irresponsible. After all, they had betrayed fellow Jews for reasons that seemed rather unimpressive after the fact. They had also—unintentionally, to be sure—inspired and condoned the crass brutality and even torture that was perpetrated against some abducted members of the Irgun. In the final analysis, their relatively benign attitude toward the Mandatory regime proved unjustified. In fact, the posture taken by the Jewish Agency and the Haganah ensured that when the Irgun revolt later broke out again in full force, it would have the support of a large segment of the Yishuv, despite the denunciations by its official leadership.

NOTES

1. *Palestine: A Study of Jewish, Arab, and British Policies*, vol. 2, p. 1021.
2. *The New Judea*, March–April 1940, p. 77.
3. Michael J. Cohen, *Palestine: Retreat from the Mandate*, p. 100.
4. *Palestine: A Study of Jewish, Arab, and British Policies*, vol. 2, p. 1022.
5. Ibid., p. 1023.
6. Cohen, *Palestine*, p. 102.
7. *Palestine: A Study of Jewish, Arab, and British Policies*, vol. 2, p. 1024.
8. Christopher Sykes, *Crossroads to Israel*, p. 207.
9. *Palestine: A Study of Jewish, Arab, and British Policies*, vol. 2, p. 1025.
10. Ibid., p. 1034.
11. J. Borisov, *Palestine Underground*, pp. 19–20.
12. Yaacov Banai, *Hayalim Almonim*, p. 72.
13. Gerold Frank, *The Deed*, p. 107.
14. J. C. Hurewitz, *The Struggle for Palestine*, p. 140.
15. Arthur Koestler, *Promise and Fulfillment*, p. 60.
16. *Jewish Frontier*, September 1941, p. 23.
17. Chaim Weizmann, "Palestine's Role in the Solution of the Jewish Problem," *Foreign Affairs*, January 1942, p. 337.
18. *Palestine: A Study of Jewish, Arab, and British Policies*, p. 1030.
19. Hurewitz, *The Struggle for Palestine*, p. 141.
20. *Jewish Frontier*, May 1942, pp. 3–4.
21. Chaim Weizmann, *The Letters and Papers of Chaim Weizmann*, series A, vol. XX, p. 388.
22. Norman A. Rose, *Chaim Weizmann: A Biography*, pp. 378–379.
23. Ibid., p. 379.
24. Yehuda Bauer, *From Diplomacy to Resistance*, p. 407, n. 4.
25. Menachem Begin, *The Revolt*, pp. 42–43.
26. *The Times*, October 12, 1944.
27. Borisov, *Palestine Underground*, p. 35.
28. Bauer, *From Diplomacy to Resistance*, pp. 323–324.

29. Government of Palestine, *A Survey of Palestine*, p. 73.
30. David Ben-Gurion, *Rebirth and Destiny of Israel*, pp. 149–150.
31. Ibid., p. 146.
32. Borisov, *Palestine Underground*, p. 41.
33. Begin, *The Revolt*, p. 151.
34. Ibid., p. 152.

8

The United Resistance

As World War II drew to a close, it became increasingly evident that the United States would have a major, perhaps the most important, voice in the future of Palestine, and both the Arabs and Zionists turned their focus on Washington. As the March 31, 1944, deadline for the cessation of Jewish immigration, in accordance with the provisions of the 1939 White Paper, drew near, Zionist lobbying reached a feverish pitch. It soon led to the introduction of identical resolutions in both houses of Congress calling upon the U.S. government to take appropriate measures to bring about the rescinding of the White Paper by Britain and the ultimate establishment of Palestine as a Jewish state.

The draft resolutions generated vociferous protests from the Arab governments in the Middle East. Because of their vehement opposition, the War Department convinced the Congress to defer consideration of the resolutions because "further action on them at this time would be prejudicial to the successful prosecution of the war."[1] President Franklin D. Roosevelt softened the blow to the Zionists with his assurance that "when future decisions are reached full justice will be done to those who seek a Jewish national home, for which our Government and the American people have always had the deepest sympathy and today more than ever in view of the tragic plight of hundreds of thousands of homeless Jewish refugees."[2] Facing a presidential election that year, the Democratic and Republican parties included statements in their respective platforms that called for the reconstitution of Palestine as a Jewish commonwealth.

In October 1944, Secretary of War Henry Stimson withdrew his objections to the pro-Zionist resolutions that had been tabled by Congress earlier in the year, pointing out that the military considerations no longer outweighed the political. However, when the resolutions were reintroduced in December, action was deferred once again. This time it was because the State Department objected on the basis that "the passage of the resolutions at the present time would be unwise from the standpoint of the general international situation," whatever that meant other than that the Arabs were adamantly opposed to it.[3] It soon became clear that the Roosevelt administration was simultaneously giving contradictory assurances to both Jews and Arabs regarding the future position of the United States with respect to Palestine.

Similar developments were taking place in the British political arena. In April 1944, the Labour Party's executive issued a statement on international policy that, among other things, called for a removal of the ban on further Jewish immigration into Palestine, and went on to recommend that

the Arabs be encouraged to move out as the Jews move in. Let them be compensated handsomely for their land and let their settlement elsewhere be carefully organised and generously financed. The Arabs have many wide territories of their own: they must not claim to exclude the Jews from this small area of Palestine. . . . Indeed, we should re-examine also the possibility of extending the present Palestinian boundaries, by agreement with Egypt, Syria, or Transjordan.[4]

This statement was endorsed without change by the national party conference in December of that year. The Liberal Party, in formulating its political platform in February 1945, included a statement calling upon the government to abandon the White Paper and "carry out faithfully its obligations under the Mandate and the Balfour Declaration."[5]

The victory in Europe soon brought matters to a head by removing all previous constraints on the brewing crisis in Palestine. This was already evident at the Conference on International Organization that was held in San Francisco (April 25–June 26, 1945). The delegates from the Arab League states attempted to have the articles dealing with trusteeship in the proposed U.N. Charter worded in a manner that would have restricted Jewish rights in Palestine exclusively to the existing Jewish population. This would have eliminated the special status of the Jewish Agency under the Mandate, and have left the community without effective formal international representation. However, the proposal failed to gain acceptance. As the full scope of the disaster that had struck European Jewry became known, demands for abandonment of the White Paper grew both in tempo and in temper.

In May 1945, Weizmann wrote to Churchill, insisting that the Jews could no longer tolerate the continuance of the policies of the White Paper. He demanded that the British government take immediate action to establish Palestine as a Jewish state, and to turn over to the Jewish Agency the authority to regulate immigration and the development of the country's resources. Churchill responded in early June that the Palestine question could not be fully resolved until a peace conference took place. Shortly afterward, the Jewish Agency submitted a second memorandum pleading for 100,000 immigration certificates for European Jews as an immediate emergency measure. No action was taken on the request. At the end of July, Churchill was swept out of office by a Labour Party landslide victory in the first postwar British election. However, once in office, notwithstanding their reaffirmation of the Labour Party's pro-Zionist policy position as recently as May 1945, the new Labour government leaders quickly backtracked and adopted a heavily one-sided pro-Arab policy, although it took some months for this to become fully evident.

Prime Minister Clement Attlee resuscitated the cabinet committee on Palestine, which promptly accepted the strategic argument that Palestine had to remain under exclusive British control for the foreseeable future. The idea of partition as a possible solution to the Arab-Jewish problem was viewed as incompatible with Britain's broad political and military interests. A committee paper of July 2, 1945, declared: "It is indispensable to imperial security in the Middle East, as also for the discharge of our responsibilities in this region to the new world order, that Palestine should be administered by Britain as an undivided whole . . . the Middle Eastern Defence Committee is unanimous in the opinion that the partition of Palestine would, from the military standpoint, spell irremediable disaster."[6]

In August 1945, a world Zionist conference was called in London that was attended by more than 100 delegates and observers from 17 countries. With most of the branches of the Zionist movement either destroyed or driven underground in the areas under Russian occupation, the principal centers of the world movement were now Palestine and the United States. The delegates were split between supporters of Weizmann, who still promoted a gradualist line, and partisans of Ben-Gurion, who demanded an activist approach if the White Paper were not promptly rescinded by the British. For the moment, the balance of power in the movement remained with Weizmann, particularly in view of the recent accession to power of the ostensibly pro-Zionist Labour Party. The conference concluded with a note of despair: "The remnants of European Jewry cannot and will not continue their existence among the graveyards of the millions of their slaughtered brethren. . . . Their only salvation lies in their speediest settlement in Palestine."[7] The demands of the Jewish Agency previously communicated by Weizmann to Churchill were now reiterated to Attlee.

Within days, the Labour government revealed the direction it was to take with regard to Palestine. Overriding the opposition of its own party's national executive, the cabinet adopted the recommendations of the special cabinet committee on Palestine, headed by Foreign Secretary Ernest Bevin. That committee had concluded that Britain was unable to adopt an openly pro-Zionist stance. Bevin proposed that until matters could be further clarified, Jewish immigration could continue at a maximum rate of 1,500 per month for an indefinite period.

The Colonial Office informed Weizmann of the cabinet's decision on August 25. The proposal on immigration was promptly rejected as inadequate. At about the same time, the new American president, Harry Truman, urged Attlee to allow as many Jewish refugees as possible into Palestine. Attlee responded by suggesting that Britain would be willing to do so as long as the United States was prepared to assume joint responsibility there, including the use of American troops, if necessary, to maintain peace in the country. This, Truman was unwilling to do. Attlee finally proposed to Truman, as a compromise between the positions of their respective governments, that a joint investigation and assessment of the Palestine problem and related matters be undertaken. The proposal was accepted at the end of October 1945, although the Anglo-American Committee of Inquiry membership was not announced until December 10. A few days later, both houses of Congress belatedly passed pro-Zionist resolutions over the objections of Truman and Secretary of State James F. Byrnes.

While Attlee was deferring action on the Palestine question by initiating another commission of inquiry, this time drawing in the Americans, tensions in Palestine were mounting daily. Jewish anger at yet another British betrayal, this time by the Labour government, could be felt in the air. On September 27, an emergency meeting of Jewish leaders in Jerusalem issued a proclamation September 27 declaring that a continuation of the restriction on immigration after the end of the war was "tantamount to a death sentence upon . . . those liberated Jews . . . still languishing in the internment camps of Germany. . . . Jewish immigrants will stream to Palestine by all means. . . . The Hebrew Book of

Books will, by its eternal strength, destroy the White Paper. . . . The Jewish State will be established."[8] The estimated 150,000 attendees at a Zionist demonstration in New York heard the president of the American Zionist Organization declare: "We refuse to recognize as 'illegal' any Jewish immigrant who enters Palestine without a certificate. . . . Illegal is the hand and the Government that attempts to bar the Jew from the Jewish national home."[9]

The determination of the Yishuv to offer mass resistance to the White Paper soon became evident. In May, the Irgun and Lehi effectively began a full-scale guerrilla war against the British, attacking police stations, blowing up telephone and telegraph poles, and interrupting the Iraq Petroleum Company pipeline. A brief truce was called during August and the beginning of September as the Labour government took office. When it became clear that Attlee was going to uphold the White Paper, the war resumed with increased intensity. Frustrated by the continued passivity of the Haganah, a number of Palmah fighters joined the Irgun. Representatives from the Jewish Agency soon approached the Irgun with the proposal that it merge with the Haganah, notwithstanding the hysteria of the leftist press, which called for a renewal of the "Season." However, this simply was no longer possible, given the increasingly anti-British mood of the Yishuv.

A merger, from the standpoint of the Jewish Agency, would effectively bring the Irgun under Haganah control and eliminate a potentially powerful political rival in a single stroke. Menachem Begin was not averse to very close cooperation with the Jewish Agency, but he was seriously and justifiably concerned about the constancy and reliability of the official leadership, which had an established record of vacillation and radical shifts of policy. If the Irgun surrendered its identity in a merger, it might be too difficult to reconstitute if the now defiant and activist Jewish Agency was once again overcome by a wave of moderation, or simply lost its nerve.

Instead of a merger, the Irgun suggested the establishment, under a unified command, of a united resistance movement in which each organization would retain its separate identity. This would effectively give the Jewish Agency a veto, which would be exercised on its behalf by the Haganah representatives in the unified command, over any operations not to its liking. The proposal was deemed acceptable to the Haganah command, and the united Tenuat Hameri (Resistance Movement) came into being. However, the Jewish Agency and Histadrut politicians were reluctant to enter into such an agreement with the Irgun, which did not serve the political purpose they had in mind when they proposed the merger. Accordingly, they procrastinated in giving their approval. If they could not directly control the Irgun and Lehi, they preferred to see them destroyed.

In the meantime, the situation in the country became increasingly volatile with the Haganah also beginning to take direct action against the British. In September 1945, a Jewish village on the Lebanese frontier resisted attempts by police to enter it in search of illegal immigrants. On October 9, the Haganah began broadcasting from its clandestine station Voice of Israel, silent since 1940, and warned the British that they were deluding themselves if they thought there could be peace in Palestine if Jewish immigration remained restricted. The message that was being sent, not clearly articulated but nonetheless implicit, was that a few angry Jews could prove more dangerous than a larger number of less well-organized and -trained Arabs.

The following day, the Haganah set free 208 illegals who were being held in a detention camp at Athlit, near Haifa, awaiting deportation. The authorities fined two villages suspected of having participated in this action, but they refused to pay. On October 11, the Haganah broadcast a call for an active resistance movement to assist the immigration of Jews from Europe. A coastal patrol boat was sunk and two others damaged. British patrols did succeed in capturing 21 out of a shipload of some 200 refugees who were without visas. The Haganah retaliated by blowing up two coast guard stations. British searches of Jewish villages met stiff resistance, resulting in some 100 casualties, including nine dead Jews and a dozen wounded British security personnel.

Moshe Sneh, head of the national command of the Haganah, was particularly anxious to use the Tenuat Hameri for a major operation. He wanted to give the British a sample of what they might expect in heavier doses if they were not more forthcoming in meeting Zionist demands, especially with regard to lifting the restrictions on immigration. Even though the Mapai politicians had not yet agreed to endorse the alliance with the Irgun and Lehi, an interim agreement was worked out for Sneh's major operation, which was to take place on the night of October 31. The Haganah was to focus its efforts on disruption of the Palestine railway system, the Palmah was to attack coast guard installations, the Irgun was to attack the Lydda railway station, and the Lehi was to attack the Haifa oil refinery. If carried out successfully, the coordinated attacks would disabuse the British of any remaining doubts about the Yishuv's determination to achieve its national aspirations.

On the night of October 31 explosions rocked the country. The Haganah detonated some 500 explosive charges, producing 153 breaks in the railway lines and numerous instances of collateral damage to railway installations and facilities all over the country. The Palmah sank two small police vessels in Haifa and another in Jaffa. The Lehi assault on the Consolidated Refinery installation in Haifa was aborted as a result of a premature explosion of a suitcase filled with primed detonators. The Irgun attack on the Lydda station destroyed one locomotive and damaged six others.

Sneh's message to the British had been successfully delivered, but apparently was not fully understood. On November 5, Attlee insisted that there was no excuse for violence in Palestine and that nothing would be gained by it. The following day, more British airborne units moved into Haifa. On November 8, Lieutenant General Sir Alan Cunningham arrived to replace Lord Gort as high commissioner. It soon became abundantly clear that the British had made the basic policy decision to use force to implement Bevin's Palestine policy. The Haganah and the Irgun prepared themselves for the challenge. The Irgun replenished its munitions stocks by the straightforward method of directly approaching the British Imperial Chemical Industries in Haifa with a phony purchase order from the municipality of Hebron for nearly five tons of Chilean nitrate, which went directly to the Irgun's munitions factory. In addition, on November 23, two truckloads of arms were stolen from a Royal Air Force installation.

On November 25, the Haganah took action once again with a raid on the police station at Givat Olga and a simultaneous attack on the coastal patrol station at Sydna-Ali near Herzliya; both facilities were used for the detection and apprehension of illegal immigrants. In the attacks, six British and eight Arab policemen were wounded. The following day, the British mounted a massive 10,000-man cordon and search operation in the Sharon plain and in the Samarian foothills, in an attempt to root out arms caches and underground fighters. They met with unexpectedly violent resistance from the settlers. By the close of the day, eight Jews had been killed and seventy-five wounded. The British reported sixty-five soldiers and sixteen police injured. Only a handful of arms were found, and 337 Jews were arrested and detained. The effort was a gross failure that served primarily to aggravate relations between the Yishuv and the British. On November 28, Ben-Gurion declared to the British at an extraordinary session of the Elected Assembly: "We do not want to die, we believe we have the right to live as individuals and as a nation like you English and others, but there are some things dearer than life. We are prepared to be killed for the right to come here and build, for the right of independence in our own country."[10] The decision to sponsor large-scale illegal immigration was formally endorsed by the Jewish Agency Executive, the Smaller Actions Committee, and the Elected Assembly. Open defiance of Britain was now the national policy of the Yishuv and the Zionist movement.

While the Irgun concentrated on targets calculated to destabilize British rule in the country, the Haganah focused all its energies on the major task of bringing large numbers of illegals through the British naval blockade of Palestine. The blockade had been complemented by the virtually complete sealing by the Arab countries of all overland routes to Palestine. On December 25, the Haganah managed to bring all 252 illegals aboard the *Hannah Senesh* safely ashore near Nahariya, and then moved them to Haifa, where they melted into the population.

The Haganah command, however, was reluctant to agree to any actions not directly related to the support of illegal immigration, even if they were to be carried out by the Irgun or Lehi. Frustrated by this situation, the Irgun and Lehi decided to mount a series of attacks outside the framework of the Tenuat Hameri. On December 27, coordinated attacks were made on the Jerusalem and Jaffa C.I.D. headquarters that resulted in the death of ten British security men and the wounding of a dozen. Understandably, the British were furious, and promptly mounted a major cordon and search operation. Ben-Gurion and Sharett were brought to the high commissioner's office for a lecture and browbeating. A 4 P.M. to 8 A.M. curfew was imposed in Jerusalem. Some 1,500 males between 16 and 50 were interrogated, and 559 were detained, but not a single member of the underground was discovered. Even the ritual condemnation of the Irgun by the leftist press was muted this time. There was very little sympathy in the country for the hated C.I.D.

By the beginning of 1946, Palestine had become an armed camp, and imposed a heavy financial burden on the British treasury. The entire 20,000-man Sixth Airborne Division was now on station there, raising British troop strength to 80,000 in addition to thousands of police, units of Transjordan's Arab Legion, and other elements assigned to security duty. In addition to coast guard and naval radar and communications bases ashore, there were two cruisers, three destroyers, and numerous smaller ships operating off the Palestinian coast. The ratio of British security forces to the Jewish population reached the exceptional figure of approximately one to five. There were armed guards everywhere, and for their own safety the British turned their headquarters and facilities into fortified and sandbagged compounds. Sentry blocks and rings of concertina and barbed wire surrounded government buildings. The Tenuat Hameri, and most especially the Irgun, had forced the British to transform the Mandatory regime into a garrison state under a self-imposed siege. For Begin and his colleagues it was a question of who would crack first, the British regime or the Yishuv. As they saw it, if the Yishuv could hold out, the ultimate prize would be a Jewish state in all of Palestine.

In January 1946, British naval units intercepted a ship loaded with over 900 illegal immigrants. The British were now forced to face the dilemma they had long feared. They were concerned that if they should attempt to deport the 900, the Haganah might be pushed into abandoning its current restraint and take up a full guerrilla war, possibly joining forces with the Irgun and Lehi. The Haganah had already signaled what might be expected by blowing up another coastal patrol facility and by attempting to damage the radar stations at Haifa. On the other hand, if they permitted the immigrants to remain, they would seriously damage their credibility with the Arabs. The British decided to risk Arab displeasure and announced that it had been decided "for cogent reasons that they must allow immigration to continue provisionally at the proposed rate of 1,500 a month."[11] The British tried to compensate the Arabs by rescinding the exclusion order against Jamal al-Husseini that had been in effect for some five years. But it was generally perceived that they had given in to the threat of a general Jewish rebellion.

The Jewish Agency promptly rejected the 1,500 per month formula once again and demanded that the gates to Palestine be opened unconditionally. Throughout January, attacks by both the Irgun and Haganah, each against the targets deemed appropriate to their separate missions, continued at an accelerated pace. The Tenuat Hameri campaign had not yet become a major threat to British rule in Palestine, but it had definitely passed the mere nuisance stage.

At the end of February 1946, the Haganah, Palmah, Irgun, and Lehi carried out a series of jointly planned assaults on British installations used to impede illegal immigration. On February 20, the Haganah attacked radar installations in Haifa, wounding eight RAF personnel in the process. The following day, the Palmah attacked police stations at Shefa Amir, Sarona, and Kfar Vitkin. On the evening of February 25, the Irgun and Lehi simultaneously raided three military airfields at Lydda, Kfar Syrkin, and Qastina. The British estimates of the damage done, which were somewhat lower than the Irgun estimates, were a total of fifteen aircraft destroyed and eight damaged. The extent of popular approval of the assaults was demonstrated by the participation of some 50,000 people, including the chairman of the Vaad Leumi Executive, in the funeral procession in Tel Aviv for the four Palmah members killed in the raid on Sarona.

Tensions reached a new height on April 25, 1946, when, in the process of an arms raid in Tel Aviv, seven British paratroopers were killed and three wounded by the Lehi. In retaliation, a group of British soldiers went berserk in Natanyah and the village of Beer Tuviah, where they smashed windows, burst into houses, destroying furniture, and assaulted innocent people. The Arabs were quick to point out that during the Arab rebellion of 1936–1939, many Arabs were sentenced to death, numerous houses were blown up, and collective fines and other measures were imposed. However, they complained, none of these measures had been applied to the Jews, notwithstanding the current extent of their rebellion.

In the meanwhile, the Anglo-American Committee of Inquiry arrived in Jerusalem on March 6, 1946, after full committee meetings and hearings in Washington, London, and Cairo. Initially, the Jewish Agency Executive was sharply divided over whether to present testimony before the committee. Abba Hillel Silver and Moshe Sneh were adamantly opposed to the idea. Nahum Goldmann and Moshe Sharett, on the other hand, argued that since the United States was actively participating in the inquiry, all current diplomatic efforts had to focus on the committee. It would not be wise, in their view, to slight the committee by refusing to appear before it. Although Ben-Gurion leaned toward a boycott, primarily because he was concerned that the committee might lend its support to the early abandonment of the Mandate by Britain, something for which the Yishuv was not adequately prepared, he was indecisive. However, the boycott approach had already been defeated within Mapai by a 16–2 vote, and shortly thereafter by a 16–11 vote in the Smaller Actions Committee.

The testimony at the committee hearings was predictable. The Arabs would not budge an inch from their demands, while the Zionists hinted at an acceptable partition scheme as the solution to the impasse. The committee, which was not overly impressed by the Zionist presentations, left Palestine at the end of March for Lausanne, where it prepared its final report. As a last resort, in order to overcome the sharp differences in view between and among the British and American delegations, the committee unanimously concluded that the overwhelming majority of the displaced surviving Jews of Europe wished to go to Palestine. It also noted that no substantial assistance could be expected from any quarter in settling these Jews anywhere outside of Palestine. The report therefore recommended that 100,000 Jews be allowed into

Palestine as soon as possible. Subsequent levels of Jewish immigration would have to be worked out between the Jews and Arabs. However, the report also concluded that because of its special religious character which made it holy to Christianity, Islam, and Judaism, Palestine should not be the exclusive territory of any single race or religion. The committee therefore strongly endorsed the concept of a binational state based on parity between Jews and Arabs.

Since it was clear that neither the Arabs nor the Jews were prepared to accept such a solution, it was recommended that the Mandate be converted into a U.N. trusteeship for the purpose of preparing both communities for a binational future. It was evident that the committee, notwithstanding its conscientious effort to arrive at an equitable solution to the Palestine dilemma, was hampered from the outset by the necessity to make its findings coincide with the public positions already staked out by the American president and the British prime minister. Truman had called for the admission of 100,000 Jews into Palestine, and this arbitrary number, originally proposed by Weizmann to Churchill as an interim emergency measure, took on a subsequent political significance that had little to do with the level of actual need. Similarly, the British members of the committee were well aware that the Attlee government was committed to the conversion of the Mandate to a trusteeship. The latter was necessary in order to preserve the British position in the Middle East. To enhance its influence with the Arab states, Britain was soon to begin withdrawal of its forces from Egypt and Iraq, and was about to terminate its Mandate over Transjordan. Palestine thus became increasingly important as a strategic base in the region. Haifa could serve as a substitute for the naval base at Alexandria, and British control of the Negev would assure ready access to the Suez Canal in the event of emergency. Given these conflicting goals, the Anglo-American Committee of Inquiry produced a report that satisfied no one.

The British clearly had no intention of making an early withdrawal from Palestine. This was quite evident from the fact that they had just erected large permanent military bases near Gaza, and had decided to construct a new oil pipeline, 60 percent larger than the one already operating between the Iraqi oil fields and Haifa. Accordingly, they showed little real interest in finding a solution to the Palestine problem that would result in sufficient stability to allow them to withdraw from the country. It would serve British interests far better to preserve the status quo, providing violence in the country could be kept to an acceptable level. As a consequence, the binational solution proposed by the committee, which was designed to accommodate the political imperatives of both governments, had little to do with the realities in Palestine. Binationalism was never acceptable to the Arabs, and no longer commanded the interest of the majority of the Jewish leadership, who had become proponents of statism since the adoption of the Biltmore Program in 1944.

At about the same time, Haj Amin al-Husseini, the grand mufti of Jerusalem, reappeared on the Arab scene. Captured by the French at the end of the war, he was placed under limited police surveillance in Paris. Despite the pressure on the British to have him tried as a war criminal for his collaboration with the Nazis, the Labour government declined to prefer any charges against him or even to request his extradition. In the spring of 1946, the mufti escaped from France and appeared in Cairo at the end of May. The divided leadership structure of the Palestinian Arabs was soon dissolved by order of the Arab League Council, to be replaced by a new Arab Higher Executive under the chairmanship of the mufti. Since he was not permitted to enter Palestine, the Arab Executive was represented in dealings with the British government by Jamal al-Husseini, who was recognized as acting chairman of the body for that purpose. However, the Arab Executive, which shortly was renamed the Arab Higher Committee, was run by the mufti from Cairo with British complicity.

In June 1946, Bevin defended his Palestine policy before the Labour Party conference in anti-Semitic terms that infuriated the Zionists, further limiting the influence of the moderates among them. He flatly refused to carry out the recommendation of the Anglo-American Committee of Inquiry with regard to the admission of 100,000 Jews to Palestine. He suggested that the Americans had come up with this idea because they "did not want too many of them in New York." He stated that he opposed a Jewish state because, as he put it, he did "not believe in the absolutely exclusively racial states."[12] He made no reference to the strategic motives of British policy, which were by now obvious to the Zionist leadership in Palestine. The latter became more determined than ever to block realization of the British scheme.

As an indication of the Yishuv's resolve and ability to interfere with British plans, a series of attacks was mounted on the country's transportation system. On June 10, the Irgun attacked three trains in the vicinity of Lydda, burning ten coaches, blowing up one engine, and derailing a second engine. Four days later, the Palmah destroyed or damaged four rail and vehicular bridges on Palestine's frontiers, disrupting traffic with the neighboring states. Then, on June 16–17, a joint Irgun-Lehi operation destroyed eleven road and railway bridges. However, a more serious drama began on June 13 when two Irgunists, Joseph Shimshon and Itzhak Ashbel, captured during a raid on the Army base at Sarafend on March 6, were sentenced to death. On June 18, the Irgun raided the British Officers' Club in Tel Aviv in broad daylight and kidnapped five British officers. Another British officer was similarly taken in Jerusalem the following day. The officers were held as hostages against implementation of the death sentence on the condemned Irgunists.

The audacity of the Irgun's act threw the whole country into an uproar. Official Jewish leadership circles went into panic for fear of what the British might do in retaliation. The Jewish Agency Executive and the Vaad Leumi promptly issued a statement condemning the kidnappers for having committed an insane act. Ben-Gurion, in London at the time to see the colonial secretary, voiced his distress and horror. Notwithstanding the pleas of the Jewish Agency to release the hostages, the Irgun refused to free the officers (one managed to escape). A few days later, the Irgun released two of the captives along with a message to be conveyed to the government. The message was unequivocal: if the Irgunists were executed, the remaining three officers would be executed as well. The Jewish Agency and Haganah quickly announced that the release of the two officers was due to their successful intervention, a statement the Irgun denied. The officers were released to serve as reliable messengers who could attest to the fact that the Irgun was serious about its threat to execute the hostages.

In response to the serious deterioration in the situation, the British cabinet finally authorized a major crackdown. The problem was that the Palestine administration didn't know where and upon whom to crackdown. They decided to put the pressure on the Jewish Agency and other prominent leaders. The Yishuv was placed under virtual military siege on June 29. For almost two weeks, British troops and police carried out intensive searches in Tel Aviv, the Jewish sections of Haifa and Jerusalem, and twenty-seven collective settlements. The kidnapped officers could not be found, and the searches produced little else. Only one sizable Haganah arms cache was discovered in a settlement near Haifa. Jewish Agency offices in Jerusalem and Tel Aviv were occupied by troops, and the Jewish Agency's files were confiscated. Communications with the outside world were severed and rigid censorship was imposed on the press. Approximately 2,700 people were arrested, including four members of the Agency Executive: Rabbi J. L. Maimon (acting chairman in Ben-Gurion's absence), Itzhak Gruenbaum,

Sharett, and Bernard (Dov) Joseph. Four Jews were killed and eighty injured. However, the attempt to intimidate the Yishuv and its leadership failed to achieve its purpose. The Irgun would not release the hostages.

The arbitrariness of the British actions caused unintended strains in relations with the United States. In a meeting with Zionist leaders, President Truman indicated that he had no prior knowledge of the British military operation and that he hoped the members of the Jewish Agency who had been arrested would soon be released. To make matters worse for the British, a proposed loan to Britain had been approved by the Senate in May and was coming up for debate in the House of Representatives. American Zionist leaders now threatened to organize mass Jewish appeals to Congress to prevent the loan from going through. On July 3, the death sentences for Shimshon and Ashbel were commuted to life imprisonment by the high commissioner. The Irgun had frontally challenged the British Empire and had prevailed. The following day, the three British officers were released.

One clearly unintended consequence of the mass arrests was to weaken the generally pro-British position of the moderate official Jewish leadership. Even Chaim Weizmann, the most pro-British of the Zionist leaders, felt compelled to comment with apparent bitterness about the fact that "the Mufti of Jerusalem, a 'war criminal and sworn enemy of Britain,' sat in a palace at Cairo, while Moshe Shertok [Sharett], who raised an army of 25,000 Jewish Palestinians to fight shoulder to shoulder with Britain in World War II, was imprisoned in Latrun detention camp."[13] Nonetheless, Weizmann remained determined to bring an end to armed opposition to the British. He dispatched his faithful American agent, Meyer Weisgal, to Palestine with an urgent message for Moshe Sneh, demanding that all underground military operations cease.

If you continue your operations this will be the equivalent of a declaration of war on Great Britain. I am certain Britain will fight back and everything we have worked for may be destroyed. I am still the president of the Zionist Movement and in democracies it is generally accepted that the President is the Commander of all the armed forces. . . . I am now using this authority. I demand that you stop all operations by all three underground groups.

Weizmann put it to him as an ultimatum, threatening to resign if Sneh did not comply with his demand, and warning, "My resignation will harm the movement. It will split the leadership and our people. I would like to avoid it but I am certain that military operations would be even more damaging."[14]

Sneh fundamentally disagreed with Weizmann. He believed it essential to continue the armed struggle in order to convince the British that if they elected to pursue a political solution in Palestine that was not favorable to the Jews, they would have to face the prospect of a major armed uprising. He was also confident that Weizmann overstated his own influence and that his resignation would not traumatize the Yishuv, the majority of whom would support the Haganah. On the other hand, the moderate politicians did support Weizmann, and his rejection of the ultimatum would cause a split between the political and the military leadership. Sneh's response to Weisgal was: "I can't answer yes or no immediately. The Jewish Agency has given me general authority to conduct a military struggle. I am facing a conflict between my responsibilities to Dr. Weizmann and to national bodies that have authorized certain military actions. Others have collaborated with us. I cannot act alone. I must have time to think and consult. You'll have my answer as soon as possible."[15]

Sneh referred the matter to the five-person policy committee (Committee "X") that oversaw Haganah operations. The committee voted three to two to respect Weizmann's ultimatum and to cancel further operations. Sneh, who cast one of the dissenting votes, resigned his position on July 16 and prepared to go to Paris, where he hoped to convince Ben-Gurion to overrule Weizmann. He did not tell Begin or the Lehi leaders about what had happened, hoping that if he was successful in Paris, the Tenuat Hameri could continue its scheduled operations. He merely asked them to delay a major operation they had planned for a few more days, without really explaining why.

As far as Ben-Gurion was concerned, until the recent affair of the hostage officers, he saw some benefit from the campaign mounted by the Tenuat Hameri; it applied pressure on the British administration, attracted international attention, and kept the restless members of Palmah from defecting to the Irgun. However, he now considered it to have become a liability. Since the British could not get to the military leadership of the underground, they were lashing out at the political leadership, which was becoming progressively weakened. He thought it might be best to stop the military campaign, dissolve the Tenuat Hameri, and satisfy the demands for action by the Haganah and Palmah by an enhanced focus on illegal immigration. This would leave the Jewish Agency free to carry on the political struggle as it saw fit, without having to bear the onus of responsibility for the actions of the Irgun and

Lehi. What Ben-Gurion did not know at the time was that on July 1 the joint command of the Tenuat Hameri had authorized an Irgun operation against the British secretariat, the hub of the Palestine administration, which was housed in Jerusalem's well-protected King David Hotel.

Begin delayed the King David Hotel operation in accordance with Sneh's request, transmitted to him by Israel Galili on July 17. However, once the explosives had arrived in Jerusalem and still no word came from the Haganah, he became fearful after several days that word of the planned action would leak out. He decided that he could not safely postpone the operation any longer.

The Irgun mounted the highly complex operation on July 22. Having created a number of diversions to limit traffic in the area of the hotel, it managed to place seven milk cans loaded with explosives around the central pillars supporting the southwest section of the building, the area occupied by the British secretariat. A message was then received by the telephone operator, warning that a bomb would go off in thirty minutes and urging that the building be evacuated. The message was given to the hotel management and then relayed to the superintendent of police. No action was taken to evacuate the building. A few minutes later the explosives were detonated, and the southwest section of the hotel was turned into a mass of rubble. The total number of casualties was ninety-one killed and forty-six injured. The dead included twenty-one first-rank government officials.

Tel Aviv was sealed off for three days while an extensive hunt went on for Irgun and Lehi leaders. Some 120,000 people were interrogated and 787 arrested, but there were no underground leaders among them. General Evelyn Barker rejected the protestations of innocence from the official Jewish leadership, stating in a letter to his officers: "Without the support, actual or passive, of the general Jewish public the terrorist gangs who actually carried out these criminal acts would soon be unearthed, and in this measure the Jews in this country are accomplices and bear a share of the guilt. . . . I repeat that if the Jewish public really wanted to stop these crimes, they could do so by acting in co-operation with us."

There was in fact substantial truth to Barker's charge. Notwithstanding the official Zionist position that argued to the contrary, there was wide-ranging support for the Irgun among the Yishuv. In fact, if this were not the case, the underground could not have existed. This support, of course, did not come from the Labor movement but rather from the broad center and right of the political spectrum, including many in the religious and Sephardi sections of the community. It was this same support that made the Haganah's "Season" a failure. The reality was that the official Zionist leadership in Palestine did not hold office on the basis of their views on how best to carry out the struggle for the Jewish homeland. The leadership represented political parties that, with the general exception of the Revisionists, were primarily based on other considerations, such as different varieties of socialism, religious belief and practice, and economic and social interests. Indeed, it is not unusual in democratic societies, because of the factors that go into making different political parties, for a government to be widely opposed by the electorate on a specific issue. This was clearly the case in the Yishuv.

Barker, however, wanted to impose collective punishment on the Jewish community. He therefore declared "all Jewish establishments, restaurants, shops, and private dwellings" to be out of bounds for all British military personnel. The purpose of this restriction was to punish "the Jews in a way the race dislikes as much as any, by striking at their pockets and showing our contempt for them."[16] This plainly anti-Semitic statement should have brought Barker's removal from his command, but it did not. It in fact reflected how many in the British military had viewed the Jews since the time of the military administration of 1918–1920. However, in the case at hand, the shock of Barker's letter served to detract from the Yishuv's concern over the King David Hotel disaster.

In London, the official government reaction to the attack was one of understandable outrage. Attlee condemned the operation as a brutal and murderous crime, and noted sanctimoniously that "The British Government have stated and stated again they will not be diverted by acts of violence in their search for a just and final solution to the Palestine problem."[17] The British insisted that no warning had been given, and that the heavy loss of life was intended as a deliberate act of terror. The Irgun insisted that the truth was quite the opposite; that it was sheer British arrogance in refusing to evacuate the hotel that caused the extensive death toll. Given the choice of absolving itself by blaming either the British or the Irgun for the disaster, most of the Yishuv establishment, politicians and press alike, preferred to blame the Irgun. In Paris, Ben-Gurion announced to a reporter for *France Soir*, "[T]he Irgun is the enemy of the Jewish people."[18]

Ben-Gurion's self-serving disclaimer made little impression on the British. On July 24, the British government published a new White Paper spelling out Haganah's role within the Tenuat Hameri and the ultimate responsibility of the Jewish Agency for the Irgun operation. Now everyone in the official leadership ran for cover. Ben-Gurion wanted the Tenuat Hameri dissolved, retroactively if possible. The Haganah wanted knowledge of its approval of the operation to be quietly suppressed. Israel Galili contacted Begin and requested that the Irgun take sole responsibility for the fiasco.

Sneh left for Paris on July 23 to try to convince Ben-Gurion to allow the Tenuat Hameri to continue to function. His appeal was rejected. Ben-Gurion was determined to end cooperation with the Irgun. The Tenuat Hameri was formally dissolved on August 23, with the withdrawal of the Haganah from the joint command. While Begin and the Irgun high command were disappointed, they were hardly surprised, since they had never had much faith in the Jewish Agency's ability to persevere under heavy pressure. Begin also understood that Ben-Gurion had now positioned himself to benefit politically from the pressure that would continue to be placed on the British administration as a result of the Irgun's actions, which he surely knew would continue with or without Haganah's cooperation. Since the Irgun had no political backers who were in a position to negotiate with the British, whatever new concessions might be wrung from the British as a consequence of the Irgun's revolt would be claimed by Ben-Gurion and the Jewish Agency Executive. There was little that Begin could do about it; he certainly wasn't going to relent in the struggle in order to undercut Ben-Gurion.

The growth of public support in the Yishuv for the fighting underground was aided considerably by the gross political incompetence of the British government in its handling of the immigration problem. Until June 1946, the numbers of illegal immigrants apprehended fell within the 1,500 per month immigration quota announced by the government. Thus, after a brief period of detention, the illegals were released. A new crisis arose in July when three ships carrying more than 4,000 illegals were intercepted by the British Navy, and even larger numbers were anticipated in succeeding months. In early August, the government decided to tighten the blockade of Palestine. European governments were requested to block the transit of Jews without proper travel documents. Italy and France responded favorably to the request, while the Soviet Union and the East European countries refused to comply. The military commander of the British zone in Germany sealed the frontier against Jews in transit and the U.S. commander, General McNarney, followed suit in the American zone.

On August 11, two ships with some 1,300 refugees arrived in the waters off Palestine. That same day the British announced that henceforth all illegal immigrants, including those who had arrived in July, would be deported to Cyprus or elsewhere. The announcement coincided with the meeting in Alexandria of the Arab foreign ministers, who indicated that the British action was clearly a step in the right direction. On the day of the first deportations, some 1,000 unarmed Jews tried to force their way into the port area in Haifa. The ensuing struggle with the British troops resulted in the deaths of three demonstrators and the hospitalization of seven. The following week, bombs damaged the two ships that were being used to ferry the deportees to Cyprus. Whatever residual feeling against open conflict with the British there may have been in the Yishuv, particularly in the aftermath of the King David Hotel incident, quickly dissipated in face of the demonstrated British insensitivity to the plight of the survivors of the holocaust.

In the wake of the failure of the Anglo-American Committee of Inquiry to come up with a realistic plan, it was decided to try a bilateral approach once again. An American cabinet committee met in London with its British counterpart in July and produced another unacceptable report, the Morrison-Grady plan. This scheme proposed converting the Mandate into a trusteeship and dividing the country into an Arab province, a Jewish province, and two separate districts of Jerusalem and the Negev. Ostensibly, the plan could ultimately lead to either a binational or a partitioned state. The central government, under a British high commissioner, would directly govern the Jerusalem and Negev districts and would have exclusive authority over virtually everything else of any significance other than religious and intercommunal affairs. It was clearly a British plan, one that the American negotiators were apparently unable to influence very much. That the plan represented a blatant move to retain Palestine under British control for the foreseeable future was fairly obvious. It led Churchill to comment: "His Majesty's Government by their precipitate abandonment of their treaty rights in Egypt, and, in particular, the Suez Canal zone, are now forced to look for . . . a jumping-off ground in Palestine in order to protect the Canal from outside Egypt. By this unwisdom . . . we can now be accused of having a national strategic motive for retaining our hold on Palestine."[19]

The Jewish Agency Executive, meeting at Paris in August (it would have been arrested in Palestine), rejected the Morrison-Grady plan as completely unacceptable because it would have denied the Jews any rights in 85 percent of the country. However, the continuing British pressure and the growing loss of official American interest in the Zionist position had already taken their toll on the determination of the Jewish Agency leadership. Nahum Goldmann, who now emerged in the front rank of the Zionist leadership, administered the final blow to the Jewish Agency's resolve. Goldmann told his colleagues that he had just received a telephone call from David Niles, President Truman's assistant for Zionist affairs. Niles had cautioned that unless the Zionists could come up with a reasonable alternative to the Morrison-Grady plan, the president would wash his hands of the whole business. Goldmann warned the Executive: "Unless we are ready to tell the President that we are ready to accept the Jewish State in an adequate part of Palestine, it is no use going to Washington and trying to obtain these improvements. I felt for years that partition of Palestine is the only way out. Biltmore is no realistic policy at the moment, because we have no Jewish majority and we cannot wait until we have a majority to get the State."[20]

The Jewish Agency Executive, violating one of the cardinal rules of successful negotiation, now abandoned its demand for a Jewish state in all of Palestine and adopted a secret resolution in favor of an independent Jewish state in a partitioned Palestine, without having achieved any prior concessions from the British. In other words, it had negotiated against itself and offered a major concession for which it received nothing in return. Some Zionist leaders, including Abba Hillel Silver and Moshe Sneh, regarded this as a colossal blunder. They were concerned, with good reason, that the "moderates" in the Jewish Agency Executive, such as Goldmann, Eliezer Kaplan, and Sharett, would be willing to compromise still further and perhaps even agree to the cantonization of Palestine. Ben-Gurion, the principal force behind the Biltmore Program, now abandoned it without a struggle and without protest.

The details of the Jewish Agency Executive's new proposal were submitted to the American and British governments a few days later. The scheme proposed that the Jews receive the Galilee, the coastal plain, and the Negev. The Arabs would get the hill districts of eastern central Palestine, Jaffa, and a corridor connecting the two. The British then invited the Jewish Agency Executive on August 15 to participate in a conference on Palestine, to be held at London in September. The Palestinian Arabs refused to participate, and after some inconclusive wrangling over the terms of the agenda and the composition of the Jewish delegation, the Jewish Agency refused to attend as well. The London conference therefore opened on September 10, 1946, with only the British government and the Arab states in attendance.

While the conference was in session, the pace of the underground war against the British in Palestine continued to increase, and the toll of British as well as Jewish killed and wounded continued to mount.

However, not all of these casualties were the result of Irgun or Lehi actions. The Haganah was also responsible for a sizable share. On November 26, Haganah resistance to the deportation of 3,900 illegal immigrants resulted in two Jews killed and forty-five hospitalized, in addition to thirty British casualties. It seemed clear that, notwithstanding the presence of 80,000 troops, the British could not pacify the country. Negotiations were renewed with the Jewish Agency Executive, which now agreed in principle to attend the second stage of the London conference, but only after its decision would be confirmed by the Twenty-second Zionist Congress that was to convene in Basel on December 9.

The course and consequences of the world war had brought dramatic changes in the size and shape of the Zionist movement. The United States, with almost half of the organization's world membership, had replaced Poland as the primary Zionist center. The wartime conversion of the Zionist leadership to statism helped bring the Revisionists back into the fold in the spring of 1946. The continuing crisis in Palestine had caused the merger of many splinter groups into more coherent parties. The long bifurcated "A" and "B" factions of the General Zionists were now reconstituted into a single General Zionist Party; the Hashomer Hatzair absorbed its urban affiliate, the Socialist League; and the Ahdut Avodah merged with the Left Poalei Zion into a single party bearing the name of the former. These changes were reflected in the Yishuv by the affiliations of delegates elected to the Zionist Congress in October.

The three Labor parties continued to constitute a majority, together receiving more than 60 percent of the votes. However, they were ideologically divided more than ever before and had great difficulty in working together coherently. Consequently, though Mapai continued to be the strongest individual party, it was able to capture only twenty-eight of the seventy-nine delegates from the Yishuv. The Revisionists, with eleven delegates, formed the second largest party, followed by the other two Labor parties in third place, with ten delegates each. The General Zionists, who won only four delegates from Palestine, nonetheless dominated the Zionist Congress because of the party's strength in the United States, which gave it 123 of the total of 385 delegates. The Union of Zionist Labor (Mapai) took second place with a total of 101 delegates, losing the predominant position it held for more than thirteen years. Mizrahi took third place with fifty-eight delegates, and the Revisionists now ranked fourth with forty-one delegates. The two other Labor parties tied for fifth place with twenty-six delegates each.

The issue of partition split virtually all the parties. Only Hashomer Hatzair, which continued to advocate a binational state, and the Revisionists, who continued to demand a Jewish state on both sides of the Jordan, maintained their internal unity while totally rejecting the idea of partition. The "moderates," led by Weizmann, Sharett, and Wise, supported Jewish Agency participation in the London conference and endorsed the partition proposal developed by the Jewish Agency Executive in August. The "activists," led by Ben-Gurion and Abba Hillel Silver, agreed with the moderates in principle but argued that for tactical reasons the partition proposal should come from the British rather than the Zionists. Accordingly, they were opposed to participation in the London conference unless there was a significant change in the situation. The activists carried the day by a close vote of 171 to 154, and the second phase of the London conference opened on January 27, 1947, without Jewish participation. However, it was unable to come up with a scheme that would satisfy the Arab, Jewish, and British interests. With the government under continuing international pressure to resolve the problem, the conference was terminated abruptly with the announcement on February 14 that "His Majesty's Government had decided to refer the whole problem to the United Nations."[21]

While the Zionist Congress was debating the question of partition, events in Palestine were taking a dramatic turn that seriously undermined the British position in the country. Two members of the Irgun, who were apprehended on September 13 for carrying arms in violation of the emergency security regulations, were sentenced to fifteen years' imprisonment and eighteen lashes with a whip. Begin was furious. He wrote later: "What was the purpose of this bestial punishment? Did the regime want to demonstrate that it regarded us as natives; that it would teach these impudent Jews in the orthodox fashion how to behave towards their benevolent masters?"[22] The Irgun immediately put up wall posters warning the British that such punishment of its soldiers was unacceptable. If the flogging were to be carried out, every British officer in the country would be liable to similar treatment. To humiliate the Irgun, on December 27 the flogging of seventeen-year-old Benjamin Kimhi was carried out. The following day, a British major was seized from the lobby of the Metropole Hotel in Natanyah. He was taken to a spot outside the town and given eighteen lashes. Before the hundreds of troops and police that descended on the hotel could begin to look for him, he was returned. In Rishon le-Zion, a British sergeant was taken at gunpoint from a cafe and given eighteen lashes at a spot nearby. In Tel Aviv, two sergeants were removed by force from the Armon Hotel to a spot near the Tel Aviv zoo where each received eighteen lashes and was then released. The next morning, another Irgun warning was posted: "If the oppressors dare in the future to abuse the bodies and the human and national honour of Jewish youths, we shall no longer reply with the whip. *We shall reply with fire.*"[23]

The British attempt to humiliate the Jews had backfired. They were humiliated instead. The other Irgun prisoner was not whipped but granted amnesty instead, along with sixteen Arabs. Churchill, concerned about British prestige, accused the government of not knowing how to "behave like men. You whip a Jewish terrorist and the terrorists catch a British major and three non-commissioned officers and whip them the next day. You then cancel the whipping of another terrorist. Do you know what this means?"[24]

NOTES

1. *New York Times*, March 18, 1944.
2. Ibid., March 10, 1944.
3. Ibid., December 12, 1944.
4. *Manchester Guardian*, April 24, 1944.
5. *New York Herald-Tribune*, February 4, 1945.
6. Michael J. Cohen, *Palestine: Retreat from the Mandate*, p. 160.
7. J. C. Hurewitz, *The Struggle for Palestine*, p. 228.
8. *Palestine Post*, September 28, 1945.
9. Hurewitz, *The Struggle for Palestine*, p. 232.
10. *Palestine Post*, November 29, 1945.
11. *New York Times*, January 26, 1946.
12. Ibid., June 13, 1946.
13. Hurewitz, *The Struggle for Palestine*, p. 256.
14. Thurston Clarke, *By Blood and Fire*, p. 108.
15. Ibid., p. 109.
16. Harry Sacher, *Israel: The Establishment of a State*, pp. 62–63.
17. *Palestine Post*, July 24, 1946.
18. J. Bowyer Bell, *Terror Out of Zion*, p. 173.
19. Hurewitz, *The Struggle for Palestine*, p. 258.
20. Michael J. Cohen, "The Zionist Perspective," in William Roger Louis and Robert W. Stookey, eds., *The End of the Palestine Mandate*, p. 86.
21. *New York Times*, February 15, 1947.
22. Menachem Begin, *The Revolt*, p. 231.
23. Ibid., p. 234.
24. Ibid., p. 235.

9

The United Nations
Special Committee

The year 1947 began most inauspiciously, with the British taking stringent steps to improve their position in Palestine. An additional 248 people suspected of underground connections had been detained since the flogging incident of the previous December. Four of the Irgun members involved in that incident had been captured and sentenced, three of them to be hanged, and one, on account of his youth, to life imprisonment. This had no apparent impact on the Irgun, whose attacks continued unabated.

On January 2, Ben-Gurion explained to the new colonial secretary, Arthur Creech-Jones, that the decision of the Zionist Congress disapproving Jewish Agency participation in the London conference did not preclude him or his colleagues in the Jewish Agency from participating informally. Since there was no practical difference between official and unofficial participation, Ben-Gurion had simply ignored the decision of the Zionist Congress that he himself had played a major role in getting adopted. However, there was in fact little to discuss at the London meeting. The course of British policy had already been determined for the most part.

On January 13, Field Marshal Montgomery, chief of the Imperial General Staff, advised Attlee and Bevin that it was "essential to retain the right to station forces in Palestine."[1] Except for the Suez Canal zone, most of Egypt was being evacuated, and there was no other area that could serve as a base for a Middle East reserve force. Such a reserve was regarded as essential for deterring any threat to the canal or to the oil installations in the region. Furthermore, air bases were required for the purpose of maintaining effective air communications with the empire in Asia. Lord Tedder, chief of the Air Staff, added: "Our whole military position in the Middle East depended on the cooperation of the Arab states."[2] He later explained to the cabinet that the retention of Britain's existing position of influence in the Middle East was one of the essential underpinnings for the defense of the British Empire. Attlee then called attention to the promise of the Palestinian Arabs that if they were assisted in attaining independence and majority rule in Palestine, they would grant Britain the military facilities it sought. It thus seemed that only a solution to the Palestine problem which suited Arab purposes would serve British interests.

On January 14, Bevin completed a policy paper in which he spelled out his intention of developing a proposal that would give the Arabs majority rule in a unitary state, with local autonomy and some Jewish cantonal enclaves. The price that the Arabs would be asked to pay would be their immediate agreement to the issuance of a large final batch of immigration certificates. This would serve the purpose of placating the Americans, since Truman had made the issuance of 100,000 certificates a goal of U.S. foreign policy. Afterward, there would be no further Jewish immigration without Arab approval. Bevin was fully convinced that the Arabs would reject any partition proposal and, he suggested, "There can be little doubt that in this event the Soviet group would align itself with the Arabs." He then concluded: "I cannot conceive of the British government, even aided by the United States, being able to carry partition with the requisite majority."[3] He also anticipated that the announcement of this policy would precipitate a major rebellion by the Jews in Palestine. However, this, too, would serve British interests, since it would happen during the transition to Arab majority rule, while Britain was still responsible for maintaining order. The British Army would have to bring the situation under control, further enhancing its position with the new Arab state.

Bevin's argument against partition was recapitulated by one of his deputies, Robert Howe, in a memorandum of January 21:

To how great an extent partition would result in an estrangement between Great Britain and the Arab peoples it is not possible to estimate. But the consequences of such an estrangement would be so grave that the risk of it should be a major consideration in the examination of partition as a possible policy. The loss of Arab good will would mean the elimination of British influence from the Middle East to the great advantage of Russia. And this in turn would greatly weaken the position of the British Commonwealth in the world.[4]

The military chiefs of staff also opposed partition in their presentation on the question to the cabinet. Partition, in their view, would destroy the British military position in the Middle East. It would create indefensible borders. Moreover, although British troops could impose a solution by force on one of the two contending communities in Palestine, they could not do so on both simultaneously. Strategic requirements dictated that Britain retain a commanding position in the country. They argued:

It was essential to our defence that we should be able to fight from the Middle East in war. . . . In future we should not be able to use India as a base for . . . deployment of force: it was the more essential, therefore, that we should retain other bases in the Middle East for this purpose. Palestine was of special importance in this general scheme of defence. In war, Egypt would be our key position in the Middle East; and it was necessary that we should hold Palestine as a screen for the defence of Egypt.[5]

At a minimum, the military chiefs wanted to retain the naval base at Haifa, at least two army garrisons, and a major air base.

When Bevin's paper was distributed to the cabinet the following day, it ran into unexpected opposition from a number of quarters, including Arthur Creech-Jones, the new colonial secretary. Creech-Jones submitted his own paper, which explained that though Bevin's plan could be defended theoretically, it was impracticable. He thought that even the Jewish moderates would fight it with all their strength. "It would spell the cessation of immigration, the arrest of Jewish development in Palestine, and the permanent subjugation of the national home, with its highly organized European population and its extensive commercial and industrial interests, to a backward Arab electorate, largely illiterate and avowedly inimical to its further progress."[6] He was convinced that the only viable solution was partition. Although the cabinet had made no decision, a few weeks later Creech-Jones told Weizmann that Britain was backing partition.

In the meanwhile, on January 15, the high commissioner announced that the British Third Division was to be moved to Palestine in three stages, bringing the total troop strength there to 100,000. Severe restrictions were placed on the movement of security forces in the country in order to reduce their vulnerability to attack. Soldiers were instructed not to move about in groups of less than four. All cinemas, large public areas, and cafes were placed off-limits. Security zones were expanded and bolstered with sandbag emplacements, barricades, wire, and additional guards. All British personnel were relocated inside the security zones. For the sake of security, the British administration created a massive military prison in Palestine and made its own forces the prisoners.

On January 24, the British military commander, General Evelyn Barker, confirmed the death sentence of Dov Gruner, an Irgun member who was wounded and captured after the attack on the Ramat Gan police station on April 23, 1946. The confirmation of sentence came as a surprise, given the unequivocal threat by the Irgun to retaliate in kind. The Irgun insisted that its men were soldiers and, if captured, were to be treated as prisoners of war. General Barker refused to accept this proposition, and was determined to teach the Irgun and all other terrorists a lesson. He apparently was also convinced that the stringent security measures he instituted would prevent any serious Irgun reprisals. It seemed that Barker was right, at least in this regard. The Irgun searched for a vulnerable officer who could be kidnapped, but was unable to find one. Instead, on January 26, they kidnapped a retired British major who had various business interests in the country. The next day they walked into the Tel Aviv courthouse and came out with a British judge, who promptly vanished.

The British were beside themselves with anger. Tel Aviv and large parts of Haifa and Jerusalem were placed under curfew, and before the House of Commons the colonial secretary threatened the imposition of martial law. These measures had no discernible effect. Then the Jewish Agency was advised informally by the administration that the death sentence against Gruner would not be carried out. When this message was passed on, the judge was released on January 28. The retired major, apparently an intelligence officer, was let go the following day. Gruner's execution was duly postponed, pending a new appeal to the Privy Council. The British had apparently capitulated to the Irgun once again.

The Jewish Agency was both relieved and disturbed. It was relieved because of its fear that had the Irgun actually executed its hostages, the country would have been placed under martial law with an inevitably harsh reaction against the Yishuv in general, and the Zionist leadership in particular. On the other hand, they were upset that the Irgun had forced the government to back down. This meant that the Irgun was setting the pace for developments in the country, undermining the importance of the Jewish Agency as the political voice of the Yishuv.

Begin, of course, saw matters rather differently. For one thing, he did not believe that the British had any intention of leaving Palestine at any time in the foreseeable future. The expansion of the British presence and the strengthening of its position in the country seemed to be clear evidence of this. On the political level, the British had practiced the principle of divide and rule, and helped to create the situation in which the impasse between the Jews and Arabs had become nonnegotiable, thus assuring a continuing justification for their occupation of the country. Their announced readiness to turn the political problem over to the United Nations was a very clever ploy that only served to emphasize this reality. By so doing, they could have their base in Palestine without the burden of political responsibility for the country. If Britain did go to the United Nations, it would be for the contrived purpose of remaining in the country for its own strategic purposes. Such a move would enable it to get rid of the Mandate and the explicit obligation to facilitate the development of the Jewish national home, an obligation on which it had clearly and intentionally defaulted.

It was Begin's understanding of what Bevin was up to that proved to be prescient, although no one in official Zionist circles would admit it. After all, Creech-Jones had just promised Weizmann that Britain would support partition and that the Jews would have their state. However, while Weizmann was exulting at Creech-Jones's promises, the colonial secretary had already reversed himself and had become a determined opponent of partition and a Jewish state. On February 6, he formally endorsed Bevin's plan. He and Bevin also agreed that if the Arabs objected to the plan, in addition to the Jews who would most assuredly be opposed to it, Britain should turn the Mandate back to the United Nations and pursue its strategic interests in Palestine as it saw fit. As anticipated, both the Arabs and the Jews rejected the plan, and Bevin decided to pursue the alternate plan for ridding Britain of its liabilities under the Mandate. The idea that Britain would turn the Mandate back to the United Nations, as successor to the League of Nations, was very upsetting to the Jewish Agency and the Zionist leadership. It meant the final defeat of decades of diplomatic effort. It also meant the loss of influence in Zionist affairs to the Revisionists and other hard-liners.

While it was impossible to predict what the General Assembly of the United Nations might do, it seemed highly unlikely that the necessary two-thirds majority required for the adoption of a proposal for partition could be mustered. Both the British and the Zionists knew this. Perhaps the major obstacle would be the opposition of the Soviet Union, which had repeatedly declared its categorical opposition to Zionism ever since the emergence of Bolshevism as the Soviet state ideology. The Soviets would never permit the emergence of a Jewish state. Indeed, Bevin had made the assumption of staunch Soviet opposition to partition the cornerstone of the January 14 paper that he submitted to the cabinet. Together with their East European allies and the Arab and Muslim states, the Soviets had the votes to block passage of a partition resolution. This would create a political stalemate at the international level and in Palestine. Under such circumstances, for the Zionists to achieve anything, they would have to reach an accommodation with Bevin on terms acceptable to the Arabs, which meant the end of Jewish immigration and the end of the dream of a Jewish state. The best that the Zionists could hope for would be a cantonization scheme, providing the Arabs could be convinced to concede even that much.

By contrast with the Jewish Agency, the Irgun was more curious than concerned about Creech-Jones's threat to impose martial law. Begin could not envision how it would change the prevailing situation in any practical way. Security could hardly be any tighter than it already was, nor could the British do much more to prevent the emergence of a Jewish state. The blockade of Palestine was being intensified as more and more Jews tried to reach its shores. On February 8, the motorized sailing ship *Mercia*, with 664 refugees aboard, was stopped by a British destroyer and boarded by force in international waters nine miles off Caesarea. The passengers were taken to Cyprus. The same thing happened to the 807 refugees aboard the *San Miguel* on February 16; the *Haim Arlosoroff* on February 27, with 1,416 refugees; and the *Abril* on March 8, with 601 on board. The Haganah, constrained by its own policy of active operations only to assist immigration from Europe, was making itself irrelevant in Palestine. While it was busily and successfully engaged in helping to organize the exodus of Jews to Palestine, it could do nothing to stop the interception of the ships carrying those Jews on the high seas, and would do nothing to retaliate against the British for these actions in Palestine itself.

The Irgun decided to escalate the level of its unilateral campaign to make the British presence in Palestine too costly to be tenable for very long. On March 1, 1947, the Irgun carried out sixteen significant operations, the most upsetting of which was an attack on the British Officers' Club in Goldschmidt House, located in the midst of the supposedly most secure compound in Jerusalem, known as the "Bevingrad" complex. The ferocious attack, during which most of the building was destroyed by satchel bombs thrown by the raiders, who broke through the barbed wire barrier surrounding the area, left twenty killed and some thirty wounded. London was in an uproar, with the press taunting the government to either rule Palestine or get out.

The following morning, martial law was proclaimed and a curfew imposed on most Jewish areas. The country came to a virtual standstill. Security vehicles were the only ones that moved. Food had to be distributed by the army. Soldiers were given police authority, and anyone could be shot for disobedience to orders of any kind. A 10,000-man cordon and search operation was mounted in Tel Aviv, and a similar one took place in Jerusalem. From a military perspective, the Irgun was right. Martial law produced no changes of any consequence. During the two weeks following the imposition of martial law, Irgun and Lehi attacks continued unimpeded, penetrating the British security zones almost at will. On March 17, the cordon and search operations were called off and martial law was rescinded. The British claimed to have arrested seventy-eight terrorists, but could identify only fifteen of them as members of Lehi and a dozen others as Irgunists. Martial law had proven to be a dismal and very expensive failure.

In the meantime the pressure on the British from the continuing flow of illegal immigration was about to reach the breaking point. On March 9, High Commissioner Alan Cunningham reported to London that he had received information that an additional 25,000 Jews were ready to leave Europe for Palestine as soon as ships could be found for them. This number of refugees would stretch British resources to their limits; they simply would not be able to cope with the problem. No more than 7,000 more internees could be accommodated in the Cyprus detention camps. In addition, there were neither enough planes to do the necessary reconnaissance nor enough destroyers to intercept the number of ships that might be used to carry that many refugees at one time. In Cunningham's view, the only feasible way of alleviating the problem was to increase the existing quota of 1,500 per month. The alternative was a collapse of the deportation system, with the resulting chaos and an inevitable increase in terrorism. The Foreign Office acknowledged the severity of the problem and queried its missions in the Arab capitals about whether an increase in the immigration quota to 4,000 per month might be acceptable now that the problem of the Mandate was being turned over to the United Nations. The answers received were uniformly negative.

Cunningham, of course, was right. The system was starting to break down. On March 12, the *Susanna*, with some 700 refugees, was beached successfully by the Haganah, and the army was able to capture only half of the illegals, the rest quickly melting into the Jewish community. The following day, Cunningham appealed to Creech-Jones once again, pointing up the humanitarian issue, but to no avail. On March 30, the *San Felipe* was intercepted and another 1,750 refugees were transferred to Cyprus. As the Cyprus camps began to reach their capacity, the promise of a new and serious crisis loomed just over the horizon.

Presumably as a result of their intense frustration at being unable to exercise unchallenged control of events in Palestine, the British authorities decided to raise the stakes by an attempt to intimidate the Irgun through use of the gallows. Dov Gruner's death sentence was still awaiting review by the Privy Council when three other Irgunists, Yehiel Drezner (Dov Rosenbaum), Mordechai Alkochi, and Eliezer Kashani, who were captured during the December flogging incident, were sentenced to death on February 10 for carrying arms. On March 17, Moshe Barazani was sentenced to death for carrying a hand grenade during an assault on a British installation several days earlier. On April 3, Meir Feinstein, who lost an arm during an attack on the Jerusalem railway station, joined his comrades on the condemned list. Then, on April 14, Gruner, Drezner, Alkochi, and Kashani were transferred from Jerusalem to death row in Acre prison. The government's information officer announced at a special press conference that there was no special significance to the transfer. The explanation was accepted without challenge, since Gruner's sentence was still under appeal. What the press had not been told was that the British had that very morning secretly enacted a retroactive regulation abolishing the right of appeal from the judgment of a military court.

The British went out of their way to make everything appear normal. Gruner's sister, who had come from the United States to see him in Jerusalem, and his attorney were told that visiting privileges would be continued in Acre. The British appear to have assumed that by carrying out the death sentences secretly, the Irgun would not have the time or opportunity to take hostages. In this way Begin's ability to prevent the executions would be preempted. Apparently very little if any thought was given to what the repercussions might be. On April 16, the four condemned men were hanged. The following day, announcement of the executions was accompanied by the imposition of a curfew for an indefinite period.

Whatever motivated the British to begin executing their Irgun prisoners, the reaction of the Irgun could not have been what they had hoped for or anticipated. An Irgun broadcast aimed specifically at the British authorities spelled out the new ground rules for the Irgun's conduct of its battle against them:

We will no longer be bound by the normal rules of warfare. In future every combatant unit of Irgun will be accompanied by a war court of the Jewish Underground Movement. Every enemy subject who is taken prisoner will immediately be brought before the court, irrespective of whether he is a member of the Army or Civilian Administration. Both are criminal organizations. He will be tried for entering illegally into Palestine, for illegal possession of arms and their use against civilians, for murder, oppression and exploitation; there will be no appeal against the decision of the people's court. Those condemned will be hanged or shot.[7]

To emphasize the seriousness of what had happened, Irgun headquarters issued orders to kidnap British soldiers, who were to be hanged in retaliation. The British, to prevent this from happening, placed virtually the entire garrison in the country on full alert and restricted almost all personnel to barracks or secure compounds. The gambit seemed to be working. Irgun patrols were unable to find any soldiers they could grab. Tension was increased further by the knowledge that Barazani and Feinstein were scheduled for execution on April 21. Escape or a break-in was impracticable, and the two condemned men knew it. They smuggled out a request for hand grenades with which they might kill themselves and their executioners on the way to the gallows. The Irgun managed to smuggle in two grenades, and on the night before their impending execution, to cheat the British of their victory, Barazani and Feinstein blew themselves up in their cell.

The executions had no deterrent effect whatever on the pace of the war being conducted by the Irgun. If anything, they contributed to an increase in the intensity of the anti-British struggle. Throughout the rest of the month, incessant attacks contributed significantly to the rapidly rising toll of casualties among British troops and police. On April 23, a train on the Cairo-Haifa railway was ambushed, resulting in eight dead and twenty-seven wounded. The following day four soldiers were wounded. On April 25, four more were killed and six wounded in an Irgun attack on the Sarona police station. The next day the C.I.D. chief in Haifa was mortally wounded, and in Tel Aviv a police inspector and three constables were killed. Together with Lehi, the Irgun planted bombs and land mines all over the country, and the British were helpless to do anything about it.

On April 28, the U.N. General Assembly met in a special session that was convened at the request of Britain. Bevin had put forward his plan to rid himself of the burdens of the Mandate into motion. Against the tragic background of the holocaust and the many thousands of Jews remaining in displaced persons camps, eloquent appeals were made for

justice for the Jew and recognition of the Zionist claim for Jewish independence in Palestine. The Arab spokesmen continued with their usual
stance of total intransigence: Palestine was Arab, and there was nothing
further to discuss. Anxious to find a compromise and not knowing
what else it could in fact do, the General Assembly appointed a Special
Committee on Palestine (UNSCOP) to investigate the Palestine problem and submit recommendations for its consideration. The official Zionist bodies geared up their propaganda machines to exploit whatever
possibilities U.N. involvement might present for strengthening the Zionist case for a Jewish state. The Irgun and Lehi, on the other hand,
were unimpressed by the establishment of yet another investigative
committee. They remained convinced that, notwithstanding the international posturing, the British would not leave Palestine unless they
were forced to do so, and that the decisive pressure could come only
from the Yishuv.

On May 4, the Irgun staged its most dramatic operation yet, shooting its way into the apparently impenetrable Acre fortress, and shooting
its way out again with 251 escapees, including 131 Arabs and 120 Jews.
Although the assault party took relatively heavy losses—four killed and
five apprehended—the feat captured international attention. In Britain, criticism of the government increased significantly. Churchill declared in a speech the following day: "The prestige of England has been
impaired in all parts of the world and her influence is waning with shat-
tering swiftness. What a shame, and disgrace, when we consider that we
have over 100,000 soldiers in Palestine."[8] The *Daily Express* editorial-
ized: "We must leave Palestine even before the resolution of the U.N."[9]
Members of Parliament began openly expressing the view that the government had erred by imagining that it could any longer impose order
in Palestine by force alone. Yet such was indeed the obvious intention of
the government.

The Irgun had failed to find suitable candidates for its planned reprisals for the hangings in April. The probability that at least three of the
five men captured in the Acre raid would be executed (the other two
were too young and would receive long prison terms) made the need to
take hostages critical. The opportunity finally presented itself on May 9,
when two policemen were kidnapped from a swimming pool. The Jewish Agency was in an uproar that such an act had taken place just as the
UNSCOP was about to be formally announced. The Haganah appealed to the public for assistance in uncovering where the policemen
were being held. It seemed that for the sake of creating what they imag-
ined would be a good impression on UNSCOP, they were prepared

once again to collaborate with the British. The coming crisis was avoided for the moment when the kidnapped policemen managed to escape the following day, after having been left alone by their captors. Shortly afterward, the Haganah discovered that the Irgun was planning an attack against Citrus House in Tel Aviv, the area military headquarters, and took steps to foil the operation. A Haganah member, Zeev Werba, was killed in the process. The British newspapers were effusive in their praise of the Haganah and the heroism of Werba. British officers even attended Werba's funeral and, in token of renewed cooperation with the Haganah, the administration released thirty-two of its members who were being held prisoner for concealing arms.

It was at this time that Bevin's plans for Palestine received a lethal blow from a most unexpected source—the Soviet Union. Soviet opposition to Zionism was an integral part of Bevin's strategy. He had every reason to believe that Soviet opposition to partition was unshakable. Communists all over the world, including Palestine, had long expressed their adamant opposition to such a scheme. Indeed, earlier in the year, the idea of partition had been definitively rejected by the Communist British Empire Conference in London. As late as April 27, an article in Moscow's *Red Fleet* dismissed partition as a bourgeois Jewish aspiration and called for an independent Arab Palestine. Then, without warning, on May 14 Andrei Gromyko addressed the General Assembly and put forth the argument that the Jews' aspiration to have a state of their own was a consequence of the failure by Western Europe to guarantee their elementary rights. Accordingly, he argued: "It would be unjustifiable to deny this right to the Jewish people, particularly in view of all they have undergone during the Second World War."[10] Gromyko took the position that if it were not possible to establish a unitary state in Palestine that would assure equal rights to both Arabs and Jews, then perhaps the only viable alternative might be to consider a partition of Palestine into separate and independent Arab and Jewish states.

Gromyko avoided definitively committing the Soviet Union to the support of partition. However, the fact that he opened the possibility of such support had far-reaching consequences. Bevin, who had been so certain of Soviet opposition and had sold his plan for turning to the United Nations to the British cabinet on the basis of that certainty, was flabbergasted. Of course, what he failed to grasp was that the Soviets understood that the creation of a Jewish state in Palestine meant a significant loss of British prestige in the Middle East. It also assured a British withdrawal from Palestine and the loss of the strategic benefits afforded by bases and facilities there. Accordingly, the Soviets were prepared to consider sacrificing their intrinsic opposition to Zionism for the opportunity of forcing a British withdrawal in the Middle East. Needless to say, this turn of events gave new and unanticipated significance to UNSCOP, which was formally constituted on May 15, and its subsequent recommendations to the General Assembly.

Gromyko's speech had interesting repercussions in the Yishuv. The Mapai saw it as a mixed blessing. Of course it meant that the Soviets would probably support partition and the creation of a Jewish state. But it also meant that the Mapai leadership was now to be deprived of one of the main justifications for its moderate, Western-oriented socialism: traditional Soviet anti-Zionism. Now the extreme left could, in good conscience, join with the Ahdut Avodah, which was the dominant party in the kibbutzim. As a result, instead of moving to the right in the socialist spectrum, the radical left pulled the Ahdut Avodah sharply to the left. And with the Ahdut Avodah went the Palmah, whose members for the most part came from the collective settlements. This deprived Ben-Gurion and the Mapai-dominated Histadrut of the political allegiance of the Yishuv's largest fully trained operational military force.

On June 16, 1947, the day of UNSCOP's arrival in Palestine, three of the five Irgun men captured in the raid on Acre—Meir Nakar, Yaacov Weiss, and Avshalom Haviv—were sentenced to death by hanging. The British stubbornly refused to recognize that their Palestine policy was not working, and that their liberal use of the gallows would not restore order in the country. At the trial, Avshalom Haviv made this clear in an address to the court when he drew a parallel between the struggle in Palestine and the one that took place earlier in Ireland:

You set up gallows, you murdered in the streets, you exiled, you ran amok and stupidly believed that by dint of persecution you would break the spirit of resistance of free Irishmen, the spirit of resistance which is God's gift to every man worthy of the name. You erred. . . . If you were wise, British tyrants, and would learn from history, the example of Ireland or of America would be enough to convince you that you ought to hurry out of our country.[11]

The point was made even more bluntly by his comrade Meir Nakar, who delivered a scathing attack on the British Palestine government: "British rule in Eretz Israel is bankrupt. . . . A Government whose officials have to sit in barbed-wire ghettoes—is that a Government? A Government which spends about half its budget on police purposes and yet remains helpless in face of the anger of the people in revolt—is that a Government?"[12]

Some of the members of UNSCOP were taken aback by the severity of the sentences. After all, since no British were killed in the Acre raid, the death sentences seemed rather extreme. One member, Jorge Garcia-Granados of Guatemala, approached General Sir Gordon Mac-Millan on the matter. MacMillan's response reflected the mindless rigidity with which the Palestine government attempted to maintain the British position in the country. He explained to Garcia-Granados: "You don't understand the situation here nor the psychology of the terrorists. They would interpret a generous gesture as a sign of weakness." When Garcia-Granados would not accept the reasonableness of this position, MacMillan told him: "You people may do as you see fit in Latin America, but British officials are bound to respect the law. When an act is designated as a crime under our laws, then whoever commits that act and violates those laws is a criminal no less than any other criminal. In any case, the political implications cannot concern me. I am a soldier and I have my duty to do."[13]

Garcia-Granados was now convinced that UNSCOP should attempt to intervene. With the assistance of Enrico Fabregat of Uruguay and Josef Brilej of Yugoslavia, and the deciding vote of the chairman, Emil Sandstrom of Sweden, UNSCOP agreed to cable the U.N. secretary-general. The message to Trygvie Lie stated: "The UN Commission expresses the concern of the majority of its members over the regrettable consequences liable to result from the carrying out of the three death sentences which the military court pronounced on June 16, and over the difficulties of fulfilling the responsibilities which the UN has imposed upon it."[14]

Secretary-General Lie subsequently contacted the British government regarding the executions and the concerns expressed by the commission. The British were furious at UNSCOP's intervention. They had no intention of allowing the United Nations to have any real voice in what took place in Palestine. To make matters worse, Sandstrom, Ralph Bunche, and Victor Hoo of UNSCOP had a secret meeting with Begin and two colleagues on June 24. Subsequently, Garcia-Granados and Fabregat also met with Begin. While they indicated that they were fully supportive of the Irgun's aims, they had a problem in making this known publicly. As Garcia-Granados put it, "We cannot be more extreme than the Jewish Agency. The members of the committee see in the Jewish Agency proposal for partition a compromise between your demands and those of the Arabs. There is no chance of a decision that will grant more than is demanded by the official Jewish representatives."[15] The British government rejected the UNSCOP plea for leniency for the condemned Irgunists on July 2. The death sentences were confirmed a week later. The Irgun again threatened to retaliate in kind for the hangings.

The Irgun found its long-sought opportunity to capture British hostages on the night of July 11, when it managed to snatch two police sergeants off the street in Natanyah. This time the captives were placed where there could be no escape, and also where the Haganah would not be able to find them. Martial law was imposed immediately on Natanyah and twenty settlements in the area. Some 5,000 troops began cordon and search operations with the full cooperation of the official Yishuv authorities and the active participation of the Haganah. More than 1,400 Jews were interrogated. No one knew anything. The hostages could not be found, and the Irgun had already warned in a broadcast that they would not be released until the death sentences were commuted. Unable to come up with anything, the cordon and search operation was effectively called off on July 16, although it officially lingered on a bit longer.

The following day a new crisis arose that severely shook the Yishuv. Handbills were passed out and posted by youngsters all over the country alerting the Yishuv to the fact that a refugee ship, *Exodus 1947*, was heading for Palestine with 4,554 passengers on board. The British had spotted the ship, and a naval force of a cruiser and five destroyers was closing in on her to prevent her from reaching Palestine. In the early hours of July 18, while the ship was in international waters about twenty miles west of Gaza, British destroyers deliberately rammed her repeatedly. A boarding party from one of the destroyers then tried to take control of the vessel. The battle for control of the ship lasted for hours. When some of the British sailors managed to get control of the wheelhouse and attempted to steer the ship toward Haifa, they found that the steering cables had been uncoupled. From the radio room, Reverend John Grauel, an American volunteer, directed a broadcast to Palestine:

This is the refugee ship *Exodus 1947*. Before dawn today we were attacked by five British destroyers and one cruiser at a distance of 17 miles from the shores of Palestine, in international waters. The assailants immediately opened fire, threw gas bombs, and rammed our ship from three directions. On our deck there are one dead, five dying, and 120 wounded. The resistance continued for more than three hours. Owing to severe losses and the condition of the ship, which is in danger of sinking, we were compelled to sail in the direction of Haifa, in order to save the 4,500 refugees on board from drowning.[16]

Later that afternoon, the *Exodus 1947* limped into Haifa harbor. Three prison ships were moored on the opposite side of the pier. As the refugees came down the gangway of the *Exodus 1947*, they were searched and hustled aboard the prison ships. By six o'clock the following morning the last of the refugees was apparently on the way to detention in Cyprus. The Yishuv was outraged. The Haganah, understandably, was especially furious. After all, it had just recently turned on its fellow Jews in the underground in a new spirit of cooperation with the British. For the first time since the demise of the Tenuat Hameri, the Haganah took offensive action, twice attacking radar installations at Haifa and sinking the *Empire Lifeguard* in Haifa harbor, wounding nineteen soldiers. The Irgun and Lehi mounted a seemingly unending series of assaults. The last two weeks of July saw over 100 incidents with thirteen members of the security forces killed and twenty-seven wounded. As the end of the month approached, attention was once again focused on Acre prison, where the three Irgunists awaited execution. There was widespread hope, following the debacle of the *Exodus 1947*, that the British would relent and commute the sentences.

Expectations of reasonableness were disappointed. To his credit, Major Charleston, the superintendent of Acre prison, refused to hang the prisoners because no British lives were lost in the escape operation. He was dismissed from his position and sent back to England. A replacement was brought from Nablus, and the three men were duly executed in the early morning of July 29. Within hours, the Irgun carried out its threat of retaliation and hanged the two police sergeants who were being held as hostages.

The British were horrified. In London, Creech-Jones, not without considerable self-righteousness, declared: "In the long history of violence in Palestine there has scarcely been a more dastardly act than the cold-blooded and calculated murder of these innocent young men after holding them hostage for more than a fortnight. I can only express the deep feeling of horror and revulsion shared by all of us here at this barbarous crime."[17] There were anti-Jewish demonstrations in London, Liverpool, Manchester, and Glasgow. In Tel Aviv, British soldiers ran amok, attacking cafes, smashing shop windows, and assaulting people on the streets. Armored cars fired into buses and cars.

The Jewish Agency was panic-stricken. From Geneva, Sharett announced: "It is mortifying to think that some Jews should have become so depraved by the horrible iniquities in Europe as to be capable of such vileness."[18] However, Sharett and his colleagues, who had long placed such high hopes on Britain, were soon to observe a lesson in British callousness that shattered any lingering expectation that an accommodation could be reached on Palestine. They were to discover that the painful drama of the *Exodus 1947* was far from over. Contrary to expectations, the refugees were not taken to detention camps in Cyprus when they were deported from Palestine on July 18. The British foreign secretary had announced a new policy with regard to illegal immigration to Palestine. The illegals were no longer to be interned in Cyprus. Henceforth they were to be returned to the countries from which they came, and *Exodus 1947* had sailed from France.

France was willing to allow the refugees to disembark, but only if they chose to do so voluntarily. The British therefore had the ships sail aimlessly around the Mediterranean in the midst of a summer heat wave for nine days, and then dropped anchor on July 29, with the expectation that the passengers would gladly debark. After all, the passengers on the three prison ships had been confined in wire cages, without space, privacy, or adequate sanitation facilities. The British tactic did not work. Only a few agreed to leave the ships. The nine days of searing heat were followed by four days of torrential rains, but still the refugees refused to disembark. The Jews declared a hunger strike. News reports started to leak out, and a wave of indignation began to swell around the world. Finally, the British announced to the refugees that unless they disembarked by the evening of the following day, August 22, the ships would take them to Hamburg. The survivors of the holocaust would be returned to Germany by the government of democratic Britain in order not to further upset the Arabs. The Haganah sent a boat equipped with loudspeakers alongside to urge the refugees not to leave the ships. They remained on board.

The ships arrived in Hamburg on September 9, with the international press corps waiting to greet them. There were also some 1,000 fully armed British troops backed by 1,500 German police with another 1,500 in reserve. They were equipped with high-pressure water hoses, steel-tipped truncheons, and riot shields. The refugees on the *Empire Rival* left the ship without trouble. In fact, they hurried off because they had set a large time bomb in the hold of the vessel. The story was quite different with the other two ships, the *Ocean Vigour* and the *Runnymede Park*. The 1,500 Jews on the latter put up fierce resistance and turned back the 400-man boarding party with anything they could get their hands on, including clubs wrapped in barbed wire. The British forced their way on board with the high-pressure hoses and began clubbing the refugees and removing them by force. The British then confined the survivors of the holocaust in German concentration camps at Poppendorf and Amstau.

While this tragedy was being played out under British direction, it slowly began to dawn that the Irgun's unprecedented reprisal for the hanging of its people was having repercussions quite the reverse of what the Jewish Agency feared. As noted by one student of the period: "It might have appeared that the death of the two sergeants vitalized British resistance to the Irgun rebellion, smeared all Jews with the terrorist label, and set back the dream of a state. This was not so; in fact, it was rather the reverse: the two sergeants were the straw that broke the Mandate's back."[19] However, it would still take more time and the spilling of more blood before Bevin would reluctantly abandon his no-win strategy in Palestine, but there could no longer be any doubt that the British were on their way out.

The British newspapers began to voice as much revulsion at British policies and tactics in Palestine as at those of the Irgun and Lehi. The price of empire in Palestine was simply becoming too costly in blood, and there seemed to be no way to contain the violence that continued unabated, notwithstanding British attempts at repression. The newspapers began to suggest that it was time to get out. This view was given further poignancy by the deteriorating economic conditions in Britain. As an economy measure, Attlee was recalling 200,000 of the 450,000 British troops stationed abroad. More than a third of those remaining overseas were in Palestine—a disproportionate commitment in terms of Britain's overall national security interests. In brief, as personally painful and politically impossible as it would have been for Ben-Gurion and the rest of the official Zionist leadership to admit, Begin's strategy for making the British position in Palestine untenable was working where endless propaganda and diplomacy had failed.

Given the direction of events, Ben-Gurion began to move to put his own stamp on them. On August 8, he voiced his opinion that the time had come to demand the immediate termination of British rule in Palestine. On August 17, he accused Britain of conducting a war against the Jews. On August 26, he observed that it appeared that Bevin was determined to remain in Palestine no matter what the cost. Begin was convinced that Ben-Gurion was now rushing to establish a record for the history books, one that would make it appear that it was his defiance which drove the British out. However, since the Irgun had no comparable political and propaganda machine at its disposal, there was little that could be done about it.

In anticipation of an UNSCOP report that was not supportive of their demands, the Palestinian Arabs began to engage in violence for the first time since the Irgun revolt started. An Arab group attacked a cafe in Tel Aviv, killing five and injuring twelve (one was mortally wounded and died later). On August 14, another incident took place along the dividing line between Tel Aviv and Jaffa that resulted in three Jews and one Arab killed, and nine Jews and seven Arabs hurt. On August 16, the Haganah retaliated against the group to which the Tel Aviv attack was traced, killing eleven including a family of seven.

The UNSCOP, unable to reach unanimity among its members, issued two reports to the General Assembly on August 31. The majority report, which reflected the Jewish Agency position, proposed partition of the country. The Jewish territory was to include the eastern Galilee, the central coastal plain, and the Negev. The Arabs were to receive the western Galilee, central Palestine, and the northern and southern ends of the coastal plain. Jerusalem and the surrounding area were to become an international zone. There was to be a two-year probationary period during which Jewish immigration would be limited to 6,250 per month. After the two-year period, the rate would be reduced to 5,000 per month. The minority report, which essentially proposed a cantonization scheme with a single capital at Jerusalem, called for a three-year period of U.N. administration. It provided for no quotas on Jewish immigration.

Once the UNSCOP reports were submitted, the Jewish Agency reoriented all its assets to focus on the United Nations. A massive propaganda campaign was undertaken in favor of the partition proposal during the two weeks between August 31 and September 16, when the General Assembly convened. Three days after the U.N. session began, the Arab League held a secret meeting at Sofar, Lebanon, at which it was agreed that the Arab states would intervene in Palestine if the General Assembly voted for partition. The Arab Higher Committee for Palestine swore that the "Arabs would never recognize the validity of partition or the authority of the United Nations to implement it."[20]

On September 23, Creech-Jones blithely informed the General Assembly that Britain would not carry out the recommended partition of Palestine. While it was unclear to many just what this meant, this was not the case as far as Begin and the Irgun command were concerned. The adoption of partition, without a British commitment to assure its peaceful implementation, raised the prospect of direct military intervention by the armies of the Arab states. If Britain would not take responsibility for assuring the peaceful establishment of Jewish and Arab states in Palestine, no one else would.

As far as Begin was concerned, Britain's intentions were transparent. Its forces would occupy key strategic positions in the country while allowing the armies of its Arab allies to invade and occupy the remainder of Palestine. Certain that the British still intended to remain in the country and would assure this by making a deal with the neighboring Arab states, Begin decided to continue the Irgun assaults on the British while the General Assembly was still debating partition. At the same time, the Irgun did what it could together with the Revisionists to discredit the partition idea, accusing Ben-Gurion and the Jewish Agency of betraying the Jewish people. This led to sporadic and sometimes bloody clashes with the Haganah, which sought unsuccessfully to contain the Irgun and Lehi. In the meanwhile, tacitly acknowledging the validity of Begin's analysis of British intentions, Ben-Gurion ordered the Haganah to develop a general mobilization plan in preparation for a full-scale war with the Arab states. A secret military procurement mission was dispatched abroad to begin purchasing the necessary arms.

As the debate continued at the United Nations, it became increasingly evident that the British were not acting in good faith or responsibly as a major power. Although the British spokesmen declared their opposition to partition, they offered no alternatives. They also made clear that they would not undertake to implement any solution that was not acceptable to both Arabs and Jews. Given the categorically intransigent position of the Arabs, this meant that Britain would do nothing at all to help resolve the problem. Moreover, there was increasing evidence that the British intended to stay in Palestine for a long time to come. In Britain, a campaign to recruit candidates for service in the Palestine police continued to be pursued vigorously.

At the United Nations, the subcommittee on partition labored to make the partition proposal acceptable to a two-thirds majority of the General Assembly. In the process, the size of the proposed territory to be allocated to the Jews was whittled down from some 6,000 square miles to about 5,500 by the removal from the plan of part of the Negev and the city of Jaffa. The subcommittee proposed that the Mandate be brought to an end on May 1, 1948, and that the transfer of power to the Arabs and Jews take place on July 1. Once it became clear that the Soviets and Americans had mutually agreed to back partition, the British cabinet gave Attlee, Bevin, and Creech-Jones blanket authority to establish a timetable for the inevitable British withdrawal. On November 13, the British ambassador to the United Nations, Alexander Cadogan, announced that British troops would not leave until August 1, and that until then the United Nations would not be permitted to exercise any jurisdiction in Palestine. The subcommittee revised its timetable accordingly and proposed that the Mandate end on August 1, but it also suggested that a U.N. commission should administer the Mandate during the period of transition. Cadogan then announced that Britain alone would determine when the Mandate would come to an end.

The reason for Britain's unwillingness to cooperate with the United Nations went beyond mere peevishness. It appeared that Bevin was in fact doing what Begin accused him of; that is, he was engaged in plotting a virtually total collapse of order in Palestine, with or without partition, to justify continued British intervention.

Finally, after some hectic maneuvering by the Zionists and their supporters to influence the General Assembly vote, on November 29, 1947, the proposal for a partition of Palestine passed by a vote of 33 to 13 with ten abstentions. In effect, the United Nations had given its blessing to a Jewish ministate in Palestine.

NOTES

1. Nicholas Bethell, *The Palestine Triangle*, p. 292.
2. Ibid.
3. Ibid., p. 293.
4. William Roger Louis, "British Imperialism and the End of the Palestine Mandate," in William Roger Louis and Robert W. Stookey, eds., *The End of the Palestine Mandate*, p. 17.
5. Ibid., p. 16.
6. Bethell, *The Palestine Triangle*, p. 294.
7. Jan Gitlin, *Conquest of Acre Fortress*, p. 113.
8. Itzhak Gurion, *Triumph on the Gallows*, p. 144.
9. Ibid., p. 145.
10. Bethell, *The Palestine Triangle*, p. 313.
11. Menachem Begin, *The Revolt*, p. 284.
12. Ibid., p. 285.
13. Jorge Garcia-Granados, *The Birth of Israel*, pp. 54–55.
14. Gurion, *Triumph on the Gallows*, p. 165.
15. Shmuel Katz, *Yom Ha'Esh*, p. 295. In his memoirs, Garcia-Granados changed his statement to sound more neutral and diplomatic, but there is no reason to doubt the version of Katz, who was present at the clandestine meeting.
16. Ruth Gruber, *Destination Palestine: The Story of the Haganah Ship Exodus 1947*, p. 18.
17. J. Bowyer Bell, *Terror Out of Zion*, p. 238.
18. *Palestine Post*, August 4, 1947.
19. Bowyer Bell, *Terror Out of Zion*, p. 238.
20. Bernard Postal and Henry W. Levy, *And the Hills Shouted for Joy*, p. 109.

10

The Troubled Birth
of the Jewish State

The U.N. resolution favoring the partition of Palestine gave new immediacy to the expectation of a war between the Jews and the Arab states. Among the latter, it was the state best equipped and prepared for such a war, Transjordan, that had the most to gain or to lose. It was also the only Arab state that had any clear view of what its objectives would be in a general Palestine war. The British had already dissuaded King Abdullah from actively pursuing his dream of a Hashemite Greater Syria, and he made an announcement to that effect on October 14, 1947. He now turned his attention to the more immediate prospect of creating a Greater Transjordan. His success would depend upon the shrewdness with which he exploited the historic opportunity about to be created by the withdrawal of the British from Palestine. According a Palestinian friend of the king, Abdullah explained his position to him on October 1, 1947, before the U.N. vote took place:

The Mufti and Kuwatly want to set up an independent Arab state in Palestine with the Mufti at its head. If that were to happen I would be encircled on almost all sides by enemies. This compels me to take measures to anticipate their plans. My forces will therefore occupy every place evacuated by the British. I will not begin the attack on the Jews, and I will only attack them if they first attack my forces. I will not allow massacres in Palestine. Only after quiet and order have been established will it be possible to reach an understanding with the Jews.[1]

Soon afterward, Abdullah held a secret meeting with Golda Meir, head of the political department of the Jewish Agency, at Naharayim in the Jordan Valley. Abdullah tried to make his position clear. He had hoped to be able to take control of the territories assigned to the Arabs under the anticipated partition plan without having to fight for them. Mrs. Meir recalled: "He would not join in any Arab attack on us. He would always remain our friend, he said, and like us, he wanted peace more than anything else. After all, we had a common foe, the Mufti of Jerusalem, Haj Amin el-Husseini. Not only that, but he suggested that we meet again, after the United Nations vote." Returning to Tel Aviv with Ezra Danin, who had met with Abdullah on a number of occasions, she asked him what he thought of Abdullah's remarks. Danin was dubious about his reliability. "It was not, he told me, that Abdullah was a liar, but that he was a Bedouin, and that the Bedouin had their own ideas about truth—which they saw as something much less absolute than we did. At any rate, he said, Abdullah was certainly sincere in his expressions of friendship, although they would not necessarily be at all binding on him."[2] Danin's assessment turned out to be prescient.

Once the partition resolution passed, the looming threat of a full-scale war with the Arabs had an evidently sobering and unifying effect on the Yishuv and its supporters. The guerrilla war that had already started drew together the diverse elements of the Jewish community, from the Communists to the Agudat Israel. In January 1948, the binationalist labor parties Hashomer Hatzair and Ahdut Avodah merged into a new party, Mapam (United Labor Party). Its founding platform declared that it "has determined to support the establishment of a Jewish state and its defence under present conditions despite its rejection, in principle, of the Partition solution."[3] At the other end of the nationalist spectrum, the Irgun and the Revisionists continued insisting upon a Jewish state on both sides of the Jordan, but did nothing to impede the emergence of a state within the area assigned to the Jews under the partition scheme.

The British government, on the other hand, sought to be as obstructive as possible. It informed Parliament in mid-December that the Mandate would be terminated on May 15, 1948. However, it refused to allow the members of the Palestine Commission appointed by the United Nations to enter the country before May 1. It also refused to accede to the requests made by the commission, in accordance with the requirements of the partition resolution, regarding matters such as the delineation of frontiers, immigration, and the establishment of armed militias. The British reluctantly admitted that hundreds of armed Arabs were entering Palestine from nearby states. They excused their failure to stop this by contending that the character of the terrain made the detection and prevention of such infiltration difficult, especially at night. The commission subsequently reported that, to some extent, the Palestine administration was arming the Arabs.

The United States also retreated from its strong position in favor of partition and a Jewish state almost as soon as the resolution passed. Within days, reacting to pressures on and by American oil companies and other private commercial interests in the Middle East, the State Department announced an embargo on shipments of arms to the Near East, an ostensibly evenhanded approach to limiting potential violence in the volatile area. Of course, the State Department was well aware that since the Arabs were receiving arms from the British, the embargo was in effect directed primarily against the Yishuv.

On February 24, the U.S. representative to the U.N. Security Council, Warren Austin, stated that while the United States would consider the use of armed force to restore order in Palestine, it would not agree to such in order to enforce partition, thereby seconding the obstructionist British position. Then, on March 19, Austin proposed that further action on implementing partition be suspended and that the General Assembly be called into special session to consider the establishment of a temporary trusteeship over Palestine, "without prejudice . . . to the character of the eventual political settlement."[4] This American betrayal of its undertakings to the Zionists, had it been carried through, would have meant the aborting of the Jewish state. There is more than a little irony in the fact that it was the Soviet Union that effectively blocked it, availing itself of the opportunity to assail the Western powers for undermining the authority of the United Nations.

At the same time, the British were pursuing a new understanding with Transjordan that would continue to ensure the protection of some of their interests in the region. Negotiations on a new Anglo-Transjordanian treaty opened at London in March 1948. The Transjordanian delegation included Prime Minister Tawfiq Abul Huda, Foreign Minister Fawzi al-Mulqi, and Brigadier John Bagot Glubb, commander of the Arab Legion. After the treaty negotiations were completed, Abul Huda and Glubb met privately with Bevin to discuss the question of the Arab state that would arise in the territory of Palestine designated for the Arabs.

Abul Huda made the argument that as soon as the British withdrew in May, the Jews would immediately establish a state. The Arabs of Palestine, however, were too disunited and unprepared to establish an Arab state. In Abul Huda's view, the vacuum that would occur in the Arab zone after British withdrawal might tempt the Zionists to ignore

the boundaries set forth in the partition plan and to occupy the territory, perhaps as far east as the Jordan River. The other possibility was
the seizure of control of the territory by the mufti. Neither situation
would serve British or Transjordanian interests. Accordingly, Abul
Huda suggested that the easiest way to assure that neither of the two
possibilities took place would be for the Arab Legion to quickly occupy
the territories assigned to the Arabs under the partition scheme. Glubb,
aware of the limitations of the Arab Legion, interjected that it would
prove impractical for the legion to attempt to occupy either the Upper
Galilee or the Gaza area. It could take effective control only of the areas
immediately adjacent to the existing frontier along the Jordan. Abul
Huda agreed to these constraints. Bevin's reply, as recorded by Glubb,
was "It seems the obvious thing to do, but do not go and invade the areas allotted to the Jews."[5]

The five months between the passage of the partition resolution at
the United Nations and the end of the Mandate witnessed a continuation of hostilities between the Irgun and Lehi and the British authorities, which resulted in the death of another thirty policemen.
Nonetheless, the main struggle now shifted to one between Jews and
Arabs. The British, for their part, were singularly unhelpful in maintaining public order or interposing themselves between the two groups.
The high commissioner's efforts were largely restricted to issuing
warnings that the violence had to cease or else the British security forces
would act against all, Jew or Arab, who broke the law. Such threats were
understood to be hollow. It was important to the British to make it clear
to the Arab states that they were doing nothing to assist the birth of a
Jewish state in Palestine. Indeed, the naval blockade of Palestine was
continued in order to stop the influx of more manpower and arms for
the Haganah.

The anticipated outbreak of full-scale civil war in Palestine raised the
serious possibility that the Jewish state could be stillborn. There was
much expectation in London that the local Arabs, with some aid from
the outside, might create sufficiently chaotic conditions to make a continued British presence in the country, even after termination of the
Mandate, an evident necessity. The prime ministers of the seven member states of the Arab League met in Cairo on December 7, 1947, and
announced that they would back the Palestinian Arabs with arms,
money, and troops. They promised that their armies would be committed to the struggle against the Jewish state as soon as the Mandate came
to an end. In the meanwhile, an Arab army of liberation was being

formed in Damascus under the command of Fawzi al-Qawkaji, and was being trained by the Syrian Army.

At the same time, there was still very little evidence that the British really expected to withdraw from Palestine in the near future. As late as December 1947, the British continued constructing military bases in the southern part of the country.

Incredibly, even at this late date, some Jewish Agency members preferred to believe that the British would ultimately honor their long neglected obligations to the Jews, or that the United Nations would somehow intervene to protect the Yishuv from an Arab onslaught and allow the Jewish state to emerge intact. Ben-Gurion was not among these. He was confident that such was not to be the case. Together with Israel Galili, head of the national command of the Haganah, he began to prepare for the massive effort that would be required to get the Haganah ready for a conventional war with the Arab states, as well as a nonconventional struggle with Palestinian Arab guerrillas.

The Haganah was by no stretch of the imagination an army at this point. It had only about 400 full-time personnel. The Palmah forces under the command of Yigal Allon numbered some 3,100, but could not be fully mobilized at any one time. As for the remaining 32,000 Haganah members, there were not enough rifles and sidearms for them, and only a handful of machine guns and mortars were available. They had no armor, artillery, or airpower. To make matters worse, there was only enough ammunition to sustain a conventional war for about three days. The need of the Yishuv for additional arms was desperate, and Ben-Gurion dispatched a special agent, Ehud Avriel, to Europe to locate the needed war matériel.

Given the dire military posture of the Haganah, some difficult defense policy decisions had to be made, and Ben-Gurion undertook to make them. Effectively shunting aside his colleagues, he quickly came to personify the unborn state. His critics were to insist not only that many of his decisions were militarily unsound, but also that some reflected a failure on his part to grasp objective realities. He insisted that under no circumstances could there be a retreat, irrespective of the extent of isolation of a settlement, the vulnerability of a section of a city, or the simple defenselessness of a position. Everything possible was to be done to hold on. This basically defensive approach effectively precluded the concentration of the forces and matériel necessary to take the offensive action required for vital military goals.

There was at the time a real concern among the official leadership that open suppression of Arab violence by the Haganah might be seen as deliberate acts of provocation, and a violation of the peace by the Jews. This, it was feared, might lead to a revocation of the partition decision by the United Nations on the basis that the country was in a state of civil war, and therefore not ready for independence. Begin rejected this line of reasoning and saw Ben-Gurion's defensive strategy simply as a new version of the old policy of havlagah, or self-restraint. The Irgun decided to continue to act on its own.

Early on the morning of December 1, 1947, a large number of Arabs gathered quietly in the Manshieh quarter of Jaffa, along the line dividing it from Tel Aviv. Soon afterward, they swept into Tel Aviv and began attacking nearby shops, burning and looting as they advanced. Haganah and Irgun forces soon arrived on the scene and engaged the Arab mob. The British security forces that were also there stood aside and did nothing. By the end of the day five Jews and three Arabs had been killed. The fighting continued the following day, leaving a toll of six Arabs killed and twenty-three wounded, fourteen Jews killed and twenty-one wounded. However, the Arab attempt to break into Allenby Street, leading to the heart of Tel Aviv, was stopped. The following day, in conjunction with a three-day general strike called by the Arab Higher Committee to protest the partition decision, there was an assault on the Jewish quarter of the Old City in Jerusalem that soon spread into the New City. Sporadic fighting broke out all over the country.

The Arab strategy was determined from the outset by the character and pattern of Jewish settlement in the country. The Jewish population was concentrated for the most part in the cities of Tel Aviv, Jerusalem, and Haifa, and in some 700 settlements spread throughout the country, many of them in predominantly Arab areas. Consequently, the coherence of the Yishuv as an organized community depended heavily on its control of the roads connecting the diffuse points of Jewish concentration. The Arabs were similarly concentrated in some 760 villages and 25 towns, in addition to their relatively large populations in Haifa, Jaffa, Safed, and Tiberias.

Operating in an offensive mode, the Arabs were well positioned to interrupt the Yishuv's vital road links in many parts of the country. By occupying positions on the heights and hillsides commanding the roads, small forces and snipers could effectively cut off and isolate whole sections of the Yishuv, which could be choked out of existence later. As a result, there was a good deal of Arab sniping at virtually anything that moved through the countryside. It was expected that one by one the more remote settlements in the Galilee and the Negev would have to be abandoned or surrendered. A similar fate would await Jeru-

salem, which was particularly vulnerable because the roads that connected it to the rest of the Yishuv meandered through winding passes
where they were readily subject to interdiction. The road from Jaffa-Tel
Aviv to Jerusalem was especially dangerous in the area near Latrun,
where it snaked through the Bab al-Wad, a narrow passage through the
hills. Consequently, the struggle with the Arabs was to become primarily one for control of the network of roads.

The military situation in the Jerusalem area was particularly bleak for
the Jews. The Arabs had set up commanding positions on the hilltops
near the neighboring villages, and established roadblocks throughout
the city; sniping at Jews was rampant. The 1,700 Jews isolated in the
Jewish Quarter of the Old City were in danger of being totally cut off
from the outside. On December 10, a Jewish convoy attempting to
reach the isolated Etzion bloc of settlements (Kfar Etzion, Massuot
Yitzhak, Ein Tzurim, and Revadim) was ambushed on the Jerusalem-
Hebron road, leaving ten dead and four wounded.

In Haifa, six Arabs were killed and thirty-two wounded by the Haganah. The following day, the Irgun attacked the village of Tireh, near
Haifa. After warning the women and children to get out, the main
house in the village was blown up, killing thirteen and wounding six.
Ben-Gurion praised the operation—until he discovered it was the Irgun and not the Haganah that carried it out. Then it was considered a
senseless provocation. Irgun attacks also took place at a number of
other centers of guerrilla activity, such as Yazur near Tel Aviv, Shaafat
near Jerusalem, and Yehudiyeh near Lydda (Lod). On December 15,
the Arabs blew up the pipes bringing water into Jerusalem. The following day two settlements in the Negev came under Arab attack.

By December 17, the countrywide death toll since the partition vote
had reached 106 Arabs and 96 Jews. Golda Meir complained to the
high commissioner that "the main activity of the government has been
directed at weakening the standing force of the Jews through searches
of arms and almost daily arrests. . . . Policemen and soldiers were standing around while shops were set on fire and Jews were being attacked,
behaving as if it had nothing to do with them."[6] She also hinted that
some of the security forces were actually helping or equipping the Arab
attackers. On December 27, a Jewish convoy was ambushed along the
Jaffa-Jerusalem road, producing another seven casualties, two of them
fatalities. Two days later, a bomb was detonated at the Damascus Gate
in Jerusalem, killing fifteen and wounding more than fifty Arabs. Three
days after that, a bomb was thrown at a crowd of about 100 Arabs
standing outside the Haifa oil refinery. A riot broke out inside the refin-

ery, where the 2,000 Arab workers sought to kill every Jew they could get their hands on. On that occasion, forty-one Jews were stabbed or beaten to death. Six Arabs also were killed during the riot.

The increasing threat of a full-scale war caused a number of members of the Jewish Agency to conclude that the Yishuv could no longer afford the luxury of dividing its military capabilities between the Haganah and the Irgun. Begin had already proposed a union of the two forces. Accordingly, a meeting was arranged on December 15 between Begin and his aides and a delegation from the Jewish Agency, Mapai, and Mizrahi. Aside from some minor technical agreements, nothing much came of the initiative. The critical factor was that such unification did not have the support of Ben-Gurion or the key Haganah commanders. Ben-Gurion did not trust Begin, and was not interested in an alliance that might give the latter recognition as a legitimate leader of the Yishuv. Indeed, Ben-Gurion's inclinations went in the opposite direction from unification.

To the surprise and dismay of many in the Yishuv, the Haganah suddenly decided to renew the "Season," and a number of anti-Irgun incidents took place, including kidnappings and beatings of Irgun members. The Haganah soon agreed to cease the kidnappings, but violated the agreement at the beginning of January 1948, when a Haganah unit in Haifa kidnapped an Irgun officer. The Irgun retaliated by kidnapping a Haganah intelligence officer in Haifa. On January 12, the local Irgun commander received a letter from his Haganah counterpart suggesting a prisoner exchange. The Haganah man was released. The Haganah claimed it had similarly released the Irgun man, but he never returned home. Three days later he was found dead in the Arab village of Tireh. The following day, the Haganah changed its story and claimed that their prisoner had escaped before he could be released. Begin demanded that the Jewish Agency organize a public inquiry into the matter. This was begun, but was postponed in early February when an even more provocative incident took place.

As the British began to withdraw from the Jewish sectors, the Irgun began to come into the open. At a rally to raise funds for arms purchases held in Tel Aviv, Haganah men threw hand grenades into the crowd, causing some serious injuries. Luckily, no one was killed. Notwithstanding the Haganah's culpability in these and numerous other less serious counterproductive acts, the Irgun took no retaliatory steps. Begin continued to press for a settlement and promised to disband the Irgun when the state came into being.

On January 5, 1948, the Haganah took offensive action against the Arab paramilitary organization Najada by blowing up most of the Semiramis Hotel in Jerusalem, which served as its headquarters. However, the only casualty of the attack was a Spanish consular officer who lived in the hotel. The Haganah was instructed to be even more careful in its operations in Jerusalem. That same day the Lehi took its first major action against the Arabs rather than the British. With the benign neglect of the latter, Arab volunteers from other countries were pouring into Jaffa. The Lehi decided to undermine Arab morale by destroying their military headquarters in Jaffa, which the Arabs considered to be relatively impregnable because of the concentration of British troops there. Two Lehi members casually drove a truck full of explosives covered with a load of oranges into Jaffa and parked it near the Arab headquarters. The resulting explosion caused over 100 casualties. The effect on Arab morale was very serious, resulting in an upsurge in emigration.

Matters took a further turn for the worse when an estimated 900 uniformed Arab volunteers crossed the Syrian border and attacked the nearby settlement of Kfar Szold on January 10. The assault was repelled with the aid of a British armored unit that happened to be nearby, reflecting the lack of coherency in British policy even among the military. This was followed six days later by a new treaty between Britain and Iraq that committed Britain to supply Iraq with arms and equipment. On February 6, the British secretary of defense, Albert V. Alexander, told the House of Commons that he had no reason to suppose that any of the arms being supplied to the Arab countries would find their way to Palestine. In mid-March the British admitted that as many as 5,000 Arabs had crossed into Palestine from Syria and Iraq. These raised the number of Arab irregulars in the country to about 15,000. The irregulars were placed under the command of General Sawfat Pasha of Iraq, who had been appointed to the post by the Arab League.

It was becoming increasingly apparent to Ben-Gurion that the Irgun's assessment of British intentions, argued by Begin a year earlier, was correct. On March 8, he confronted High Commissioner Alan Cunningham and told him that he was convinced that British intended to sabotage the U.N. decision on partition. Three days later, he wired Moshe Sharett in New York:

It is becoming clear that the termination of the Mandate means merely giving up any formal obligation and responsibility under national or international law, leaving free arbitrary [hand] for British troops for indefinite period in indefinite areas of the country. Further sabotaging UN policy, helping Arab

League in carrying out its designs against [Jews]. . . . These dangers must be brought immediately to the attention UN authorities and US Government.[7]

In early February, Ben-Gurion appointed David Shaltiel the new Haganah commander in Jerusalem. This made any close collaboration with the Irgun especially difficult because Shaltiel, as the former head of Haganah intelligence, had played a significant role in the "Season." He was distrusted by the Irgun and Lehi, which saw him as more of a stooge of Ben-Gurion than a military commander, notwithstanding his impressive military credentials.

On February 12, British soldiers arrested four Haganah men in Jerusalem and turned them over to an Arab mob in the Old City. One was killed immediately; the other three were beaten, castrated, and then hacked to death. Although this was not the first time such an incident had occurred, it brought an end to Haganah passivity and the policy of havlagah. The Haganah soon joined in taking the offensive by blowing up houses to encourage Arab evacuation from selected areas, attacking Arab villages, and ambushing Arab patrols.

Even though a political settlement between the Jewish Agency and the Irgun was beyond reach, given Ben-Gurion's opposition to anything short of a complete capitulation by Begin, an operational agreement was eventually concluded on March 8. In defensive matters, the Irgun would be under Haganah orders, but would operate under its own officers. Offensive operations against the Arabs or reprisal actions against the British were to be approved by the Haganah. Other points dealt with lesser matters such as fund-raising for arms purchases. The agreement was to go into effect as soon as the Zionist General Council ratified it.

The Zionist General Council had convened at the beginning of April, primarily to consider the decision taken a month earlier by the Zionist Executive and Vaad Leumi to establish a provisional government and parliament, in advance of the termination of the Mandate and the British withdrawal. Under the U.N. resolution, the Palestine Commission was supposed to form a provisional government council before April 1, or to inform the Security Council if it was unable to do so. On March 25, Sharett contacted the Palestine Commission and recommended the formation of a provisional council with twenty-five members, submitting a proposed list of candidates. The Palestine Commission rejected the recommendation, and the British warned the Yishuv against any attempt to establish institutions of a future Jewish state as long as the Mandate remained in operation. The Zionist General Council decided to ignore the British and proceeded to do what it thought necessary to prepare for the fateful day. On April 12, after an extensive debate that lasted ten days, the council agreed by a majority of 40 to 18 (the minority, which was made up of the Mapam and the Revisionists, objected to the wording of the statement) to the following resolution: "In accordance with the decision of the World Zionist Organization and with the approval of Jews everywhere we resolve that with the termination of the British Mandate and the end of foreign rule, the Jewish people will establish an independent regime in their Homeland."[8]

On the basis of this resolution two governing institutions for the embryonic state were established, a thirty-seven-member Provisional State Council and a thirteen-member National Administration. All decisions regarding security, defense, and mobilization were entrusted to the National Administration, which was henceforth to be accountable to the Provisional State Council. The Zionist Executive retained responsibility for immigration, information and propaganda, and fundraising. Since the Zionist General Council had now transferred jurisdiction over security matters to the National Administration, which was headed by Ben-Gurion and which had no Revisionist representation, Ben-Gurion was able to have his way and once again scuttled the Haganah-Irgun agreement.

The situation in Jerusalem began to deteriorate. Access to the city by road was blocked for all practical purposes, and stocks of supplies were dwindling rapidly. In February, only two convoys managed to break through the Arab blockade. Efforts to break the siege were doubled in March but produced little success. Notwithstanding the U.N. resolution, it seemed increasingly unlikely that Jerusalem would be internationalized. Indeed, it began to look like the city and its large Jewish population might be lost to the Arabs. Accordingly, on April 1 the Haganah command, critically short of adequately trained and armed forces, reluctantly agreed to mount an offensive to open the road to Jerusalem. This required the launching of a major operation to capture the heights controlling the road at critical points along its route.

In Jerusalem itself, where Shaltiel was directing the defense of the city, the shortage of fighting men was such that he was forced to seek help from Mordechai Raanan, the Irgun commander there. Shaltiel had earlier made a similar approach to the Lehi commander in Jerusalem, Yehoshua Zettler, but it quickly ended in a quarrel between the two. The meeting with Raanan had a similar result. Neither the Irgun nor the Lehi commander was willing to place himself under Shaltiel's control because they simply did not trust him. They considered him to be

234   Pangs of the Messiah

an arrogant and basically incompetent flunky of Ben-Gurion. Raanan and Zettler therefore decided to take joint action by themselves to help alleviate the difficult military situation. With very limited resources at their disposal, they concluded that the most reasonable target for them was the small Arab village of Deir Yassin, west of Jerusalem. The village was a base for Arab snipers and was the home of four clans that had been actively anti-Jewish since the 1929 riots.

On April 6, the Haganah launched Operation Nahshon, the offensive intended to open the road to Jerusalem. It involved assaults from both ends of the road simultaneously. The fighting was especially heavy around the village of Kastel, about five miles west of Jerusalem. Kastel dominated the road for some three miles, and its capture was critical to the success of the whole operation. The Haganah had managed to take it two days earlier, but was under continuing counterattack by the Arabs. When Shaltiel learned that the Irgun and Lehi were planning an attack on Deir Yassin, which if successful would relieve the pressure on Kastel, he had little choice but to suppress his hatred for both groups and grudgingly hope for their success. On April 7, he sent the following message to Raanan and Zettler:

I have no objection to your carrying out the operation provided you are able to hold the village. If you are unable to do so I warn you against blowing up the village, which would lead to the flight of the inhabitants and the occupation of the destroyed and empty houses by foreign forces. This situation would increase our difficulties in the general struggle and a second conquest of the place would require heavy sacrifices. Furthermore, if foreign forces took over, this would upset our general plan for establishing an airfield.[9]

That same day the Arabs retook Kastel, placing the success of Operation Nahshon in jeopardy.

On April 9, the Irgun and Lehi assault on Deir Yassin took place. Their plan was simple. The village would be surrounded on three sides, and then an announcement would be made over a loudspeaker warning the inhabitants that the village was under attack by superior forces. The villagers would be encouraged to flee by the road leading to Ein Karim, which would be left open for their use. As it happened, the plan went awry. The village was far more heavily defended than expected, and the level and din of battle were such that it was uncertain if the broadcast message was heard by most of the inhabitants. In any case, what was expected to be a relatively easy operation turned into a difficult house-to-house battle, with many of the houses not only full of Arab irregulars but also containing numerous women and children. When the smoke cleared after the village was finally secured, it became apparent that there were a large number of women and children among the 116 Arab dead. According to the original Arab accounts there were 100 killed out of a population of 1,000; this was embellished in some Jewish accounts to as many as 250 out a total population of 500. The survivors were loaded on trucks and taken to Jerusalem, where they were released. The protracted battle, which lasted almost an entire day, had cost the lives of about 40 percent of the attacking force.

Later that same afternoon, Raanan went to Givat Shaul to report on the battle and to request that the Haganah take over the village from the exhausted Irgun and Lehi forces. Shaltiel sent his operations chief to Deir Yassin with Raanan to estimate how many men would be needed to hold the village. When the two returned to see Shaltiel, the Haganah man told him that they would need 100 men to hold the town. Without explanation, Shaltiel insisted to Raanan: "I want you to hold the village for another 48 hours. I warn you, if you leave the village before then, the Haganah will not enter there at all."[10]

It appears that Shaltiel was upset that the fighting had taken as many lives as it did, and wished to distance himself from any connection with the assault. Two days later, on April 11, Raanan went to Haganah general headquarters in Bet HaKerem to plead for relief for his exhausted men. Haganah forces arrived about midnight and blockaded the village, preventing the Lehi men who were still holding the place from leaving. The Irgun had turned the village over to the Lehi on the previous day as part of a rotation system they had worked out for holding the village until the Haganah sent replacements. Finally, after some harsh exchanges the following morning, the Haganah took control of the village. In the meantime, Shaltiel took the occasion to absolve himself of any responsibility for Deir Yassin by putting out a patently false and duplicitous statement:

This morning, the last Lehi and Etzel soldiers ran from Deir Yassin, and our forces entered the village. We were forced to take command of the village after the splinter forces opened a new enemy front and then fled, leaving the western neighborhoods of the city open to enemy attack. The splinter groups did not launch a military operation. . . . For a full day, Etzel and Lehi soldiers stood and slaughtered men, women, and children, not in the course of the operation, but in a premeditated act which had as its intention slaughter and murder only. They also took spoils, and when they finished their work, they fled.[11]

On April 11, without even hesitating to ascertain the facts, Ben-Gurion sent a message to King Abdullah on April 11 expressing his horror and regret at the outrage that took place at Deir Yassin, fearing that what had happened might preclude reaching a peaceful accommodation between them. The Jewish Agency issued a statement that made "an earnest appeal to all parties that if armed conflict in Palestine can indeed not be avoided, it should at least be conducted in accordance with the rules of civilized warfare and that in particular the rights of the civilian population should be scrupulously respected."[12] Even the chief rabbis were swept up in the general hysteria and pronounced a ban of excommunication upon those who had participated in the assault.

Ben-Gurion must have appeared and felt rather foolish after Raanan and Zettler promptly released Shaltiel's letters to them, clearly demonstrating that the latter had lied about the incident. Nevertheless, Ben-Gurion kept his peace. His condemnation of the attack on Deir Yassin had served as a confirmation of the false reports of slaughter, rape, and mutilation that had been concocted by survivors of the battle. Others, who similarly wished to discredit the Irgun and Lehi in the eyes of the Jewish public for partisan political purposes, subsequently embellished the reports.

One unanticipated consequence of the false report and Ben-Gurion's confirmation of it was that it lent credence to the hysterical Arab propaganda about the fictitious atrocities, which served to frighten the Arabs rather than strengthen their resolve to resist. These false reports, coupled with fears generated by the general Haganah offensive, caused thousands of Arabs to begin to flee the areas of Jewish settlement, and in many cases Palestine. When the British withdrew from Tiberias on April 18, the entire Arab population of about 6,000 fled, leaving behind an open city. When the Haganah attacked in Haifa on April 20, a mass exodus of more than 60,000 Arabs took place.

At this same time the Irgun decided to undertake the conquest of Jaffa. Although the city was outside the partition boundaries of the proposed Jewish state, Arab control there posed a continuing threat not only to the security of Tel Aviv but also to the road to Jerusalem. The assault began on April 25 and met with very heavy resistance as the Haganah began its own operation to outflank and seal off the city. The following day, Galili and Yigael Yadin, chief operations officer of the Haganah, met with Begin and agreed to cooperate under the terms of the March 8 Haganah-Irgun agreement. It had been approved some two weeks earlier by the Zionist General Council, but was ignored by Ben-Gurion, who would not be bound by any collective decisions with which he disagreed. As the Irgun moved forward, the British decided to block its advance by force. British tanks started toward the Manshieh district but soon ran into unanticipated Irgun resistance. Irgun men were knocking the tanks out of action by creeping up and planting dynamite on them. When the British realized, after a couple of hours of engagement, that they were unlikely to break through the Irgun lines and that their paths of retreat were being closed behind them, they abandoned the assault and withdrew.

The British retreat, coupled with a murderous mortar barrage, threw the Arabs of Jaffa into a panic, and they, too, began to flee. Before long, only some 4,000 of the previous 70,000 Arab residents of Jaffa remained in the city. Nonetheless, the presence of large numbers of British troops in the still uncaptured sections of Jaffa prevented the occupation of the city by Jewish forces for another two weeks. On April 30, having effectively completed the conquest of northern Jaffa, thereby assuring the security of Tel Aviv, the Irgun turned the city over to the Haganah. The city formally surrendered on May 13, the date of the British withdrawal.

Elsewhere in the country the news was mixed. Despite the odds against it, Safed remained under Jewish control, as did the isolated kibbutzim in the Negev. The Palmah had cleared additional areas in the Galilee and a small Haganah force captured Acre. The situation around Jerusalem, however, had deteriorated once again. The Arab Legion, under British command, was intervening in an attempt to clear out the Etzion bloc of four settlements that commanded the road from Jerusalem to Hebron. The apparent aim was to create a situation in which the Arab Legion, as a British force, would withdraw a day before the end of the Mandate, as promised by the colonial secretary. It would then return unimpeded the following day as an "independent" Arab force, still under Glubb's command, to complete the conquest of Jerusalem, even though this went beyond the understanding reached with Bevin in March.

However, events in the previous two months had radically changed the situation, precluding the peaceful takeover of central Palestine by the Arabs. First, the attempts of the Palestinian Arabs to close the road to Jerusalem had brought Jewish forces into areas assigned to the Arabs under the partition plan in order to keep the road open. It was hardly likely that the Jews would simply turn these strategically vital footholds over to the Arab Legion. Second, notwithstanding his repeated assurances to the Jews, by the first week of May, Abdullah had already committed himself to joint military action with the Arab League. Several days before the Mandate was to come to an end, the political committee of the Arab League convened in Amman to work out final arrangements for inter-Arab coordination during the coming war.

At the same time, attempting to pursue the earlier understanding reached with the British in London, Glubb sent Colonel Desmond Goldie to meet with a representative of the Haganah at Naharayim. His mission was to try to reach an understanding with the Haganah that would relieve the Arab Legion of the necessity to fight to gain control of the areas earmarked for the Arabs. Goldie proposed to the Haganah representative, Shlomo Shamir, that the Arab Legion be permitted to occupy the Arab zones unopposed, while both the Haganah and the Arab Legion would stay out of Jerusalem. In return, the Legion would be prepared to wait two or three days before crossing into Palestine, to give the Haganah time to consolidate its control of the Jewish sectors of the country. Goldie received assurances from Shamir that if the Legion did not attack Jerusalem, the Haganah would also refrain from doing so. As for the rest of Goldie's proposal, Shamir promised to report it to his superiors. The proposal must have struck the Haganah leadership as rather bizarre, since Abdullah was certainly in no position to control what the other Arab states would do. Moreover, once open fighting broke out, it was unlikely that Glubb and the Legion would be allowed to observe any agreement that he might have worked out with the Haganah.

Notwithstanding the improbability of success, the National Administration decided to try one last time to dissuade Abdullah from joining in the war. A meeting with Abdullah was arranged, and Golda Meir made a secret trip to Amman on May 11, accompanied once again by Ezra Danin. Upon her return from the meeting with Abdullah, she handed Ben-Gurion a note that stated: "I had a friendly meeting [with Abdullah]. He is very worried and looks terrible. He did not deny that we had agreed on a mutually satisfactory arrangement. According to his plan, this would mean a united country with autonomy for the Jewish section, and then, after a year, he would take over the Arab section. But now he is only one of five. It will be one country under his rule."[13]

Abdullah evidently became increasingly concerned over the uncertainties of the outcome of a war with the Jews. He sought to reach some sort of accommodation with the Zionists that would satisfy the other Arab states and thereby avoid the coming conflict. Abdullah inquired if "the Jewish leaders would be prepared to cede to him some of the land allotted to them in the partition scheme, so as to persuade the Arab world to accept the division of Palestine." This sort of tactic did not sit very well with Ben-Gurion and his colleagues. Even the staunchest advocates of partition had accepted it as the only practical means of obtaining international support for a Jewish state in Palestine. However, it was one thing to appease the United Nations and quite another to appease the Arab states that had no legitimate claim on Palestine in the first place. The kind of bargain that Abdullah sought was out of the question. In fact, Ben-Gurion, as well as some of the other leaders, had concluded that if the Arabs did not accept the partition scheme as it was, he would not be bound by it either. In such a case, he would feel free to redivide the country in accordance with the opportunities that were presented by the impending military struggle. Accordingly, the Zionist response to Abdullah was "that the acceptance of the boundaries described in the plan approved by the United Nations Organization was subject to the partition scheme being implemented as a whole and in a peaceful fashion. If the Arabs went to war the Jews would retain anything they could win."[14]

As the end of the Mandate approached, there was uncertainty as to whether the Jewish state would be declared as previously anticipated, particularly in view of American pressure to postpone the decision. At issue was an American truce proposal that, if accepted, would have nullified many of the gains made through hard fighting to protect the communications links between the various segments of the territories earmarked for the Jewish state. The National Administration was sharply divided over whether or not to accept the truce. In accordance with one of the specific articles of the truce proposal, acceptance would have necessitated a temporary postponement in declaring the independence of the state. On the other hand, the truce would have afforded a respite to build up the Haganah for the full-scale war that was clearly coming. Jewish defense forces had been mauled by the Arab Legion, and there was concern about the readiness of the Haganah to battle other regular armies without further reinforcement and training. There was no disagreement that the conflict with the Arabs would ultimately be resolved on the battlefield. The question was whether to accept a temporary but risky setback in exchange for a needed respite, assuming that the Arabs would abide by the terms of the truce.

Ben-Gurion, who was opposed to accepting the truce on the basis of the terms offered, stated to the members of the National Administration: "I am not moved by the disaster of the Etzion bloc. Unfortunately, I have expected such things to happen and fear there will be more difficult trials. The decision will be made when we wipe out the greater part of the Arab Legion, because the extermination of an enemy force is the determining factor. . . . It is a question of a decision by force of arms."[15]

On May 12, the National Administration voted 4 to 6 in favor of rejecting the truce, thereby effectively confirming the decision to proceed with the proclamation of the Jewish state on May 15. Several days before the vote, Ben-Gurion sent Eliezer Liebenstein to see Begin. Begin later recalled: "He told me that Mr. Ben-Gurion 'appreciated very much' our proclamations demanding the establishment of a Jewish Government; they were helping him overcome the opposition from various quarters. But he asked us to emphasize in our further statements the *positive* point—that if a Government were established we would support it with all our strength."[16]

Begin, however, was not entirely convinced that Ben-Gurion would not reverse himself, as he had done so often in the past. Just in case, the Irgun high command made preparations to unilaterally declare a Jewish state in Jerusalem. They published a statement that declared:

The Hebrew Government will certainly arise. There is no "perhaps." It will arise. If the official leaders set it up, *we shall support it with all our strength*. But if they surrender to threats or allow themselves to be cajoled, our strength and that of the fighting youth, will be behind the free Government which will arise from the depths of the underground and which will lead the people to victory in the war for freedom.[17]

Begin's admonitions proved unnecessary. On Friday afternoon, May 14, the Jewish state was proclaimed by Ben-Gurion eight hours before the end of the Mandate, in order to avoid making the declaration on the Sabbath. The newborn state, severely troubled by internal contradictions and external pressures, would continue to struggle for viability for the next half-century, and perhaps beyond.

NOTES

   1. Jon Kimche and David Kimche, *A Clash of Destinies*, p. 59.

   2. Golda Meir, *My Life*, p. 215.

   3. J. C. Hurewitz, *The Struggle for Palestine*, p. 311.

   4. Ibid., p. 312.

   5. John B. Glubb, *A Soldier with the Arabs*, p. 63.

   6. Nicholas Bethell, *The Palestine Triangle*, p. 352.

   7. Michael J. Cohen, "The Zionist Perspective," in William Roger Louis and Robert W. Stookey, eds., *The End of the Palestine Mandate*, p. 90.

   8. David Ben-Gurion, *Israel: A Personal History*, p. 70.

9. Dan Kurzman, *Genesis 1948*, p. 140.

10. Yardena Golani, *HaMitos shel Deir Yassin*, p. 72.

11. Kurzman, *Genesis 1948*, p. 148.

12. Bernard Postal and Henry W. Levy, *And the Hills Shouted for Joy*, p. 115.

13. Ben-Gurion, *Israel*, p. 91.

14. Alec Kirkbride, *From the Wings: Amman Memoirs, 1947–1951*, pp. 21–22.

15. Zeev Sharef, *Three Days*, p. 123.

16. Menachem Begin, *The Revolt*, p. 347.

17. Ibid.

Selected Bibliography

Abboushi, W. F. *The Unmaking of Palestine*. The Cottons, U.K., 1985.

Abdullah, King of Jordan. *Memoirs*. London, 1950.

———. *My Memoirs Completed*. Washington, DC, 1954.

Abramov, S. Zalman. *Perpetual Dilemma: Jewish Religion in the Jewish State*. Rutherford, NJ, 1976.

Ahad Ha'am. *Nationalism and the Jewish Ethic: Basic Writings of Ahad Ha'am*. Edited by Hans Kohn. New York, 1962.

Allen, Richard. *Imperialism and Nationalism in the Fertile Crescent*. New York, 1974.

Almog, Shmuel, ed. *Zionism and the Arabs*. Jerusalem, 1983.

Antonius, George. *The Arab Awakening*. New York, 1965.

Arlosoroff, Chaim. *Jerusalem Diary*. Edited by Z. Sharef. Tel Aviv, 1949.

Arlosoroff, Chaim, ed. *Hechalutz*. New York, 1929.

Ashbee, C. R. *A Palestine Notebook, 1918–1923*. New York, 1925.

Avineri, Shlomo. *The Making of Modern Zionism*. New York, 1981.

Avishai, Bernard. *The Tragedy of Zionism*. New York, 1985.

Banai, Yaacov. *Hayalim Almonim*. Tel Aviv, 1948.

Barbour, Nevill. *Nisi Dominus: A Survey of the Palestine Controversy*. Beirut, 1969.

Bardin, Shlomo. *Pioneer Youth in Palestine*. New York, 1932.

Bar-Zohar, Michael. *Ben-Gurion: The Armed Prophet*. Englewood Cliffs, NJ, 1968.

Bauer, Yehuda. *From Diplomacy to Resistance*. Philadelphia, 1970.

Begin, Menachem. *The Revolt*. New York, 1951.

Bein, Alex. *The Return to the Soil*. Jerusalem, 1952.

Bell, J. Bowyer. *Terror Out of Zion*. New York, 1977.

Ben-Ami, Yitshaq. *Years of Wrath, Days of Glory.* New York, 1983.

Ben-Gurion, David. *Rebirth and Destiny of Israel.* New York, 1954.

———. *Israel: A Personal History.* New York, 1971.

———. *My Talks with Arab Leaders.* Jerusalem, 1972.

Ben-Gurion, David, ed. *The Jews in Their Land.* Rev. ed. New York, 1974.

Ben-Sasson, H. H., ed. *A History of the Jewish People.* Cambridge, MA, 1976.

Bentwich, Norman. *England in Palestine.* London, 1932.

———. *Fulfillment in the Promised Land.* London, 1938.

———. *Palestine.* London, 1946.

———. *My 77 Years.* Philadelphia, 1961.

Berlin, Isaiah. *Chaim Weizmann.* New York, 1958.

Bethell, Nicholas. *The Palestine Triangle.* New York, 1979.

Borisov, J. *Palestine Underground.* New York, 1947.

Borochov, Ber. *Nationalism and the Class Struggle.* New York, 1937.

Burstein, Moshe. *Self-Government of the Jews in Palestine Since 1900.* Tel Aviv, 1934.

Caplan, Neil. *Palestine Jewry and the Arab Question, 1917–1925.* London, 1978.

———. "The Yishuv, Sir Herbert Samuel, and the Arab Question in Palestine, 1921–25." In *Zionism and Arabism in Palestine and Israel,* ed. Elie Kedourie and Sylvia G. Haim. London, 1982.

———. *Futile Diplomacy: Early Arab-Zionist Negotiation Attempts 1913–1931.* London, 1983.

Carpi, Daniel, ed. *HaZionut* (in Hebrew). Vol. 1. Tel Aviv, 1970.

Chigier, M. "The Rabbinical Courts in the State of Israel." *Israel Law Review* 2.2 (1967).

Clarke, Thurston. *By Blood and Fire.* New York, 1981.

Cohen, Aharon. *Israel and the Arab World.* New York, 1970.

Cohen, Gabriel. "The Evacuation from Palestine as Reflected in British Policy." *Cathedra* (in Hebrew), April 1980.

Cohen, Geula. *Woman of Violence: Memoirs of a Young Terrorist, 1943–1948.* New York, 1966.

Cohen, Israel. *The Zionist Movement.* New York, 1946.

———. *A Short History of Zionism.* London, 1951.

Cohen, Michael J. *Palestine: Retreat from the Mandate.* New York, 1978.

———. "The British Decision to Leave Palestine." *Cathedra* (in Hebrew), April 1980.

———. *The Origins and Evolution of the Arab-Zionist Conflict.* Berkeley, CA, 1987.

Cohen, Mitchell. *Zion & State: Nation, Class and the Shaping of Modern Israel.* New York, 1987.

Cohen, Naomi W. *The Year After the Riots.* Detroit, 1988.

Collins, Larry, and Dominique Lapierre. *O Jerusalem!* New York, 1972.

Crossman, Richard H. S. *Palestine Mission: A Personal Record.* New York, 1947.

———. *A Nation Reborn*. New York, 1960.

Dann, Uriel. *Studies in the History of Transjordan, 1920–1949: The Making of a State*. Boulder, CO, 1984.

Derogy, Jacques, and Hesi Carmel. *The Untold History of Israel*. New York, 1979.

Documents on British Foreign Policy, 1919–1939. Vol. IV. Edited by E. L. Woodward and R. Butler. London, 1952.

———. Vol. XIII. Edited by R. Butler and J.P.T. Bury. London, 1963.

Dothan, Shmuel. "From the Cantons Proposal to the Partition Plan, 1929–1938." *Cathedra* (in Hebrew), April 1980.

———. "Religious Polemics Surrounding the 1937 Partition Plan." In Vol. 2 of *The Jerusalem Cathedra*, ed. Lee I. Levine. Jerusalem, 1982.

Duff, Douglas V. *Sword for Hire*. London, 1934.

Dunner, Joseph. *The Republic of Israel: Its History and Its Promise*. New York, 1950.

Elam, Yigal. "Haganah, Irgun and 'Stern': Who Did What?" *The Jerusalem Quarterly*, Spring 1982.

Elan, Amitzur. "When Did the British Decide to Leave?" *Cathedra* (in Hebrew), April 1980.

Encyclopaedia Judaica. 16 vols. Jerusalem, 1972.

Encyclopedia of Zionism and Israel. 2 vols. New York, 1971.

Farago, Ladislas. *Palestine on the Eve*. London, 1936.

Federbusch, Simon, ed. *Hazon Torah veTziyon*. New York, 1960.

Feiwel, T. R. *No Ease in Zion*. London, 1938.

Flapan, Simha. *Zionism and the Palestinians*. London, 1979.

———. *The Birth of Israel: Myths and Realities*. New York, 1987.

Frank, Gerold. *The Deed*. New York, 1963.

Frankenstein, Ernst. *Justice for My People*. New York, 1944.

Friedman, Menachem. *Society and Religion: The Non-Zionist Orthodox in Eretz-Israel 1918–1936* (in Hebrew). Jerusalem, 1977.

Friesel, Evyatar. "Herbert Samuel's Reassessment of Zionism in 1921." *Studies in Zionism*, Autumn 1984.

Frischwasser-Ra'anan, H. F. *The Frontiers of a Nation*. Westport, CT, 1976.

Fromkin, David. *A Peace to End All Peace: Creating the Modern Middle East 1914–1922*. New York, 1989.

Furlonge, Geoffrey. *Palestine Is My Country: The Story of Musa Alami*. New York, 1969.

Galnoor, Itzhak. *The Partition of Palestine: Decision Crossroads in the Zionist Movement*. Albany, NY, 1995.

Gaon, M. D. *Yehudei haMizrah beEretz Yisrael beAvar ubaHove*. Jerusalem, 1928.

Garcia-Granados, Jorge. *The Birth of Israel*. New York, 1948.

Gervasi, Frank. *To Whom Palestine*. New York, 1946.

———. *The Life and Times of Menachem Begin*. New York, 1979.

Getter, Miriam. *Chaim Arlosoroff: A Political Biography* (in Hebrew). Tel Aviv, 1977.

Gilbert, Martin. *Exile and Return*. Philadelphia, 1978.

Gil-Har, Yitzhak. "The Separation of Trans-Jordan from Palestine." In Vol. 1 of *The Jerusalem Cathedra*, ed. Lee I. Levine. Jerusalem, 1981.

Gilner, Elias. *War and Hope: A History of the Jewish Legion*. New York, 1969.

Gitlin, Jan. *Conquest of Acre Fortress* (in Hebrew). Tel Aviv, 1962.

Glubb, John B. *A Soldier with the Arabs*. New York, 1957.

Golani, Yardena. *HaMitos shel Deir Yassin*. Tel Aviv, 1976.

Goldberg, Giora. "Haganah, Irgun and 'Stern': Who Did What?—(Rejoinder)." *The Jerusalem Quarterly*, Fall 1982.

Goldmann, Nahum. *The Autobiography of Nahum Goldmann*. New York, 1969.

Gorny, Yosef. *The Arab Question and the Jewish Problem* (in Hebrew). Tel Aviv, 1985.

Government of Palestine. *A Survey of Palestine*. Vol. 1. 1946.

Greenberg, Louis. *The Jews in Russia: The Struggle for Emancipation*. New York, 1976.

Gruber, Ruth. *Destination Palestine: The Story of the Haganah Ship Exodus 1947*. New York, 1948.

Gunther, John. *Inside Asia*. New York, 1942.

Gurion, Itzhak. *Triumph on the Gallows*. New York, 1950.

Habas, Braha. *Sefer Meoraot 5696*. Tel Aviv, 1937.

———. *David Ben-Gurion veDoro*. Tel Aviv, 1952.

Haber, Eitan. *Menachem Begin: The Legend and the Man*. New York, 1978.

Haim, Yehoyada. *Abandonment of Illusions: Zionist Political Attitudes Toward Palestinian Arab Nationalism, 1936–1939*. Boulder, CO, 1983.

Halpern, Ben. *The Idea of the Jewish State*. 2nd ed. Cambridge, MA, 1969.

———. *A Clash of Heroes: Brandeis, Weizmann, and American Zionism*. New York, 1987.

Hanna, Paul L. *British Policy in Palestine*. Washington, DC, 1942.

Hattis, Susan L. *The Bi-National Idea in Palestine During Mandatory Times*. Haifa, 1970.

Heckelman, A. Joseph. "Deir Yassin: The 'Massacre' That Never Was." *Conservative Judaism*, Spring 1973.

Heller, Joseph. "Did the Yishuv's Struggle Influence Britain to Evacuate Palestine?" *Cathedra* (in Hebrew), April 1980.

———. *The Struggle for the Jewish State: Zionist Politics, 1936–1948* (in Hebrew). Jerusalem, 1984.

Hertzberg, Arthur, ed. *The Zionist Idea*. New York, 1966.

Horowitz, Dan, and Moshe Lissak. *Origins of the Israeli Polity: Palestine Under the Mandate*. Chicago, 1978.

Hurewitz, J. C. *The Struggle for Palestine*. New York, 1950.

Hurwitz, Haim A. *David Ben-Gurion: Ershter Premier fun Yisrael* (in Yiddish). New York, 1952.

Hyamson, Albert M. *Palestine: A Policy.* Westport, CT, 1975.

———. *Palestine Under the Mandate 1920–1948.* Westport, CT, 1976.

Ingrams, Doreen. *Palestine Papers 1917–1922: Seeds of Conflict.* New York, 1973.

Israel, Gerard. *The Jews in Russia.* New York, 1975.

Jabotinsky, Vladimir. *The Jewish War Front.* London, 1940.

———. *The Story of the Jewish Legion.* New York, 1945.

Jbara, Taysir. *Palestinian Leader Hajj Amin al-Husayni.* Princeton, NJ, 1985.

Jeffries, J.M.N. *Palestine: The Reality.* London, 1939.

Jewish Agency for Palestine. *Memorandum Submitted to the Palestine Royal Commission.* Westport, CT, 1975.

John, Robert, and Sami Hadawi. *The Palestine Diary.* 2 vols. New York, 1970.

Jones, Martin. *Failure in Palestine.* London, 1986.

Joseph, Bernard. *British Rule in Palestine.* Washington, DC, 1948.

Katz, Doris. *The Lady Was a Terrorist.* New York, 1953.

Katz, Jacob. *Jewish Emancipation and Self-Emancipation.* Philadelphia, 1986.

Katz, Shmuel. *Yom Ha'Esh.* Tel Aviv, 1966.

———. *Days of Fire.* London, 1968.

Kedourie, Elie. *The Chatham House Version and Other Middle Eastern Studies.* New York, 1970.

———. *In the Anglo-Arab Labyrinth.* Cambridge, U.K., 1976.

Kedourie, Elie, and Sylvia G. Haim, eds. *Zionism and Arabism in Palestine and Israel.* London, 1982.

Khoury, Fred J. *The Arab-Israeli Dilemma.* 3rd ed. Syracuse, NY, 1985.

Kimche, Jon. *The Unromantics: The Great Powers and the Balfour Declaration.* London, 1968.

———. *The Second Arab Awakening.* New York, 1970.

———. *There Could Have Been Peace.* New York, 1973.

Kimche, Jon, and David Kimche. *A Clash of Destinies.* New York, 1960.

Kirk, George E. *A Short History of the Middle East.* Washington, DC, 1949.

———. *The Middle East in the War.* London, 1952.

Kirkbride, Alec. *A Crackle of Thorns.* London, 1956.

———. *From the Wings: Amman Memoirs, 1947–1951.* London, 1976.

Kisch, Frederick H. *Palestine Diary.* London, 1938.

Klausner, Joseph. *Menahem Ussishkin: His Life and Work.* New York, 1942.

Klieman, Aaron S. *Foundations of British Policy in the Arab World: The Cairo Conference of 1921.* Baltimore, 1970.

———. *Divide or Rule: Britain, Partition and Palestine, 1936–1939* (in Hebrew). Jerusalem, 1983.

Knox, D. Edward. *The Making of a New Eastern Question: British Palestine Policy and the Origins of Israel.* Washington, DC, 1981.

Koestler, Arthur. *Promise and Fulfillment.* New York, 1949.

Kohn, Hans. *Nationalism and Imperialism in the Hither East.* New York, 1969.

Kolinsky, Martin. *Law, Order and Riots in Mandatory Palestine, 1928–1935.* New York, 1993.

Kurzman, Dan. *Genesis 1948.* New York, 1970.

———. *Ben-Gurion: Prophet of Fire.* New York, 1983.

Laqueur, Walter. *A History of Zionism.* New York, 1972.

Learsi, Rufus. *Fulfillment: The Epic Story of Zionism.* Cleveland, OH, 1951.

Lesch, Ann Mosley. *Arab Politics in Palestine, 1917–1939.* Ithaca, NY, 1979.

Levenberg, S. *The Jews and Palestine: A Study in Labour Zionism.* London, 1945.

Lipovetzky, Pesah. *Yosef Trumpeldor* (in Hebrew). Kovno [Kaunas], Lithuania, 1924.

Lipsky, Louis. *A Gallery of Zionist Profiles.* New York, 1956.

Litvinoff, Barnet. *Ben-Gurion of Israel.* New York, 1954.

———. *Weizmann: Last of the Patriarchs.* New York, 1976.

Lloyd George, David. *The Truth About the Peace Treaties.* London, 1936.

———. *Memoirs of the Peace Conference.* London, 1938.

Lorch, Netanel. *The Edge of the Sword: Israel's War of Independence, 1947–1949.* New York, 1961.

———. *One Long War: Arab Versus Jew Since 1920.* Jerusalem, 1976.

Louis, William Roger, and Robert W. Stookey, eds. *The End of the Palestine Mandate.* Austin, TX, 1986.

Lucas, Noah. *The Modern History of Israel.* New York, 1975.

Manuel, Frank E. *The Realities of American-Palestine Relations.* Washington, DC, 1949.

Margalit, Elkanah. "The Zionist-Socialist Labour Movement of Eretz-Israel in the 1920s." *Cathedra* (in Hebrew). July 1980.

Marlowe, John. *The Seat of Pilate.* London, 1959.

McTague, John J. *British Policy in Palestine, 1917–1922.* Lanham, MD, 1983.

Meinertzhagen, Richard. *Middle East Diary 1917–1956.* New York, 1960.

Meir, Golda. *A Land of Our Own: An Oral Autobiography.* Edited by Marie Syrkin. New York, 1973.

———. *My Life.* New York, 1975.

Merhav, Peretz. *The Israeli Left: History, Problems, Documents.* San Diego, 1980.

Mossek, M. *Palestine Immigration Policy Under Sir Herbert Samuel.* London, 1978.

Nakdimon, Shlomo, and Shaul Mayzlish. *De Haan: The First Political Assassination in Palestine* (in Hebrew). Tel Aviv, 1985.

Namier, Lewis B. *In the Margins of History.* Freeport, NY, 1969.

Niv, David. *The Irgun Zvai Leumi.* 3 vols. Tel Aviv, 1965–1967.

O'Brien, Connor Cruise. *The Siege: The Saga of Israel and Zionism.* New York, 1986.

Ofer, Pinhas. "Disappointment with the Attainments of the Jewish National Home—A Factor in the Change of British Policy in Eretz-Israel in 1930?" *Cathedra* (in Hebrew), July 1980.

Palestine: A Study of Jewish, Arab, and British Policies. 2 vols. New Haven, CT, 1947.

Palestine Royal Commission. *Report.* London, 1937.

Parkes, James. *A History of Palestine from 135 A.D. to Modern Times.* New York, 1949.

Patai, Raphael. *Nahum Goldmann: His Missions to the Gentiles.* University, AL, 1987.

Patai, Raphael, ed. *Encyclopedia of Zionism and Israel.* New York, 1971.

Patterson, John H. *With the Judeans in the Palestine Campaign.* New York, 1922.

Pearlman, Moshe. "Chapters of Arab-Jewish Diplomacy, 1918–1922." *Jewish Social Studies*, April 1944.

———. *The Army of Israel.* New York, 1950.

Perlmutter, Amos. *Israel: The Partitioned State.* New York, 1985.

———. *The Life and Times of Menachem Begin.* Garden City, NY, 1987.

Peters, Joan. *From Time Immemorial: The Origins of the Arab-Jewish Conflict over Palestine.* New York, 1984.

Pipes, Daniel. "The Year the Arabs Discovered Palestine." *Middle East Review*, Summer 1989.

Polk, William R., David Stamler, and Edmund Asfour. *Backdrop to Tragedy: The Struggle for Palestine.* Boston, 1957.

Popper, David H. *The Puzzle of Palestine.* New York, 1938.

Porath, Yehoshua. *The Emergence of the Palestinian-Arab National Movement, 1918–1929.* London, 1974.

———. *The Palestinian Arab National Movement.* Vol. 2, 1929–1939. London, 1977.

Postal, Bernard, and Henry W. Levy. *And the Hills Shouted for Joy.* Philadelphia, 1973.

Prittie, Terence. *Eshkol: The Man and the Nation.* New York, 1969.

Rabinowitz, Ezekiel. *Justice Louis D. Brandeis: The Zionist Chapter of His Life.* New York, 1968.

Rappoport, Angelo S. *History of Palestine.* New York, 1931.

Revusky, Abraham. *Jews in Palestine.* New York, 1936.

Rifkind, Simon H., et al. *The Basic Equities of the Palestine Problem.* New York, 1977.

Robinson, Jacob. *Palestine and the United Nations.* Washington, DC, 1947.

Rose, Norman A. "The Debate on Partition, 1937–38." *Middle Eastern Studies*, November 1970–January 1971.

———. *The Gentile Zionists: A Study in Anglo-Zionist Diplomacy, 1929–1939.* London, 1973.

———. *Chaim Weizmann: A Biography.* New York, 1987.

Royal Institute of International Affairs. *Great Britain and Palestine 1915–1945.* London, 1946.

Rubin, Barry. *The Arab States and the Palestine Conflict.* Syracuse, NY, 1981.

Ruppin, Arthur. *Three Decades of Palestine.* Westport, CT, 1975.

Russell of Liverpool, Lord. *If I Forget Thee.* London, 1960.

Sachar, Howard M. *The Emergence of the Middle East: 1914–1924.* New York, 1969.

———. *A History of Israel.* New York, 1976.

Sacher, Harry. *Israel: The Establishment of a State.* London, 1952.

St. John, Robert. *Ben-Gurion: The Biography of an Extraordinary Man.* Garden City, NY, 1959.

Samuel, Edwin. *A Lifetime in Jerusalem.* New York, 1970.

Samuel, Horace B. *Unholy Memories of the Holy Land.* London, 1930.

Samuel, Maurice. *What Happened in Palestine.* Boston, 1929.

———. *On the Rim of the Wilderness: The Conflict in Palestine.* New York, 1931.

Sanders, Ronald. *The High Walls of Jerusalem.* New York, 1983.

Schechtman, Joseph B. *Rebel and Statesman: The Early Years.* New York, 1956.

———. *Fighter and Prophet: The Last Years.* New York, 1961.

———. *The Mufti and the Fuhrer.* New York, 1965.

Sefer Toldot HaHaganah. Vol. 1, part 2. Vol. 2, parts 1–3. Tel Aviv, 1956–1964.

Segre, V. D. *Israel: A Society in Transition.* London, 1971.

Sereni, Enzo, and R. E. Ashery, eds. *Jews and Arabs in Palestine.* New York, 1936.

Shaltiel, Eli, ed. *Jerusalem in the Modern Period* (in Hebrew). Jerusalem, 1981.

Shapira, Anita. *Berl: The Biography of a Socialist Zionist—Berl Katznelson, 1887–1944.* Cambridge, U.K., 1984.

Sharef, Zeev. *Three Days.* Garden City, NY, 1962.

Shavit, Yaacov. *Revisionism in Zionism* (in Hebrew). Tel Aviv, 1978.

Sheffer, Gabriel. "British Colonial Policy-Making Towards Palestine (1929–1939)." *Middle Eastern Studies*, October 1978.

———. "The Principles of British Pragmatism: Reevaluation of British Policies Toward Palestine in the 1930s." *Cathedra* (in Hebrew), September 1983.

Shlaim, Avi. *Collusion Across the Jordan: King Abdullah, the Zionist Movement, and the Partition of Palestine.* New York, 1988.

Sicker, Martin. "Echoes of a Poet: A Reconsideration of Abraham Stern-Yair." *The American Zionist*, February 1972.

Silver, Eric. *Begin: The Haunted Prophet*. New York, 1984.

Silverberg, Robert. *If I Forget Thee, O Jerusalem: American Jews and the State of Israel*. New York, 1970.

Stein, Kenneth W. *The Land Question in Palestine, 1917–1939*. Chapel Hill, NC, 1984.

Stoyanovsky, J. *The Mandate for Palestine*. London, 1928.

Sykes, Christopher. *Crossroads to Israel*. Cleveland, OH, 1965.

Syrkin, Marie. *Golda Meir: Israel's Leader*. New York, 1969.

Taylor, Alan R. *Prelude to Israel: An Analysis of Zionist Diplomacy, 1897–1947*. New York, 1959.

Teveth, Shabtai. *Ben-Gurion and the Palestinian Arabs*. New York, 1985.

———. *Ben-Gurion: The Burning Ground, 1886–1948*. Boston, 1987.

Tibawi, A. L. *Anglo-Arab Relations and the Question of Palestine 1914–1921*. London, 1978.

Toldot Mihemet HaKomemiut. Israel, 1959.

Toynbee, Arnold J. *Survey of International Affairs, 1930*. London, 1931.

Trevor, Daphne. *Under the White Paper: Some Aspects of British Administration in Palestine from 1939 to 1947*. Jerusalem, 1948.

Tuchman, Barbara W. *Bible and Sword*. New York, 1956.

Urofsky, Melvin I. *American Zionism from Herzl to the Holocaust*. Garden City, NY, 1975.

———. *A Voice That Spoke for Justice: The Life and Times of Stephen S. Wise*. Albany, NY, 1982.

Wasserstein, Bernard. *The British in Palestine: The Mandatory Government and the Arab-Jewish Conflict 1917–1929*. London, 1978.

Waxman, Chaim I. "Messianism, Zionism and the State of Israel." *Modern Judaism*, May 1987.

Weizmann, Chaim. "Palestine's Role in the Solution of the Jewish Problem." *Foreign Affairs*, January 1942.

———. *Trial and Error*. New York, 1949.

———. *The Letters and Papers of Chaim Weizmann*. Series A, *Letters*. London, 1968.

———. *The Letters and Papers of Chaim Weizmann*. Series B, *Papers*. New Brunswick, NJ, 1984.

Weizmann, Vera. *The Impossible Takes Longer*. New York, 1967.

Wilson, Harold. *The Chariot of Israel*. New York, 1981.

Wise, Stephen S., and Jacob de Haas. *The Great Betrayal*. New York, 1930.

Yaari, Avraham. *The Goodly Heritage*. Jerusalem, 1958.

Yishai, Yael. "Factionalism in Labour Zionism and Religious Zionism—A Comparative Perspective." *Cathedra* (in Hebrew), July 1980.

Zaar, Isaac. *Rescue and Liberation*. New York, 1954.

Zadka, Saul. *Blood in Zion: How the Jewish Guerrillas Drove the British out of Palestine*. London, 1995.

Ziff, William B. *The Rape of Palestine*. New York, 1938.

Zionist Organization. *Reports of the Executive to the XIIth Zionist Congress*. 1921.

———. *Reports of the Executive to the XIIIth Zionist Congress*. 1923.

———. *Reports of the Executive to the XIVth Zionist Congress*. 1925.

Zweig, Ronald. "Great Britain, the 'Hagana' and the Fate of the White Paper." *Cathedra* (in Hebrew), September 1983.

Index

About the Author

MARTIN SICKER is a private consultant who has served as a senior executive in the U.S. government and has taught political science at the American University and George Washington University. Dr. Sicker has written extensively in the fields of political science and international affairs; he is the author of ten previous books, including the companion volume, *Reshaping Palestine: From Muhammad Ali to the British Mandate, 1831–1922* (Praeger, 1999).